Charles T. Call • Cedric de Coning
Editors

Rising Powers and Peacebuilding

Breaking the Mold?

Editors
Charles T. Call
School of International Service
American University
Washington, DC, USA

Cedric de Coning
Norwegian Inst. of International Affairs
Oslo, Norway

DOI 10.1007/978-3-319-60621-7

To Shayla, Dash & Jag
and
To Embla & Frida

Preface

This book emerged from a multinational research project originally called "New Actors and Innovative Approaches to Peacebuilding." With the support of the Carnegie Corporation of New York and the Norwegian Ministry of Foreign Relations, six research institutions embarked in 2014 on a two-year effort to investigate the role of the rising powers in the Global South in aiding and supporting other countries to attain and sustain peace.

The institutions were the African Centre for the Constructive Resolution of Disputes (ACCORD) in Durban; the Centre for Strategic and International Studies (CSIS) in Jakarta; the Istanbul Policy Center (IPC) in Istanbul; the Norwegian Institute of International Affairs (NUPI) in Oslo; the School of International Service of American University in Washington DC; and the United Service Institution of India (USI) in New Delhi. We explicitly sought to create an opportunity for critical thinkers from rising powers and more traditional thought-centers to shed light on their own government's practices and approaches, and to bring those ideas into international fora.

The project sought to answer one central question: What exactly is new and innovative about the peacebuilding approach of the new actors from the Global South, and what results are they having? Building on this question, we sought to achieve three more specific objectives:

1. To provide a structured analysis of the values, content, and impact of recent peacebuilding initiatives of rising powers, comparing them to one another and to approaches by Western donors and international organizations.
2. To offer new theoretical claims about the role of the rising powers in peacebuilding, rooted in empirical work.
3. To make key policy audiences aware of alternative approaches and their empirical records and theoretical underpinnings.

The latter objective reflects the policy goals of the project, whereby the partners sought to educate one another in their own concept and activities, and then to stimulate exchanges of ideas about these approaches with more traditional centers of thought regarding peacebuilding. Ultimately, the project sought to influence the exchange of ideas among rising powers in the Global South and between Northern and Southern centers of policy. We held insightful (and fun) seminars in Jakarta, Istanbul, Addis Ababa (in conjunction with the African Union), New York, Washington DC, Brussels, and The Hague to advance these policy aims.

This book reflects the outcome of the former two project objectives. It captures the inputs of the project partners and a few additional intellects, offering in-depth, comparative studies of the rising powers, with case examples, aimed at also contributing to mid-level theoretical generalizations about these phenomena. We hope you enjoy the results.

Acknowledgements

Charles T. Call and Cedric de Coning join the project participants in thanking the Carnegie Corporation of New York and the Norwegian Ministry of Foreign Relations for their support to the "Rising Powers and Peacebuilding Project" (www.risingpowerandpeacebuilding.org). We are also grateful for the material and in-kind support received from American University's School of International Service, including its Office of Financial Operations and Office of Sponsored Projects. The editors also thank Katy Collin, Manu Ramkumar, Holly Christensen, and Brandon Sims for their research and other assistance. We thank also Indonesia's Permanent Mission to the United Nations and Yvonne Mewengkang for organizing a project-related event in March 2016. We offer a special deep thanks to Chris Brandt, whose excellent management of the project helped meetings, research deadlines, finances, and the process of editing the chapters conclude remarkably smoothly.

Adriana Abdenur wishes to thank the National Council of Technological and Scientific Development and its Senior Post-Doctoral Scholarship Program, and the Centro de Pesquisa e Documentação de História Contemporânea do Brasil at Fundação Getúlio Vargas for supporting her role in this research.

Lina Alexandra and Marc Lanteigne would like to express our appreciation for the extensive support given by institutions in Myanmar and Indonesia that contributed to this research. We would like to thank current and former officials of the Indonesian Ministry of Foreign Affairs, especially Dr. Hassan Wirajuda (2001–2009); the Institute for Peace and

Democracy (IPD); the former Indonesian Ambassador to Myanmar, Dr. Sebastianus Sumarsono (2008–2013); the Indonesian National Election Commission; Indonesian parliament member (Commission I); and The Habibie Center. In Myanmar, we would like to thank the Embassies of Indonesia (especially its then-Ambassador Dr. Ito Sumardi), India, Japan, Norway, Switzerland; officials in the Strategic Studies and Training Department of the Ministry of Foreign Affairs (MOFA); Myanmar Human Rights Commission; representatives of the Myanmar Armed Forces (Tatmadaw); the commissioners from the Myanmar National Election Commission; and academics and researchers in the Yangon University, the Myanmar Development Research Institute (MDRI)/Center for Strategic and International Studies (CSIS), Myanmar Institute of Strategic and International Studies; the Mingalar Myanmar and the Shalom (Nyein) Foundation.

P K Singh would like to thank Ambassador Amar Sinha, IFS, Secretary, Ministry of External Affairs, Government of India, and former Indian Ambassador to Afghanistan, and the staff of the Indian Embassy in Afghanistan for their support to the USI team in carrying out their field work in Afghanistan and to the Afghan nationals in their Government and in civil society for giving us their time, friendship and valuable inputs for our project.

Shakti Sinha would like to acknowledge the support of the United Services Institution of India (New Delhi), in particular its Director, Lt Gen P.K. Singh (retd.) for the opportunity to work on this subject, and the American University-NUPI-USI project for its support.

Auveen E. Woods and Onur Sazak would like to thank our interviewees in Turkey and Somalia who were gracious with their time and knowledge.

Contents

List of Figures

List of Tables

CHAPTER 1

Introduction: Why Examine Rising Powers' Role in Peacebuilding?

Cedric de Coning and Charles T. Call

Despite progress since the Cold War in reaching negotiated settlements in civil wars, efforts to consolidate peace with effective governance have proven challenging in places as diverse as the Congo, Afghanistan, Haiti, Iraq, Central Africa, and the Middle East. Two decades ago international peacebuilding was understood as a centrally coordinated package of interventions aimed at resolving a conflict by addressing its root causes. International institutions were thought to have acquired the scientific knowledge and the practical expertise to "build" peace (Chandler 2012). The problem—recurring violent conflict—was usually located in weak and failing states in the Global South, and the solutions required that these states adopt liberal state practices—democratic politics, free-market policies, and rights-based approaches to Rule of Law—that have proven successful in the Western state-formation experience.

C. de Coning (✉)
Norwegian Institute of International Affairs, Oslo, Norway

Peacekeeping and Peacebuilding Unit, ACCORD, Durban, South Africa

C.T. Call
School of International Service, American University, Washington, DC, USA

C.T. Call, C. de Coning (eds.), *Rising Powers and Peacebuilding*, Rethinking Peace and Conflict Studies,
DOI 10.1007/978-3-319-60621-7_1

Over the last decade this shared understanding of peacebuilding has been significantly eroded. The belief in the transformative power of international peacebuilding has waned because many of the interventions undertaken over the preceding period, and especially those in the Balkans, Iraq, Afghanistan, and in Africa's Great Lakes and Horn regions, are widely understood to have been ineffective. It is increasingly less clear what type of problems, if any, can be resolved through international peacebuilding, and how intrusive and prescriptive such interventions should be (Richmond 2015).

Peacebuilding "successes" in Central America, Southern and West Africa, and the Balkans are plagued by problems such as criminal violence, corruption, political exclusion, or continued instability (Call and Wyeth 2008). The failure of peacebuilding to deliver sustained peace has combined with a push from rising powers against Western dominance, to produce a turn to the Global South as a source for more legitimate and effective responses to mass organized violence in the world.

At the same time, debates over and institutions associated with peacebuilding have become a central focus of post-conflict contestation. A United Nations (UN) Peacebuilding Commission created in 2005 is the sole UN organ where Northern and Southern UN member states come together to discuss peace and security issues outside of the General Assembly (Jenkins 2013). While parts of the UN's peacebuilding architecture, such as the UN Peacebuilding Fund, proved innovative and effective,[1] the performance overall of the UN's peacebuilding architecture has not met expectations (de Coning and Stamnes 2016). Two major UN reviews were undertaken in 2015, one taking stock of peace operations and the other assessing the peacebuilding architecture (Report of the High-Level Independent Panel on United Nations Peace Operations 2015; Advisory Group of Experts for the 2015 Review of the United Nations Peacebuilding Architecture 2015). Both shied away from embracing the concept of peacebuilding and instead opted for the new emerging but still vague concept of sustaining peace. As a result of these reviews, adjustments are being introduced to both the concept of peacebuilding and to how, especially, the UN Peacebuilding Commission functions.

Peacebuilding also emerged as an important new dimension in the negotiations over the post-2015 development agenda (Richmond and Tellidis 2013) and resulted in peacebuilding-related issues featuring in several of the goals of the new sustainable development goals of Agenda

2030, including especially in Goal 16, which aims to promote peaceful and inclusive societies for sustainable development, to provide access to justice for all, and to build effective, accountable, and inclusive institutions at all levels.

In another development, a group of 19 self-identified fragile states like East Timor and Liberia have been at the forefront of the New Deal (International Dialogue on Peacebuilding and Statebuilding 2017; Wyeth 2012, 7–12). It seeks to transform the way international assistance to these countries is managed by placing the countries themselves in the driver's seat when it comes to determining what causes their fragility, setting their own priorities, planning their own paths to resilience, and managing the relationship with their international partners.

Onto this stage new actors like the BRICS (Brazil, Russia, India, China, and South Africa) (de Coning et al. 2014) and a number of other prominent regional powers in the Global South like Indonesia and Turkey have emerged as new "donors" that advance their own political and technical approaches to peacebuilding (de Carvalho and de Coning 2013). Many of these countries have established development cooperation agencies that prioritize South-South technical assistance, new less conditional modes of operating, appropriate peer-provided guidance on political processes, and a celebration of national ownership and empowerment (Mawdsley 2012). These Southern approaches are seen by many as technically more appropriate and thus a further improvement to the liberal Western model (Chaturvedi et al. 2012). They are also seen as an alternative or antidote to dominant liberal approaches (Campbell et al. 2011). These approaches seem to answer the first of the two core deficiencies cited about current approaches: that they are Western dominated and that they ignore local contextual dynamics and opportunities.

Although there is a growing literature about the development roles and approaches of the rising powers, the research on their roles and approaches to peacebuilding is still underdeveloped. This book aims to make a contribution to this field because the entry of the rising powers into the peacebuilding field is likely to have significant implications for how the UN and other international and regional organizations, as well as both the traditional donors and the recipient countries, view peacebuilding in the future. Will the entry of the rising powers into the field of peacebuilding fundamentally alter how we understand and undertake peacebuilding a decade or more from now?

Our Aim with This Book

With this book, we seek to answer the following central question: What exactly is new and innovative about the peacebuilding approach of the rising powers from the Global South, and what are the implications of these new approaches for peacebuilding?

A number of related questions help to further inform our central question, such as: How are these rising powers changing the peacebuilding landscape? What influence are they having on the way the African Union (AU), Association of Southeast Asian Nations (ASEAN), European Union (EU), United Nations (UN), North Atlantic Treaty Organization (NATO), and traditional bilateral donors [Organization for Economic Cooperation and Development (OECD)] are approaching peacebuilding? To what degree does the engagement of rising powers with fragile states have peacebuilding objectives (theories of change aiming to influence relapse into violent conflict)? How do these rising powers differentiate between development and peacebuilding? How does the change model (theory of change) used by these rising powers differ from the Western liberal peacebuilding model? To what degree are peacebuilding projects undertaken by these rising powers locally grounded and owned? To what degree are their projects perceived to be successful by the recipient countries (people and governments)? What innovations, lessons learned, and best practices have come about as a result of the entry of the rising powers into the peacebuilding field? To what degree are these rising powers concerned with results, and what kind of monitoring and evaluation systems do they employ?

In our efforts to answer these questions, we provide a structured, critical analysis of the values, intent, and content of the peacebuilding initiatives of a number of rising powers. We compare them to one another and to the approaches of the UN and the EU. In our analysis, we offer new theoretical claims about the role of the Global South in peacebuilding, rooted in our empirical work on Somalia, Afghanistan, and Myanmar as well as on the specific policies and approaches of Brazil, India, Indonesia, South Africa, and Turkey.

Our Approach

We have selected five rising powers for this book, namely Brazil, India, Indonesia, South Africa, and Turkey. The rising power concept is ambiguous. All of these countries are regional powers, and some have been longstanding important or middle powers on the global stage. Some like Brazil have sought a more high-profile role over the past decade, whereas others like Indonesia have sought a low-profile role. We have opted to use the rising power concept as indicative of one of the characteristics that these countries have in common, that is their influence in the global order is increasing, or their influence (soft and hard power) has been on the rise. In some cases, such as Brazil and Turkey, domestic instability has caused turbulence for foreign policy as well. Yet the overall status of these countries as rising powers remains pertinent. This aspect is especially relevant in the context of this study in that their influence on peacebuilding is now starting to be felt. Up to now these countries had little or no influence on how peacebuilding was understood or practiced, apart from participating in debates at the UN, and even there, such debates were not initiated or framed by these countries.

Our hypothesis is that as their influence on global governance increases over time, their approaches to peacebuilding may significantly influence how peacebuilding will be understood and practiced in global governance in the future. If so, then what can we know now about how these countries understand and practice peacebuilding that may give us an indication of how they may influence the future of peacebuilding?

An alternative hypothesis we explore is that the rising powers' understanding and approach to peacebuilding may change as they engage more with peacebuilding in ways similar to that of the traditional donors. For instance, the more the rising powers engage in development cooperation type initiatives with the aim of contributing to international peace and security, the more they will come under pressure—domestically and internationally—to assess the effectiveness of their approach to peacebuilding. The rise of these countries may thus not only result in them influencing how peacebuilding is viewed as part of global governance in future, but the pressures and experiences of doing so may also influence how these countries themselves view and approach peacebuilding nationally. According to this hypothesis, the experience of taking up not just national responsibility but also international responsibility for global peace and security will influence the understanding of concepts like peacebuilding within the rising powers. It may result in their approaches to peacebuilding adjusting over time and arriving at a position that is much closer to where the traditional approach to peacebuilding is today than their current approaches. If so, we will explore if we can see any indications at this stage that would support such a maturing to a global responsibility hypothesis.

These specific countries have been selected to represent a sample of the rising power phenomenon. We are not making an argument that these countries are THE rising powers, but rather that they represent a sample, including leading examples of rising powers from Africa, Asia, Latin America, the Middle East, and South East Asia. Three of these countries—Brazil, India, and South Africa—are members of the BRICS, and three are also members of another South-South cooperation forum called IBSA (India, Brazil, and South Africa) (Abdenur et al. 2014; Piccone 2015; Stuenkel 2014). Countries like Brazil, South Africa, and Turkey are obviously important players in their regional context and have global impact on several issues, whilst India is among the major global economic and political actors.

Most of our contributors are researchers from these countries. We have consciously opted to select contributors that can assist the reader to understand these countries' approaches to peacebuilding in the context and narrative articulated by these countries themselves, rather than offer a Western interpretation. The book thus includes chapters on each of these countries—Brazil, India, Indonesia, South Africa, and Turkey—that explore how peacebuilding is understood in these countries, including in the context of their local experience, history, and culture. Each of these chapters also explains what kind of peacebuilding activities these countries undertake and discuss a few specific examples. In this way, the book will provide a more systematic understanding of the commonalities, differences, and heretofore unexposed patterns in the origins and shifts of rising powers' roles in peacebuilding.

Most of our contributors have worked extensively with (or inside) organizations like the UN and the AU, governments like India, South Africa, and the USA, non-governmental organizations, universities and think tanks, as well as in operations and programs in the field. This understanding of key audiences and actual peacebuilding and related activities has greatly facilitated the aim of helping infuse the learning and perspectives of these rising powers into global policies and practices, thereby recognizing that peacebuilding practice rests in multiple domains and levels.

The book explicitly wrestles with understanding the strategic goals and interests of these rising powers. Rather than making assumptions about the roles and motives of these countries on their new roles, the book explores the various complex motives and political divisions within these rising powers that drive their roles and approaches. Further, the book analyzes the multiple coalitions and actors within these countries, and their expressions in operations abroad offer an understanding of how much programs reflect national cultures or philosophical approaches. In addition, the book shows how ephemeral they may be depending on the government in power and its internal political calculations, and the bureaucratic politics of these countries' approaches. Without adopting strict public policy theoretical frameworks, the book interrogates these internal political and economic dimensions behind the rising powers' diverse and evolving roles in peacebuilding.

The fact that researchers from these rising powers critically interpret and analyze their own experiences ensures that the values, perspectives, and approaches of these rising powers are explicitly compared. Throughout the various chapters, our contributors explore the assumptions that underlie our chosen approaches, helping hone in on what exactly is distinctive and innovative about Northern and Southern approaches to peacebuilding.

In addition to the country chapters, the book also includes three case-study chapters. Our contributors have looked at Afghanistan, Myanmar, and Somalia as examples of countries where rising powers such as India, Indonesia, China, and Turkey have actively engaged in peacebuilding initiatives. We opted to use a "structured, focused" method for our case studies; through asking a common set of questions across the cases (George and Bennett 2005), this book provides a framework that enables comparison across the three case studies. This marks a shift from the contemporary single case study and ad hoc case study approach that dominates current research on peacebuilding.

Although there is no single "Western" or dominant template for peacebuilding, one may glean common characteristics of dominant multilateral institutions and bilateral donors. The EU approach is a good example of the traditional or established approach to peacebuilding as practiced by the donor countries that are members of the OECD. Through the OECD these countries have a codified approach to development assistance and peacebuilding, through agreed approaches such as the "The Principles for Good International Engagement in Fragile States and Situations".[2] In general, the approach of the UN Secretariat and of these European institutions can be characterized as top-down, institution-focused rather than process-focused, state-centric, and on a relatively short time horizon (Call and Collin 2015; Stamnes 2016). The policies and practices of many OECD bilateral donors also adhere to these traits, as well as conditionality on good governance. Powerful countries have thus far shaped how the concept and practice of peacebuilding are understood in the UN. Yet as the influence of the rising powers increases, the UN's understanding of and approach to peacebuilding offers a test or window into our competing hypotheses of whether rising powers will reshape the dominant multilateral and bilateral approaches, or whether they will, in turn, be shaped by the dominant approaches and discourse and come to resemble more conventional approaches.

How Do We Conceptualize Peacebuilding?

For the purposes of this book, we have opted to use a very broad understanding of peacebuilding. If not, we would have undermined our attempt to understand how the rising powers view peacebuilding by imposing a definition and approach to peacebuilding influenced by the traditional understanding and approach to peacebuilding. We have thus opted to use a broad understanding of peacebuilding to mean any deliberate program-like effort that has a conflict-resolution theory of change that is meant to influence preventing a lapse into violent conflict or to sustain peace.

We have considered using the UN definition(s) and approach to peacebuilding, as it represents a globally agreed concept, but we have found that there is a considerable gap between what many Member States view as the role of an international body like the UN when it comes to peacebuilding, and how they choose to deal with such issues domestically. For instance, whilst the USA engages in debates on peacebuilding at the UN, the concept is not prominently used domestically in the policies or approaches of the US government.

We have thus opted against using the UN definition for fear of contaminating our study of peacebuilding in the rising powers by imposing an external concept. Instead we have tasked our contributors to take a "bottom-up" approach and to seek out national concepts and understandings that approximate this broad theory of change approach to peacebuilding. Even this broad approach to peacebuilding has proven challenging at times. In our concluding analysis, we discuss these definitional and conceptual challenges in greater detail.

The Chapters that Follow

The first section of the volume presents national approaches to peacebuilding in their own contexts. The authors seek to describe, on their own terms, the national approaches to peacebuilding. Each researcher sought to specify what various national officials and other constituencies mean by the term "peacebuilding" and to identify what other terms are deployed in official documents and discourse that refer to bundle of activities that might in traditional circles be labeled "peacebuilding." In these analyses of national approaches, the authors sought to describe each approach as it has emerged and how it is bureaucratically circumscribed, in the terms of each country context. Each of these chapters was authored by researchers living in the country studied. These authors all conducted interviews with pertinent diplomatic and development officials, mainly in the capitals, but also in some cases in the missions to the UN in New York. Some of the authors of these analyses of national approaches also drew on field research in the countries where these operations are taking place.

This section begins with Abdenur and Call's analysis of Brazil, which has been among the more vocal and visible on peacebuilding policy in the UN and in fora of the Global South such as the India-Brazil-South Africa Dialogue Forum (IBSA) and the Community of Portuguese-Language Countries. It then moves to Alexandra's analysis of Indonesia, one of the newer actors in regional peacebuilding active especially in mediation facilitation in Southeast Asia. The next chapter by P. K. Singh details the long record of India in peacebuilding policy and activities from its earliest days as an independent country, explaining its strong emphasis on nationally owned, state-led development. Sazak and Woods' chapter on Turkey's role in peacebuilding reflects an expanded role in humanitarian diplomacy and its identity as a Muslim nation seeking to play a more active role in the Middle East. Finally, South African leadership seeking to support peace processes and post-conflict efforts in the continent, including peace operations, is the subject of Nyuykonge and Siphamandla's final chapter, among other national approaches to peacebuilding.

The second section of the book presents three case studies that illustrate the role of rising powers in specific countries in transition. Few people recognize India's role as the fifth largest donor in Afghanistan in the twenty-first century, and Sinha's chapter contrasts that role with the approach of traditional donors in that conflict-ridden country. The personal interest of then Prime Minister Recep Erdoğan in Somalia's strife helped Turkey take a prominent role in that country. Its humanitarian, mediation, and institution-building support helped define Turkey's approach to peacebuilding, as analyzed by Sazak and Woods in this case study. Finally, Indonesia, China, and other rising powers have been important supporters of Myanmar's transition to democracy and in efforts to address the diverse communal armed conflicts. The chapter by Alexandra and Lanteigne examines those peacebuilding efforts.

A concluding chapter analyzes these empirics, cataloging several common characteristics of what might be considered common to the diverse group of rising powers examined in this study. Some of the characteristics are stronger in some countries than others. Furthermore, we identify some of the important differences among rising powers' peacebuilding activities. These are important as they show how trends may evolve in different ways and reflect the various motives that underlie the relatively new engagement of rising powers as protagonists in peacebuilding efforts in partner countries. The conclusion also analyzes the influence rising powers' approaches have had on traditional institutions and their peacebuilding policies and practices.

Finally, we suggest some implications for theorizing about the broader political and strategic role of emerging or middle powers. As the number of armed conflicts rises and the numbers of their victims reach historic highs not seen since World War II, "peacebuilding" is an increasingly important arena for addressing global violence and its human consequences. It is also an important window on North-South relations in evolving global governance, including the identities of these countries on the world stage. As such, we anticipate that this analysis will contribute not just to policy debates about peacebuilding, but to theoretical discussions of global governance.

Notes

1. The editors, Charles T. Call and Cedric de Coning, have served in their personal capacities on the UN Secretary-General's Advisory Group for the UN Peacebuilding Fund. De Coning's term was from 2012 to 2015, while Call served two terms from 2012 to 2017.
2. In 2009 the Development Assistance Committee (DAC) of the OECD established a subsidiary body called the International Network on Conflict and Fragility (INCAF). Through INCAF, DAC members participated in the development of the New Deal for Engagement in Fragile States in partnership with the g7+, which is a voluntary association of 20 countries that are or have been affected by conflict, as well as civil society. This collaboration was done under the aegis of the International Dialogue on Peacebuilding and Statebuilding. See: http://www.oecd.org/dac/governance-peace/conflictfragilityandresilience/iefs.htm, accessed on July 1, 2016.

References

Abdenur, Adriana Erthal, Maiara Folly, Kayo Moura, Sergio A.S. Jordão, and Pedro Maia. 2014. The BRICS and the South Atlantic: Emerging Arena for South-South Cooperation. *South African Journal of International Affairs* 21(3): 303–319.

Advisory Group of Experts for the 2015 Review of the United Nations Peacebuilding Architecture. 2015. *The Challenge of Sustaining Peace*. New York: United Nations.

Call, Charles T., and Katy Collin. 2015. The United Nations Approach to Peacebuilding. Paper prepared for "Rising Powers and Peacebuilding" project. www.risingpowersandpeacebuilding.org

Call, Charles T., and Vanessa Wyeth, eds. 2008. *Building States to Build Peace*. Boulder, CO: Lynne Rienner.

Campbell, Susanna, David Chandler, and Meera Sabaratnam, eds. 2011. *A Liberal Peace?: The Problems and Practices of Peacebuilding*. London: Zed Books.

Chandler, David. 2012. Resilience and Human Security: The Post-interventionist Paradigm. *Security Dialogue* 43(3): 213–229.

Chaturvedi, Sachin, Thomas Fues, and Elizabeth Sidiropoulos. 2012. *Development Cooperation and Emerging Powers: New Partners Old Patterns?* London: Zed Books.

de Carvalho, Benjamin, and Cedric de Coning. 2013. *Rising Powers and the Future of Peacekeeping and Peacebuilding* (NOREF Report, 14). Oslo: Norwegian Peacebuilding Resource Centre.

de Coning, Cedric, and Eli Stamnes, eds. 2016. *UN Peacebuilding Architecture: The First 10 Years*. New York: Routledge.

de Coning, Cedric, Thomas Mandrup, and Liselotte Odgaard, eds. 2014. *BRICS and Coexistence: An Alternative Vision of World Order*. New York: Routledge.

George, Alexander L., and Andrew Bennett. 2005. *Case Studies and Theory Development in the Social Sciences*. Cambridge, MA: Massachusetts Institute of Technology Press.

High-Level Independent Panel on United Nations Peace Operations. 2015. *Uniting our Strengths for Peace: Politics, Partnership and People*. New York: United Nations.

International Dialogue on Peacebuilding and Statebuiding. 2017. A New Deal for Engagement in Fragile States. Factsheet available at http://www.pbsbdialogue.org/media/filer_public/07/69/07692de0-3557-494e-918e-18df00e9ef73/the_new_deal.pdf

Jenkins, Rob. 2013. *Peacebuilding: From Concept to Commission*. New York: Routledge.

Mawdsley, Emma. 2012. *From Recipients to Donors: Emerging Powers and the Changing Landscape*. London: Zed Books.

Piccone, Ted. 2015. *Five Rising Democracies*. Washington, DC: Brookings Institution Press.

Richmond, Oliver P. 2015. *After Liberal Peace: The Changing Concept of Peacebuilding*. RSIS Commentary No. 272. Singapore: S. Rajaratnam School of International Studies.

Richmond Oliver P., and Ioannis Tellidis. 2013. *The BRICS and International Peacebuilding and Statebuilding* (NOREF Report 1). Oslo: Norwegian Peacebuilding Resource Centre.

Stamnes, Eli. 2016. The European Union and Peacebuilding. Paper prepared for "Rising Powers and Peacebuilding" project. www.risingpowersandpeacebuilding.org

Stuenkel, Oliver. 2014. *India-Brazil-South Africa Dialogue Forum: The Rise of the Global South*. New York: Routledge.

Wyeth, Vanessa. 2012. Knights in Fragile Armor: The Rise of the 'G7+'. *Global Governance* 18(2): 7–12.

Cedric de Coning is Senior Research Fellow in the Peace and Conflict Studies Research Group at NUPI, and Senior Advisor on Peacekeeping and Peacebuilding for ACCORD.

Charles T. "Chuck" Call is Associate Professor of International Peace and Conflict Resolution, School of International Service, American University, Washington DC.

PART I

National Approaches to Peacebuilding

CHAPTER 2

A "Brazilian Way"? Brazil's Approach to Peacebuilding

Adriana Erthal Abdenur and Charles T. Call

Introduction

Since the early 2000s, Brazil has been a high-profile advocate of non-Western approaches to development cooperation, peace operations, and other initiatives related to peacebuilding. This avid support is associated primarily with the administration of President Lula Inácio da Silva (2003–2010). During this period, Brazil sought greater prominence on the international stage on several fronts. Brazil pressed for transformations in the multilateral system, including helping to create and then exercise leadership in fora such as the BRICS (Brazil, Russia, India, China, and South Africa) coalition and the IBSA (India, Brazil, and South Africa)

Adriana Erthal Abdenur is grateful to the Brazilian Council for Scientific and Technological Development (CNPq) and its Senior Postdoctoral Scholarship program for supporting this research through the Centro de Pesquisa e Documentação de História Contemporânea do Brasil (CPDOC) at Fundação Getúlio Vargas in Rio de Janeiro.

A.E. Abdenur (✉)
Fundação Getúlio Vargas, Rio de Janeiro, Brazil

C.T. Call
School of International Service, American University, Washington, DC, USA

C.T. Call, C. de Coning (eds.), *Rising Powers and Peacebuilding*, Rethinking Peace and Conflict Studies,
DOI 10.1007/978-3-319-60621-7_2

Dialogue Forum. It also worked to gain greater influence within the multilateral system, boosting its historic bid for a permanent seat on the UN Security Council and contesting United Nations (UN) securitization. Under Lula, Brazil almost tripled its development cooperation to $1.6 billion reais (USD$923 million at the time). Some 66.3% of this total was channeled through multilateral cooperation, and the remainder with bilateral efforts focusing on Latin America and Africa (IPEA 2011). This represented a significant surge and diversification in Brazil's role in development, including in many conflict-affected countries.

More broadly, during this period Brazil became more active in a variety of initiatives that can be considered to fall under the concept of peacebuilding. As part of its South-South development cooperation efforts, Brazil vastly expanded its technical cooperation with post-conflict countries such as Angola, Mozambique, Guinea-Bissau, and East Timor. It also sponsored and executed peace-related development projects to support the UN Stabilization Mission in Haiti (MINUSTAH), whose military command it held continuously for an unprecedented 12 years, starting in 2004. Both in its home region and beyond this vicinity, Brazil engaged in conflict mediation efforts, whether through regional organizations like the Union of South American States (UNASUR) or via ad hoc arrangements. At the UN, Brazil was instrumental in the creation of the UN Peacebuilding Architecture, and once established it assumed a broader leadership role at the Peacebuilding Commission, especially with respect to Guinea-Bissau. In UN normative debates, Brazil promoted peacebuilding as a complement and sometimes as an alternative to militarized approaches to peacekeeping, arguing that investing in political processes and socioeconomic development was essential to the promotion of peace.

This chapter describes the scope of, and trends in, Brazil's peacebuilding activities since the early 2000s, focusing on the eight-year Lula presidency and, to a lesser extent, its aftermath. It analyzes the broader context, key principles, and main mechanisms of Brazilian peacebuilding; identifies major patterns and trends; and notes some of the most important challenges and contradictions. In particular, we examine whether there is a "Brazilian" approach to peacebuilding and what its elements might be, as well as how that approach differs from dominant or Western principles and practices. The research is based on interviews conducted in mid-2015 and mid-2016 in Brasilia, Rio de Janeiro, and New York, as well as analysis of official documents from the UN and the Brazilian government.

We find that, although Brazilian stakeholders rarely use the term "peacebuilding" (in Portuguese, "*consolidação da paz*") outside UN debates, and while there is no single dedicated government agency guiding this engagement (and rather, a broad gamut of institutions whose efforts include peacebuilding activities), Brazilian efforts abroad constitute a loose but emergent approach to promoting stability and development in partner countries. Brazil has articulated clear principles of a peacebuilding approach that differs in policy and on-the-ground practice from those of Western donors. Nevertheless, Brazil's approach also shares some similarities with Western peacebuilding, both normatively and operationally. In the post-Lula years, two main elements—the economic downturn in Brazil and the political turmoil surrounding Rousseff's presidential impeachment—has reoriented Brazilian foreign policy, raising new questions about Brazil's ability to sustain its emerging role in peacebuilding.

Foundations of a Brazilian Approach to Peacebuilding

Brazil has no single document, such as a White Paper, outlining a policy framework for peacebuilding. The term *consolidação da paz*, in fact, is seldom used outside multilateral settings such as the UN and IBSA. Outside of those platforms, Brazil's approach to peacebuilding can be inferred from official speeches and statements, national security documents, diplomats' understandings, and actions along three fronts: development cooperation, international conflict mediation, and humanitarian assistance.

Despite the breadth of these initiatives, certain common principles underlie Brazil's approach to peacebuilding, and these concepts are frequently evoked by Brazilian diplomats and some academics in arguing that there is a distinct "Brazilian" approach to promoting peace and stability. While Brazilian officials and experts do not exclude the possibility that other countries embrace or reflect similar principles, they often defend the idea that these principles are based on Brazil's somewhat unique historical trajectories and experiences with peace and development, and that, as a result, Brazil's engagement with peacebuilding entails more equitable relations of power among stakeholders.

Historical Foundations

Although most initiatives that make up Brazil's peacebuilding have emerged in the past 15 years, the country's historical trajectory offers a source of inspiration for its current approach. Relevant here are (a) Brazil's status as a colony of Portugal that "shrugged off" empire and assumed independence with minimal violence; (b) its legacy as the largest slave importing state in the Americas, as well as the last nation in the Western world to abolish the practice; and (c) its position as a regional power that nurtures ambitions to become a global power yet remains sensitive to how its exercise of power in the hemisphere is perceived by its neighbors.

As a result of its own colonial experience, as well as its sheer size (Brazil is now the world's fifth largest country by territory and accounts for 48% of South America's territory), Brazil has repeatedly sought to reassure other countries in its vicinity that it would not abuse its vast geography to seek regional hegemony. According to the mainstream historiography, upon independence, in 1822, within its relations with other states Brazil adopted a "culture of pacifism" meant to prevent the newly formed sovereign country from being seen as imposing or intruding on its neighbors.[1] The 1934 constitution—which only lasted three years but was extremely influential in the drafting of subsequent constitutions—states that Brazil will "never engage in a war of conquest" and stipulates that war shall not be launched until arbitration is exhausted (Constituicao 1934). Similarly, textbooks stress the country's non-military approaches to foreign engagement—leitmotifs that have carried into contemporary discourses of foreign policy.[2] There were some early territorial wars against neighboring countries, especially over the Cisplatine province (which became, with British mediation, independent Uruguay in 1928), and coercive diplomacy was used with Bolivia and Argentina during territorial disputes. Internally, there were a handful of revolts in the Southern and Northern regions (including the Canudos War, a popular-messianic uprising that was crushed by the Brazilian Army in 1897). Despite these incidents, the country managed to avoid major interstate conflicts and, as a result, the country's pacifist mythology emphasizes that Brazil has never launched a war.[3]

Despite its relatively peaceful trajectory in defining its borders, and although the country's population is historically diverse, Brazil has a far less harmonious history when it comes to issues of ethnicity and race. The formation of Brazil as a people was the result of violent processes (Ribeiro 1995). The colonial state exterminated and marginalized indigenous people and, even after the formal end of slavery, its "whitening" immigration policies favored Europeans. Over a century of institutional denial of racial and ethnic differences has led to unacknowledged deep inequalities and discrimination that are most visible in the country's contemporary high rates of violence (a 2013 UNODC study showed that Brazil had 25.2 homicides per 1,00,000 people, among the highest in the world)

(UNODC 2013). As a result, despite its official discourse of pacifism and harmony, Brazil's internal contradictions sometimes belie the rhetoric of peace and stability that officials and others draw upon in legitimizing Brazil's role in peacebuilding. The same can be said of the country's turbulent history with democracy, with several periods of repressive military regime (including from 1964 to 1985) and a political trajectory marred by presidential coups and countercoups.

The Post–World War II Period

During the Cold War, and especially when the country was under military rule, Brazilian foreign policy largely aligned with that of the USA, even as Brazil retained its membership in the G77 and was among the most active states fighting for the inception of the UN Conference on Trade and Development (UNCTAD). Although Brazil has never been a member of Non-Aligned Movement (NAM), it has followed many of the group's initiatives as an observer, and there are strong parallels in Brazil's discourse of solidarity and that of the movement. This ambivalence in Brazilian foreign policy toward the rest of the developing world—and its resulting policy shifts—also characterized Brazil's stance toward the struggle against colonialism in the mid-twentieth century. As Portugal's empire was collapsing in the early 1970s, Brazil—which previously had mostly stood by Portugal's position against the independence of African states in UN debates—began supporting decolonization in Angola, Mozambique, and other Lusophone colonies (Pinheiro 2007). Thereafter, Brazil's foreign policy placed an even stronger emphasis on non-intervention and peaceful approaches to resolving conflict.

Outside of its immediate vicinity, Brazil engaged in issues of international security by becoming an early contributor to UN peacekeeping missions, starting with the first mission (UNEF I, in Sinai) in 1956. This participation launched a long-term commitment to UN peacekeeping, although troop contributions have varied over time; to date, Brazil has participated in more than 50 peacekeeping operations and related missions, having contributed over 33,000 military officials, police officers, and civilians (Brazilian Ministry of Foreign Affairs). This participation reflects Brazilian foreign policy's longstanding commitment to multilateralism, particularly via the UN.

Toward the end of the Cold War, even as Brazil underwent a gradual transition from military to civilian rule, it worked with Argentina to overcome a deep historical rivalry that had culminated in both countries attempting to develop nuclear weapons. The two sides successfully resolved their tensions by deepening political and economic ties (for instance, via Mercosur) and voluntarily dismantling their nuclear weapons programs, while maintaining their peaceful elements. The 1991 establishment of the Brazilian-Argentine Agency for Accounting and Control of Nuclear Materials (ABACC), a bilateral safeguards agency, marked an innovative way of institutionalizing peaceful conflict resolution between the two states and avoiding regional tensions (de Quieroz 2016). The resulting warming of ties between the two countries is often cited by Brazilian diplomats as a way of boosting Brazil's credentials in conflict prevention and resolution (Patriota and Timerman 2011).

The Post–Cold War Period

With the end of the Cold War, Brazil relied even more heavily on multilateral platforms to expand its role in international peace and security, not only through the UN but also via regional platforms such as Mercosur and, more recently, UNASUR, which was created in 2008.[4] Especially in Africa, Brazil has been active in peacebuilding through the Community of Portuguese-Language Countries (CPLP). And, since the 2000s, it helped to create new coalitions of rising powers, such as IBSA and the BRICS. Working through multilateral institutions not only provides Brazil with added legitimacy in peacebuilding, it also helps to extend its reach geographically, since other members sometimes engage in peacebuilding efforts in countries where Brazil's bilateral relations are relatively weak.

This predilection for multilateralism has been essential to understanding Brazilian efforts to promote democracy and human rights abroad. Brazil has historically eschewed direct engagement in promotion of democracy and human rights in other countries because this practice is sometimes associated with Western powers' self-interested and selective efforts, which have often yielded counterproductive outcomes. However, Brazil engages in democracy and human rights promotion when a specific demand arises via a multilateral forum, including the Organization of American States (OAS), UNASUR, and the CPLP.

Brazil has, on occasion, tried to boost its role in mediation of conflicts in South America. In 1995, it worked with the USA, Chile, and Argentina to mediate the brief border conflict between Peru and Ecuador, the Cenepa War (Biato 1999). The ensuing 1998 peace agreement, the Brasília Presidential Act, was definitive in establishing the formal demarcation of the border, putting an end to one of the longest territorial disputes in the Western Hemisphere. Despite these examples, Brazil's engagement in conflict mediation within its own region has remained sporadic and selective.

The Core Principles of Brazilian Peacebuilding

The early 2000s witnessed a new, concerted effort by Brazil to engage on peacebuilding issues. The figure of Lula was central to this surge. A former factory worker and union leader who was imprisoned briefly by the military dictatorship, Lula led the socialist Workers Party for 14 years through the country's transition from authoritarianism. Elected based on a coalition representing urban workers, peasants, and the lower middle classes, Lula sought to transform Brazil into a more equitable society while using foreign policy to boost development and expand the country's influence abroad, including in international security issues.

In foreign policy, Lula's government frequently drew on domestic policy initiatives as inspirations to combat poverty and hunger globally. To this end, the Brazilian government promoted a discourse of solidarity and horizontality, presenting its South-South development cooperation efforts as devoid of the power asymmetries resulting from Europe and the USA's colonial and imperial legacies in much of the developing world. In 2013, the director of ABC [a Brazilian Cooperation Agency, a division of the Ministry for External Relations (MRE)] underscored the principles believed to differentiate Brazil's approach from those of donors and established multilateral organizations:

> The policy of Brazilian cooperation is based on international solidarity [...] we react to the demands (we don't have previously prepared projects to be presented to partners). [...]The principle of South-South cooperation that we follow is that of no conditionality, which is the non-linkage between technical cooperation and pursuit of economic and commercial goals and benefits or concessions in areas of services in exchange for cooperation. [Another principle Brazil respects is the] non-interference or non-intromission in internal affairs. (de Abreu 2013)

These principles—solidarity, demand-driven cooperation, non-conditionality, and non-interference—are invoked by Brazilian diplomats as the hallmarks of a distinct "Brazilian way." In addition, the Lula administration emphasized national ownership of development cooperation projects abroad as part of the country's respect for sovereignty. However, some have criticized Brazil's solidarity as strictly targeting other governments (regardless of type of regime) and of equating "national" ownership with "government" decision-making, as opposed to more participatory processes that would include non-governmental and opposition voices in partner states (Abdenur and Marcondes 2016). Other traits of what might be termed a "Brazilian way" include Brazilians' proclivity for closeness to people in local communities abroad (a point that is often stressed with respect to Brazilian peacekeepers), emphasis on economic programs and job generation in post-conflict countries, and reliance on development cooperation rather than on aid.

Some of these principles resonated with, and were in turn reinforced by, Lula's initiatives in global coalition-building, especially with other rising powers. The creation of coalitions like IBSA, which brings together three diverse democracies, and the BRIC (which in 2011 expanded to include South Africa and became known as BRICS), reflected both a desire to transform the international system into a more multilateral configuration and an aspiration to open up more space for Brazil's own possibilities abroad. The BRICS adopted a highly contestatory discourse vis-à-vis certain components and norms of the established global governance architecture, and began to deepen cooperation and coordinate some positions, especially on issues related to economic cooperation and development financing. The coalition acquired a greater degree of institutionalization by launching new institutions, such as the BRICS New Development Bank (NDB) (BRICS 2014). The NDB is meant not only to help fill the gargantuan demand for infrastructure financing in the developing world, but also to place further pressure on established institutions like the Bretton Woods organizations to undertake serious reform in their decision-making processes. The new institution is relevant to peacebuilding because, at a normative level, the bank reinserts infrastructure investment at the heart of development debates, including within conflict-affected areas.

Despite its visibility, the BRICS and IBSA are not the only informal coalitions on Brazil's rising power agenda. The G20, initially launched in 1999, became more important to Brazilian foreign policy in the 2000s as a high table for global governance and economic policy. On a far lesser scale, Brazil also helped to establish and expand bi-regional summits such as the Summit of South American-Arab Countries and the Africa-South America Summit. Brazil's role in these various informal coalitions of states, which helped to expand its influence across the Global South, was decisive and influential for its peacebuilding initiatives in part because they granted Brazil greater legitimacy in engaging in a wider variety of contexts.

Within the UN System, this contestatory tone translated into demands for organizational reforms, including changes to the Security Council that would guarantee Brazil a permanent, veto-wielding seat on the UN Security Council. In this respect, Brazil has sought alignments beyond rising powers. For instance, starting in the mid-2000s, the country joined Germany, Japan, and India in the G-4, whose members seek a more democratic Council that would reflect contemporary interstate relations rather than the aftermath of World War II (Brazilian Ministry of Foreign Affairs). Although these countries helped prompt the formation of a High-Level Panel on UN Reform in 2004, its recommendations for broadening the Council's membership were not acted upon. As a Brazilian diplomat in Brasília put it, "This failure to reform added to the palpable sense of frustration among [us], thus strengthening the resolve to launch alternative routes outside the UN architecture, especially through the loose coalitions of rising powers."[5]

Nevertheless, at the UN Brazil engaged more directly in key normative debates about security and development. At the UN Security Council, where Brazil occupied a non-permanent seat in 2004–2005 and in 2010–2011 (making it, along with Japan, the member state that has occupied such a position the most times in UN history), (Ministry of Foreign Affairs) Brazil argued that the UN has neglected its original focus on conflict prevention and post-conflict reconstruction in favor of heavy-handed military interventionism, whether led by North Atlantic Treaty Organization (NATO) or otherwise. As one Brazilian diplomat states,

> In general terms the UN has focused too much on the pillar of peace and security versus development. Decisions have been toward militarized solutions.... In our view, peacekeeping and peacebuilding shouldn't be sequenced, but should be dealt with together, in tandem. When dealing with a post-conflict situation, one must deal with the causes of the conflict—institutional, political, social and environmental. (Patriota 2011)

These sentiments reflect the foreign policy principles encoded in the 1988 federal constitution, such as non-intervention, self-determination, international cooperation, and the peaceful settlement of conflicts—principles that had long guided Brazil's positions at the UN. Back in the early 1990s, for instance, Brazil proposed that the UN Secretariat produce an "Agenda for Development" to complement the influential "Agenda for Peace" published by Boutros Boutros-Ghali in 1992 (Vigevani and Cepaluni 2012). However, under Lula Brazil placed greater emphasis on the transformative agenda. When chairing the Security Council in 2011, Brazil chose to focus a debate on "security and development." Brazil emphasized the interconnectedness of these aims as reflected in the presidential statement (PRST) that the Security Council adopted: "The Security Council underlines that security and development are closely interlinked and mutually reinforcing and key to attaining sustainable peace" (President of UN Security Council 2011). The statement also recognized and called for strengthening the links between peacekeeping and early peacebuilding.

One Brazilian diplomat reflected on Brazil's efforts:

> I see that [PRST] statement as the culmination and heyday of a process of thinking about peacekeeping and peacebuilding in Brazil. From 2002 to 2011, we were learning how to be norm-setters in the international community. Haiti was formative in conceptual development but also in the coalition-building element. We learned how to twist arms to have our concepts included in the Council's resolutions.[6]

Similarly, Brazil's 2012 attempt to temper the principle of Responsibility to Protect (R2P) by proposing the concept of Responsibility while Protecting (RwP)—despite never gained significant traction—demonstrates Brazil's occasional willingness to make high-profile proposals for alternatives to Western approaches. It also shows that Brazil's primary platform for engaging with international security and peacebuilding, at least at a normative level, remains the UN. We now turn to how these broader concepts and principles play out in practice in Brazil's peacebuilding efforts.

Brazil's Peacebuilding in Practice

UN Peace Missions

When Brazil assumed the leadership of the military component of MINUSTAH, in 2004, the move represented a significant step up in its commitments to UN peacekeeping. That engagement became even more complex after the 2010 earthquake created a humanitarian crisis superimposed on an already highly unstable setting. Even before the disaster, Brazil was the single largest troop contributor country to MINUSTAH, as well as a part of the core group of countries in Port-au-Prince and in the "Group of Friends of Haiti" in New York. Brazil saw the Haiti mission as a chance to initiate an alternative approach to UN peacekeeping—in essence, a more peacebuilding-oriented approach. As one Brazilian diplomat said, "This was key in Haiti: how do we make it different? Our assessment was that the US effort in the 1990s was a failure because it invested too much in the military and not enough in development and capacities."[7]

Brazil pressed for authorization to use UN peacekeeping funds, generally restricted to funding peacekeepers and their operational needs, on development and peacebuilding-oriented programs in Haiti. As another diplomat reported, "In the Security Council and in the fifth [budget] committee, we pushed for quick-impact projects [QIPs] and community violence programs for Haiti." The UN allocated approximately USD$5 million annually to these QIPs (Ministry of Foreign Affairs). In one example that combined elements of development and peacebuilding, the "Light and Security" initiative, coordinated by Brazilian troops, installed solar lampposts in the most vulnerable parts of the capital, making those areas safer at night (UN Brazil 2013).

The Brazilian Corps of Engineers also helped to perforate wells, build bridges and dams, and carried out slope stabilization in landslide-prone areas (Ministry of Foreign Affairs 2014). One Brazilian diplomat reported that, in Haiti, "Our military engineers pushed the boundaries. The UN Secretariat wouldn't let us repair roads too far from the battalion base [i.e., not required for MINUSTAH operational needs], so we brought in our own asphalt manufacturing capability and used Embassy funds to pay for road repairs elsewhere."[8] In many of these initiatives, Brazilian troops built upon the development-oriented activities that the Brazilian Armed Forces carry out domestically, for instance in remote areas of the Amazon and border regions.

In a somewhat usual arrangement, in Haiti the Brazilian government also created a partnership with Viva Rio, a Rio-based NGO that had specialized in community peacebuilding and disarmament in urban Brazil, to carry out humanitarian and development initiatives in areas of Haiti that had been strongly affected by the earthquake and ensuing crisis. For instance, Viva Rio coordinated a reconciliation program in which it helped mediate between the Haitian national police and leaderships from different parts of Bel Air, Cité Soleil and Delmas. Viva Rio also received MINUSTAH financing to carry out sports (including *capoeira*) and culture (such as Carnaval celebrations) in strengthening this mediation initiative (Viva Rio 2015). At the same time, the Brazilian government provided bilateral technical cooperation in social policy areas like public health, agriculture, energy, and capacity-building. Through these different arrangements, Brazil worked to complement the military role in MINUSTAH with initiatives that would promote social well-being and stability in the long term.

Brazilian diplomats and analysts identify specific differences in the country's approach to peacekeeping that have led some to refer to the "Brazilian way." First among these is the warm conviviality of Brazilian culture, including the open and friendly manner of its soldiers in dealing with the Haitian population. Many Brazilian solders come from the poor favelas and communities that share traits with the most difficult communities in Haiti, and many are similarly dark-skinned, despite Brazil's complicated race relations. Related to this cultural affinity was Brazil's early decision to deploy its forces with greater contact and proximity to the populations, especially in shantytown communities like Bellaire and Cité Soleil considered to have been taken over by politicized criminal gangs opposed to the government. One analyst described a decision that, when Brazil's troops entered Bellaire in 2006, they would remove their sunglasses, look into the eyes of the people, and—in contrast to the Jordanian units—get out of their armored personnel carriers (APCs) and walk in the streets and converse with the population.[9] In addition, Brazilian forces announced their entry into the community a few days prior, letting the criminal gang leaders leave and granting Brazilian troops non-confrontational entry and continued presence in these communities. Brazil followed up these operations with social programs. Numerous analysts have evaluated and documented the more positive reaction of the inhabitants of these communities to the Brazilian units over earlier troops.

Brazil's approach in Haiti, including in Bellaire, was neither uniform nor unproblematic. Despite the discourse on Brazilian conviviality and ease in integrating with locals, its participation in MINUSTAH has not been without critics. Some note that there is a feedback loop between Brazilian security forces' heavy-handed presence in (or incursions into) the favelas in Rio and the peacekeeper's approach to urban gangs in Haiti (Muller 2016). Certain Brazilian observers have criticized the insufficient coordination among stakeholders in Haiti, including Brazil (Hirst 2010).

Others have also noted that, as a result of its Haiti's engagement, Brazil's approach to peacebuilding often relies on a heavy military component and an uneasy or incomplete relationship with both Brazilian and local civil society actors. The same can be said of Brazil's humanitarian efforts, in which Brazilian civil society and its official engagement with local non-government actors is minimal, if at all present.

Aside from Haiti and East Timor, most conflict-affected countries that Brazil has engaged with lie in Africa (Santos and Cravo 2014). During the 2000s, in particular, Brazilian peacebuilding initiatives expanded on the continent as part of Lula's broader drive to increase Brazil's presence in, and relevance to, Africa, especially the Sub-Saharan countries. Lula engaged in a highly visible presidential diplomacy, making 33 country-visits to partner states in the continent. He opened 19 embassies in the continent. His speeches tended to underscore the idea of solidarity and kinship, stressing that Brazil had a moral debt to Africa due to the heavy influence of African slavery on Brazilian society.

Development Cooperation

In its efforts to expand Brazilian cooperation with partner nations, the Lula government significantly broadened technical expert cooperation, especially in Africa and Latin America, with a focus on social policy areas such as tropical agriculture, public education and public health. During the eight years of his two-mandate presidency, Lula visited 27 African countries, opening and reopening embassies around the continent (Peixoto 2010). Brazil's expanded development and peacebuilding efforts reflected not just ideological commitments to South-South solidarity, but also a pragmatic recognition that Brazil's ambitions to transform global power would require the political support of many countries of the global South.

Brazil branded itself a policy innovator in policy areas like public health, education, and tropical agriculture, framing its own development experiences as more similar to those of partner countries than those of traditional donors. Most of this technical cooperation is coordinated by the Brazilian cooperation agency (ABC), a division of the Ministry for External Relations (MRE). The ABC's annual budget grew from 18.7 million reais in 2006 to 52.26 million in 2010, the last year of Lula's second mandate (Ministry of Foreign Affairs). In 2009 alone, half the budget was spent in African countries, while 23% was spent in South America, 12% in Central America and the Caribbean, and 15% in Asia—illustrating that Brazil's technical cooperation portfolio was not driven entirely by regional considerations (Ministry of Foreign Affairs).

The ABC coordinates works with the implementing institutions (mostly other ministries or associated institutions, such as Fiocruz, the public health institution attached to the Ministry of Health, and Embrapa, the public agriculture research and development company affiliated with the Ministry of Agriculture. Less frequently, ABC partners with non-governmental institutions like SENAI (National Service for Industrial Learning) to carry out vocational and professional education programs abroad, but local civil society entities are rarely directly involved in Brazil's technical cooperation initiatives. Although Brazil still lacks a legal framework for regulating its international development cooperation (or humanitarian assistance, examined below), its project portfolio diversified considerably during Lula's two mandates, both geographically and thematically. It also came to incorporate more trilateral cooperation arrangements, whether with donor states [for instance, Japanese International Cooperation Agency (JICA)] or with multilateral platforms like the European Union or IBSA (Brazilian agency for cooperation, Ministry of Foreign Affairs).

The majority of cooperation projects involve sending Brazil-based experts from those institutions on short missions abroad to share knowledge and experiences with their counterparts in partner states, typically drawing inspiration from initiatives inspired by Brazil's domestic experiences. This approach means that Brazilian technical cooperation lacks the thick middle layer of "development experts" that populate other countries' donor agencies and international organizations, as Brazil's providers hold expertise in their given technical field much more than in the transmission of those skills in foreign contexts. While this approach generates few knowledge-generating mechanisms and less institutional memory, it also reduces bureaucracy and some expenses, for instance the maintenance of offices and personnel abroad.

At the same time, during the Lula years Brazil expanded its humanitarian role abroad. Within the Ministry of External Relations, a separate division was created in 2004, the General Coordination of Humanitarian Cooperation and Fight against Hunger (CGFOME). The division was tasked with coordinating Brazil's humanitarian assistance, much of which focused on agricultural and nutritional issues via financial and grain donations to UN agencies and programs, as well as specific initiatives undertaken in partnership with other government divisions, such as the Ministries of Health, Defense, and Agriculture. From 2006 to 2015, Brazil channeled humanitarian assistance to 96 countries in Latin America, Africa, Asia, and the Middle East (Ministry of Foreign Affairs 2016).

There were some exceptions to this pattern of periodic missions, both in Mozambique and therefore part of broader efforts to foment stability in this post-conflict state: The first was a factory meant to produce medicine locally, especially anti-retrovirals for HIV/AIDS. The second was a triangular cooperation project, undertaken in collaboration with the JICA, to transform large swaths of Mozambique into a corridor for export-oriented production of commodities (Suyama and Pomeroy 2015). Both these projects ran into problems of scale and financing and, in the case of ProSavana, met resistance by local as well as Brazilian civil society actors. These examples have made some Brazilian diplomats and specialists form the implementing agencies reluctant to take on ambitious, costly projects abroad.

The most strategic initiatives in these settings have become labeled as "structuring projects" (*projetos estruturantes*), and they are meant to build individual and institutional capacity to catalyze sector-wide reform inspired by Brazilian policy models. For instance, Fiocruz has been engaged in the creation and expansion of national public health schools that draw inspiration not only on Brazil's own public health schools, but also on the SUS, its public health system, which is based on Brazil's constitutional right to universal access to free health care. Through these structuring projects, Brazil seems to offer state-led alternatives to models promoted by Western donors and major international organizations. However, in some instances they are implemented with little attention to local civil society, which contrasts to the very origins of those systems back in Brazil. For instance, the SUS itself resulted as much from grassroots activism during Brazil's redemocratization in the 1980s as from government efforts. As a result, when such models are used as inspiration for post-conflict settings like Mozambique and Angola, they may run into difficulties resulting from the "political disembeddedness" of the cooperation projects, which do not take into account the role of local civil society (Abdenur and Marcondes 2016).

Brazil's peacebuilding has also included economic cooperation, including via trade and investments (particularly infrastructure), which are viewed as necessary for triggering growth in partner states and essential for post-conflict reconstruction. For instance, although starting from a relatively low base in absolute numbers, there were efforts under Lula to both intensify and diversify Brazil's commercial exchanges with African states. These flows were mostly comprised of Brazil exporting manufactures and semi-processed goods and importing from Africa commodities. In addition, there was an expansion of Brazilian investments in Africa, especially by large companies—either state-affiliated ones like the oil company Petrobras or the airplane manufacturer Embraer, or private ones like Odebrecht, Camargo Corrêa, and other Brazil-based multinationals specializing in infrastructure construction. The mining purchased major concessions and planned large investments around Africa. Some of these companies' investments were partially financed by the Brazilian National Development Bank (BNDES), which created special credit lines for export incentives and even opened a regional office in Johannesburg to help coordinate these ties (BNDES 2013).

Within Africa, Brazil has engaged most deeply, although sporadically, in Guinea-Bissau. Many of the strengths, and contradictions, of Brazilian peacebuilding are evident in this case. At the UN, Brazil has long acted on behalf of Guinea-Bissau, trying to call attention from the international community to the country's problems, which concern not just recurring political instability but also chronic underdevelopment. Even as Brazil was a very active participant in the creation of the UN peacebuilding architecture, including the Peacebuilding Commission (PBC), it continued to work via the UN and the CPLP to garner resources and political dedication to trying to solve Guinea-Bissau's instability and poverty. Once the PBC was established, Brazil assumed the leadership of the Country-Specific Configuration for Guinea-Bissau, through which it has tried to mobilize political solutions, especially by helping to coordinate the role of regional states and ECOWAS in preventing further coups-d'état in Guinea-Bissau (Abdenur and Marcondes Neto 2014). After the April 2012 coup, Ambassador Antonio Patriota undertook fact-finding missions to the country, strengthened communications about Guinea-Bissau between the PBC and the UNSC (where Guinea-Bissau competes for attention with more severe crises), and was highly proactive in working with ECOWAS to prevent spillovers from the crisis (UN Secretary General Report on Peacebuilding in Guinea-Bissau 2015).

Brazil has also tried to implement bilateral cooperation efforts in Guinea-Bissau, ranging from the construction of a security forces training center to technical cooperation in areas like education and agriculture, particularly with a view to helping diversify the country's economy away from its narrow reliance on the cashew nut cash crop (Brazilian Agency for Cooperation 2012). Finally, Brazil has invested heavily in trying to boost

Guinea-Bissau's electoral system and human rights institutions, but the recurrence of coups in Bissau attests to the limitations of Brazil's approach and, more broadly, of the efforts by the broader international community.

International Conflict Mediation

Brazil also tried to expand its role in international mediation, which historically had been largely limited to South America, for instance in the successful efforts to mediate a brief border conflict (the Cenepa War) between Ecuador and Peru in 1995. In the 2000s, Brazil became more willing to engage in international conflict mediation outside its own region. For instance, in 2007, Brazil was the only Latin American country to be invited to the Middle East peace conference in Annapolis, on the Palestine-Israel peace process. Yet the most visible and controversial such attempt involved a collaboration with Turkey and the USA to temper growing tensions surrounding Iran's nuclear program. These efforts culminated in a 2010 agreement signed by Iran, Brazil and Turkey, whereby Iran would send low-enriched uranium to Turkey in exchange for enriched fuel for Iran's nuclear research reactor (CFR 2010). The deal was not implemented for a variety of reasons, including the withdrawal of US support, and the outcome made Brazilian diplomats a bit more reluctant to engage in such high-level mediation attempts. However, the experience did not stop Brazil (under Dilma Rousseff) from working through IBSA in an attempt to mediate the intensifying conflict in Syria; in August 2011, the three countries sent ministerial delegations to Damascus and were met there by President Bashir al-Assad, who promised (in vain) that his regime would act to stop the escalation of violence (Ministry of Foreign Affairs 2011).

Points of Tension

However, Brazil's peacebuilding is also marked by some points of tension between its discourse and practice. For instance, to some analysts, Brazil's longstanding commitment to non-intervention seemed to come into contradiction with its participation in MINUSTAH, a Chapter VII mission (although the Brazilian government argued that only one chapter of Resolution 1542, which created the Multinational Interim Force, was based on Chapter VII, rather than the whole resolution; Fishel and Sáenz 2007). Another point over which Brazilian peacebuilding has been criticized is that of insufficient transparency and accountability of initiatives. Although IPEA, the government think tank, has been in charge of collecting data on different aspects of Brazil's South-South cooperation, the government institutions that are invited to open up their data do so voluntarily (IPEA 2011).

More broadly, the MRE in particular has been reluctant to adopt monitoring and evaluation practices because these are considered by some Brazilian cooperation specialists to have a heavily Western bent, especially when associated with the practices of donor countries and the Organisation for Economic Co-operation and Development (OECD). However, recognizing the need for more systematic planning that establishes benchmarks for both process and outcome-based evaluations, ABC in 2016 began considering the possibility of developing "homegrown" M&E practices. It is worth noting that the public institutions from which Brazil's South-South cooperation experts are drawn, such as Fiocruz and Embrapa, have robust mechanisms for M&E that are applied to projects domestically, and that these toolboxes have not been implemented abroad partly due to the low institutionalization of Brazilian peacebuilding, but also due to political resistance.[10] At any rate, part of objective of this technical cooperation is political—the maintenance of good diplomatic relations, an element that is not readily captured by traditional M&E processes.

Also on the flip side, Brazilian arms companies like Taurus also benefitted from expanding African markets (and indirectly, from African conflicts and instability) to boost their sales of arms and military equipment, including some, such as cluster bombs, that had been banned under UN regimes. In 2013, Brazilian exports transferred some USD$10 million in small arms and accessories alone to other countries (Small Arms Survey 2014). As with other major arms-exporting countries, these transfers sometimes undermine Brazil's peacebuilding credentials abroad.

The Retraction in Brazil's Peacebuilding

Despite their close political relationship during Lula's presidency, the transition from Lula to his former chief of staff, Dilma Rousseff, saw a noticeable shift in foreign policy. Rousseff seemed to take little interest in issues of foreign policy, aside from commercial and investment relations, and her presidential diplomacy reflected this relative lack of attention (in her five and a half years of presidency, she only visited three African states, for instance—South Africa, Angola, and Mozambique). There were also strained relations between the presidency and the MRE, with abrupt switches of foreign ministers on two occasions. Although Brazilian diplomats (who are overwhelmingly career professionals) provided some continuity to political and cooperation efforts, for instance Brazil's commitment to the BRICS, there was a considerable retraction in high-visibility engagement, both in South-South Cooperation and in relations with the North. As one Brazilian diplomat remarked in 2015 about the country's role at the UN, "We learned how to be agenda makers. Now maybe we are rolling back that role."[11] Brazil's global role was also complicated by damaged US-Brazilian relations after Wikileaks documents showed widespread cyberespionage by the US government against Brazilian companies and political leaders, including the president herself.

This foreign policy shift and its economic context—a combination of falling prices in key commodities and ineffective policies—have had concrete repercussions for Brazil's peacebuilding efforts. By 2014, the Brazilian government faced serious economic challenges, as GDP growth dropped from a peak of 7.5 in 2010 to below 1% in 2014. As a recession ensued, wide budget cuts were made, including to the MRE. These cuts affected not only Brazil's South-South development cooperation at ABC, but also the day-to-day operation of its embassies and other diplomatic representations abroad. According to one source, the budget of the CGFOME dropped precipitously from 2010 to 2014.

When the Brazilian Congress first voted to impeach President Rousseff, in spring 2016, Vice President Michel Temer became an interim president and appointed José Serra, a São Paulo politician and former presidential candidate from the opposition party PSDB, as a foreign minister. In his inaugural speech, Serra indicated that the Temer government would stress different priorities than the two preceding Workers Party-led governments, notably by deemphasizing the role of South-South cooperation and seeking to deepen ties to the USA and Western Europe. Temer's government indicated that it wished to tone down the anti-Western rhetoric of both Lula and Rousseff and to deepen ties to the OECD and to northern countries (Ministry of Foreign Affairs 2016). Discussions began within Brazil about phasing out the country's role in MINUSTAH, although some have noted that such a retraction would deeply impact Brazil's visibility in international peacekeeping unless troop contributions to other UN missions were made. However, the discussions have not yet yielded a concrete plan. At the same time, some restructuring within the MRE has generated new sources of uncertainty. In August 2016, after the presidential impeachment had been completed, the government announced that the

CGFOME had been permanently closed. Although its humanitarian assistance initiatives were reallocated to ABC and the Social Policy division, this restructuring signaled the Temer government's non-prioritization of Brazil's role in humanitarian action (Valente 2016).

Although it is too soon to say what the mid- to long-term effects of the new government's reorientation will be, deep uncertainty surrounds Brazil's future role in peacebuilding, especially outside of the UN. Brazil's engagement with peacebuilding follows an arc—a steep surge followed by a seemingly, equally steep decline in its engagement abroad. This variation raises broader questions about how vulnerable the rising power's newfound roles in peacebuilding are to political winds and economic downturns. The low degree of institutionalization and questionable commitment of the state to these recent initiatives make their sustainability unclear.

Conclusion

In its peacebuilding engagement, which peaked in the 2000s, Brazil pursued both bilateral and multilateral avenues. However, in comparison with other large rising powers like China, Russia, Indonesia, India, and Turkey, much of Brazil's engagement has taken place through multilateral institutions—not only the UN, but also informal coalitions such as the G20, BRICS, and IBSA. This option reflects the central role that multilateralism has played in Brazilian diplomacy, including the belief that collective, UN-sanctioned initiatives tend to be the most legitimate course of action.

Despite the discourse of demand-driven initiatives, Brazil's peacebuilding is motivated by a combination of interests and identity. While the country's history, including its constitutional landmarks, have established a set of principles that serve as more or less stable guidelines for its foreign policy, they are not always applied in a uniform or consistent manner. Under Lula, Brazil's aspiration to accelerate the transition of the international system toward a more multipolar configuration no doubt influenced some of its peacebuilding engagements. A related objective—a permanent seat at the UNSC—was also among the drivers behind Brazil's expanding engagement with peacebuilding. In turn, these aspirations raised the expectations that other actors in the international community have about Brazil's role in peace and security, both quantitatively (for instance, in terms of financial or troop contributions) but also qualitatively, through innovative approaches to promoting peace.

Brazil has consistently argued in favor of a less militarized approach to international security issues, and most of its peacebuilding efforts rely more heavily on mediation, investment in socioeconomic development (not only through social policy and job generation, but also via infrastructure development), and coordination between national and regional actors.

One persistent question, however, concerns the sustainability of these initiatives. Will there be a resurgence in Brazilian peacebuilding? Within the UN, it is likely that Brazil's political commitment to the PBA, which has been deeply entrenched both in Brasilia and at the mission in New York, will continue. Outside of the UN, the possibility of another surge in Brazilian peacebuilding is constrained not only by the dual political and economic crisis, but also by the "spread too thin" character of Brazil's engagement during the 2000s. This overextension is particularly evident in the country's South-South development cooperation portfolio, with many projects indefinitely suspended in 2016 due to budget cuts. Combined with low institutionalization, as reflected in the lack of a dedicated legal framework and career path specializing in development cooperation within the MRE, the funding gap leads to lapses in institutional learning and feedback mechanisms that would enable improvements, such as in project planning and accountability.

Although Brazil's expanded peacekeeping role has been highly visible, thanks to its participation in MINUSTAH and MONUSCO, the way that Brazil links peacekeeping and peacebuilding initiatives differs from the approaches of the other rising powers. For instance, whereas India sees development and peacebuilding as deeply intertwined, and whereas Turkey links peacebuilding with humanitarian and peacemaking efforts, for Brazil there is a clearer (but by no means absolute) distinction between peacekeeping and peacebuilding. Brazil does embrace the distinction between those two spheres made in UN circles, but these two dimensions are more closely linked in Brazilian practice than in Western efforts. This is because Brazil views peacebuilding as a key corrective to conventional approaches to peacekeeping, especially the heavy focus on security and military-dominated initiatives. By linking civilian peacebuilding alongside peacekeeping operations, as was done in Haiti through the partnership with Viva Rio, Brazil hopes to ensure that peacekeeping missions not only meet the everyday security needs of the local population, but also helps to ensure its economic and social well-being. Brazil's main contribution, therefore, is not to enhance the Western approach to peacebuilding, but rather to use peacebuilding in order to help rebalance Western approaches in a less securitized direction. However, in order to push for deeper transformation, Brazil needs to make its own peacebuilding more sustainable, coherent, and accountable.

Notes

1. Interview with Prof. Tania Manzur, July 2015, Brasilia.
2. Interview with Prof. Tania Manzur, July 2015, Brasilia.
3. Brazil entered World Wars I and II only after its ships were attacked.
4. As of September 2016, UNASUR comprises 12 South American countries: Argentina, Bolivia, Brazil, Chile, Colombia, Ecuador, Guyana, Paraguay, Peru, Uruguay, Suriname, and Venezuela.
5. Interview with Brazilian diplomat in Brasília, November 2015.
6. CT Call personal interview with Brazilian diplomat who had worked at the mission to the United Nations and requested anonymity, August 2015, Brasilia.
7. CT Call personal interview with Brazilian diplomat who had worked at the mission to the United Nations and requested anonymity, August 2015, Brasilia.
8. CT Call personal interview with Brazilian diplomat who requested anonymity, August 2015, Brasilia.
9. CT Call personal interview with Leopoldo Paz, August 2015, Brasilia.
10. Interview with Fiocruz specialist, Rio de Janeiro, October 2016.
11. CT Call personal interview with Brazilian diplomat who requested anonymity, August 2015, Brasilia.

References

Abdenur, Adriana, and Danilo Marcondes. 2016. Democratization by Association? Brazil's Social Policy Cooperation in Africa. *Cambridge Review of International Affairs*: 1–19. doi:10.1080/09557571.2015.1118996.

Abdenur, Adriana, and Danilo Marcondes Neto. 2014. Rising Powers and the Security-Development Nexus: Brazil's Engagement with Guinea-Bissau. *Journal of Peacebuilding & Development* 9(2): 1–16.

Biato, Marcel. 1999. O processo de paz Peru-Equador. *Parcerias Estratégicas* 6: 247–247.

Brazilian Development Bank. 2013. BNDES Inaugurates its Representative Office in Africa. http://www.bndes.gov.br/SiteBNDES/bndes/bndes_en/Institucional/Press/Noticias/2013/20131206_africa.html

BRICS. 2014. Agreement on the New Development Bank. http://ndb.int/charter.php

Constituicao. 1934. Constitution of the Republic of the United States of Brazil. 16 July 1934.

Council on Foreign Relations. 2010. Joint Declaration by Iran, Turkey and Brazil on Nuclear Fuel. http://www.cfr.org/brazil/joint-declaration-iran-turkey-brazil-nuclear-fuel-may-2010/p22140 de Abreu, Fernando Jose Marroni. 2013. *Speech before the Chamber of Deputies.* Brasilia.

de Quieroz, João Marcelo Galvão. 2016. ABACC: Os Primeiros 25 Anos. *Cadernos de Política Exterior* 2/3: 45–64.

Fishel, John T., and Andrés Sáenz. 2007. *Capacity-Building for Peacekeeping: The Case of Haiti.* Potomac Books.

Hirst, Monica. 2010. O Haiti e os desafios de uma reconstrução sustentável—um olhar sul-americano. *Revista Política External* 10(1): 103–111.

IPEA. 2011. *Cooperação Brasileira para o Desenvolvimento Internacional (Cobradi).* Brasília: Instituto de Pesquisa Econômica e Aplicada.

Ministry of Foreign Affairs. 2011. Statement to the Press from IBSA about Consultations Held in Syria—Damascus. http://www.itamaraty.gov.br/en/press-releases/14334-declaracao-a-imprensa-do-ibas-sobre-consultas-mantidas-na-siria-2

———. 2014. O Brasil e os dez anos da MINUSTAH. Blog do Itamaraty. http://blog.itamaraty.gov.br/82-o-brasil-e-os-dez-anos-da-minustah

———. 2016. *Histórico da cooperação humanitária brasileira.* Brazilia. http://www.itamaraty.gov.br/pt-BR/notas-a-imprensa/2-sem-categoria/13229-historico-da-cooperacao-humanitaria-brasileira

Muller, Markus-Michael. 2016. Entangled Pacifications: Peacekeeping, Counterinsurgency and Policing in Port-au-Prince and Rio de Janeiro. In *The Global Making of Policing: Postcolonial Perspectives*, ed. Jana Honke and Markus-Michael Muller. London: Routledge.

Patriota, Antonio. 2011. Speech on the occasion of the open debate convened by Brazil as Chair of the UN Security Council. New York.

Patriota, Antonio Aguiar, and Héctor Marcos Timerman. 2011. Brasil e Argentina, Cooperação Nuclear. *O Estado de São Paulo.* http://www.itamaraty.gov.br/pt-BR/discursos-artigos-e-entrevistas-categoria/ministro-das-relacoes-exteriores-artigos/4598-brasil-e-argentina-cooperacao-nuclear-o-estado-de-s-paulo-06-7-2011

Peixoto, Fabricia. 2010. Em oito anos, Lula visitou 85 países em bisca de parceiros comerciais e políticos. *BBC Brasil.* http://www.bbc.com/portuguese/noticias/2010/12/101227_eralula_diversificacao.shtml

Pinheiro, Leticia. 2007. Ao vencedor, as batatas: o reconhecimento da independência de Angola. *Estudos Históricos* 39: 83–120.

Ribeiro, Darcy. 1995. *O Povo Brasileiro.* Rio de Janeiro: Companhia das Letras.

Santos, Rita, and Teresa Almeida Cravo. 2014. Brazil's Rising Profile in United Nations Peacekeeping Operations Since the End of the Cold War. *Norwegian Center for Conflict Resolution (NOREF) Report.* https://www.ciaonet.org/attachments/24875/uploads

Small Arms Survey. 2014. Exporter. http://www.smallarmssurvey.org/weapons-and-markets/transfers/exporters.html

Suyama, Bianca, and Melissa Pomeroy. 2015. *Picking and Choosing: Contributions of Brazilian Cooperation to More Horizontal Post-2015 Partnerships*. São Paulo: Articulação Sul.

United Nations Office on Drugs and Crime. 2013. *Global Study on Homicide: Trends, Contexts, Data*. Vienna: United Nations Office on Drugs and Crime. https://www.unodc.org/documents/gsh/pdfs/2014_GLOBAL_HOMICIDE_BOOK_web.pdf.

United Nations Security Council. 2011. Statement by the President of the Security Council. http://www.un.org/ga/search/view_doc.asp?symbol=S/PRST/2011/4

Valente, Gabriel. 2016. Itamaraty extingue departamento de combate à fome. *O Globo*. http://oglobo.globo.com/brasil/itamaraty-extingue-departamento-de-combate-fome-20101655

Vigevani, Tulio, and Gabriel Cepaluni. 2012. *Brazilian Foreign Policy in Changing Times: The Quest for Autonomy from Sarney to Lula*. Lanham, Maryland: Lexington Books.

Viva Rio. Gingando Pela Paz. 2015. http://vivario.org.br/viva-rio-no-haiti/centro-comunitario-kay-nou/gingando-pela-paz/

Adriana Erthal Abdenur is Fellow at the Instituto Igarapé and Senior Postdoctoral Researcher at the Fundação Getúlio Vargas, Rio de Janeiro.

Charles T. "Chuck" Call is Associate Professor of the International Peace and Conflict Resolution School of International Service, American University, Washington DC.

CHAPTER 3

Offering Support and Sharing Experiences: Indonesia's Approach to Peacebuilding

Lina A. Alexandra

Introduction

Compared to peacekeeping, the term peacebuilding receives relatively less attention among Indonesian policymakers and society. Indonesia's active contribution to United Nations peacekeeping since 1957, not too long after its independence, has often been showcased as one of the country's greatest achievements in the maintenance of international peace and security.

However, this should not lead to the conclusion that Indonesia is not playing any role within the peacebuilding arena. This is partly because peacebuilding has been understood in a much broader sense than peacekeeping. In the Indonesian context, peacebuilding, rather than viewed as direct efforts to prevent another lapse into conflict in post-conflict societies, is understood as different kinds of activities that can contribute to conflict prevention and conflict management. Indonesia focuses its peacebuilding efforts on sharing its experiences and knowledge in democracy as a key to sustaining peace, playing a role as mediator/facilitator/

L.A. Alexandra (✉)
Centre for Strategic and International Studies (CSIS), Jakarta, Indonesia

C.T. Call, C. de Coning (eds.), *Rising Powers and Peacebuilding*, Rethinking Peace and Conflict Studies,
DOI 10.1007/978-3-319-60621-7_3

observer, and conducting humanitarian actions that can help initiate the peace process.

While Indonesia has been involved in mediation activities for decades, this peacebuilding role developed more robustly during the ten years of President Yudhoyono's administration from 2004 to 2014. The transition from the authoritarian regime of the New Order era to a democratic government led to greater stability, marked by the ability of the government to initiate peace processes that led to the settlement of various internal conflicts, and also the implementation of the first direct presidential election in the country. Despite some problems, the transition went smoothly and the country avoided violent revolution, which was predicted by many observers. These experiences of democratic transition, which included installing the civilian government, returning the military to the barracks, and settling internal conflicts, have been considered valuable lessons which can be shared with other countries that are currently struggling with similar challenges.

This willingness to share experiences and lessons learned has been seen as part of Indonesia's soft power to be projected in order to achieve its vision of becoming a middle power. As Indonesia gradually transforms itself from an aid recipient into an emerging donor or development partner, peacebuilding has become one of the key areas in which the government assists other countries that are struggling to rebuild their core political and economic infrastructures in order to achieve sustainable peace.

This policy brief explores how peacebuilding is understood in Indonesia, including any novel insights that can be drawn from its understanding of the concept; the principles/philosophies that underlie peacebuilding, the motivating factors, and the existing debate about peacebuilding; and finally descriptions of peacebuilding activities and how the results of those activities implemented abroad have been measured. Rather than exploring Indonesia's unilateral role per se, the elaborations also include Indonesia's role in the context of ASEAN (Association of Southeast Asian Nations), since the country has often worked through the framework of the regional organization, and Indonesia is often perceived by others as the 'natural leader' of ASEAN.

The policy brief begins with a brief explanation of the historical evolution of Indonesia's peacebuilding efforts. For the purpose of this study, it traces back only to the so-called peacebuilding activities in the New Order era up to the post-reformation era under President Yudhoyono's (2004–2014) administration. This historical evolution is important to show a sense of continuity in the values and principles applied to Indonesia's foreign policy, including in peacebuilding activities abroad. However, as is often the case, pragmatism sometimes takes precedence over a values-based approach to foreign policy.

The Indonesian approach to peacebuilding is distinct in at least two ways. First, it emphasizes persuasion to encourage host countries to think of ways to create peace in their respective countries, particularly through intensive dialogues with local stakeholders. Rather than taking place solely at the formal level, such dialogues have often been conducted on an informal basis to engage non-state actors, such as think-tanks and non-governmental organizations. Second, Indonesia emphasizes the concept of 'sharing' experiences. Rather than acting as an expert conveying its success stories, Indonesia tends to apply a two-way approach in which it not only shares its own experiences, but also learns from the host country and works to understand the local context while seeking the local 'modalities' to be utilized in order to start the peacebuilding process. Indonesia does not advocate a 'one-size-fits-all' peacebuilding policy since each country has its own unique challenges and context. Respect for these conditions is considered key to successful peacebuilding.

Historical Evolution of Indonesia's Role in Peacebuilding: New Order to Post-reformation Era

Rather than understanding peacebuilding strictly as a set of activities conducted in the aftermath of conflict, Indonesia interprets the concept more broadly. In the New Order era (1966–1998) under President Soeharto, such activities were mainly focused on conflict management, which entailed mediation or facilitation roles. In the post-reformation era under President Yudhoyono, Indonesia has also shared its experiences and lessons learned in democratization and dealing with internal conflicts.

Any discussion of Indonesia's peacebuilding roles must be placed within the context of the country's overall foreign policy.

During the first decade of his term starting in 1966, President Soeharto abandoned Soekarno's flamboyant style and high-profile foreign policy, instead focusing on economic development. Foreign policy initiatives were directed to invite foreign investment, mainly from Western countries and international financial institutions to finance its development plan.

Rather than playing an assertive role like in the Old Order era under President Soekarno, from the late-1960s through the mid-1980s, Indonesia took a lower profile, focusing on economic growth and development, which was seen as the path toward a more assertive role internationally in the long term. In his remarks in August 1969, Soeharto elucidated this logic: 'Why is the voice of Indonesia no longer heard abroad? The matter is that we shall only be able to play an effective role if we ourselves are possessed of a great national vitality' (Leifer 1983). It was not until the 1980s, after the 'Asian economic miracle' and a period of sustained growth, that Indonesia started to play a more active role, initially within Southeast Asia.

Two cases are often quoted as examples of successful peace efforts by Indonesia. The first is the end of the long Cambodian armed conflict. Working within the framework of ASEAN, Indonesia hosted the Jakarta Informal Meeting I in Bogor in July 1988 and the Jakarta Informal Meeting II in Jakarta in October 1989, which culminated in the historical Paris Peace Agreement in late October 1991. As depicted by former Foreign Minister Ali Alatas, Indonesia, interlocutor for ASEAN, these two meetings sought to facilitate dialogue, first among the four Cambodian factions and second among those factions and Indonesia, Vietnam, and other concerned countries (Alatas 2001, 270). ASEAN, including Indonesia, worked hard to keep international attention on the Cambodian conflict and to end Vietnam's occupation in Cambodia. Ultimately changing international circumstances at the end of the Cold War led Vietnam to withdraw its forces in April 1989 (Narine 1998, 207).

The second case is Indonesia's involvement in facilitating the peace process between the Government of Philippines and the Moro National Liberation Front (MNLF) for two decades. According to Wiryono Sastrohandoyo, a seasoned Indonesian diplomat who once acted as a mediator of conflicts in Mindanao, soon after the rebellion broke out in late 1972, President Soeharto suggested that President Marcos settle the conflict through the mechanism of ASEAN. However, seeking to secure oil from the Middle East, Marcos decided to bring the case to the Organization of the Islamic Conference (OIC) instead. The process under OIC resulted in the signing of Tripoli Agreement in December 1976, but the agreement could not be implemented. Further discussions considering the establishment of an autonomous Muslim region in the southern Philippines were halted as hostilities among the parties resumed. The peace agreement was hampered even more as the Marcos administration insisted on implementing it without the participation of the MNLF.

Only at its Ministerial Meeting in 1991 did the OIC) decide to expand the committee to include member countries from Asia. This development was also supported by the new Philippine government of President Corazon Aquino. At that time, the OIC) Secretariat asked Indonesia to help facilitate the peace process. In 1993, Indonesia was elected Chair of the OIC) Ministerial Committee of Six, of which fellow Asian country Bangladesh was also a member. In April 1993, Indonesia hosted a second round of informal exploratory talks in Cipanas, West Java, which resulted in a 'Statement of Understanding' that called for formal peace talks that would discuss the modalities to fully implement the Tripoli Agreement. The first round of formal peace talks was held in October–November 1993, which resulted in the signing of a Memorandum of Agreement and the 1993 Interim Ceasefire Agreement. After a series of meetings at the technical level, informal consultations and formal peace talks, the peace agreement was then signed between the Government of the Philippines and the MNLF in Manila in September 1996. Ambassador Sastrohandoyo, discussing Indonesia's crucial role in forging the agreement, said:

> This is a case of preventive diplomacy, peacemaking, and peace-building in which the United Nations (UN) was not involved at all. Instead it was an international organization with a religious orientation, the OIC), which was mediating. Its efforts could make no headway, however, until two countries from the Asian region, one of them a next-door neighbour of the conflicted country, became involved. (Sastrohandoyo 2008, 19)

In the post-reformation era, the Yudhoyono government was again able to assume a more assertive role in the region after half a decade of internal domestic consolidation. Indonesia experienced serious political, security, and economic crises during the period of 1999–2003, in the aftermath of Soeharto's New Order regime. The impact of these crises was so severe that the economic growth declined and its political and military influenced waned in the immediate post-Soeharto years. Some analysts saw Indonesia as a 'wounded phoenix', unable to rise and pursue a robust foreign policy due to internal crises and lacking the strong leadership shown by Soeharto during New Order era (Weatherbee 2005).

It is interesting to observe how the post-reformation government under Yudhoyono tried to cope with its lack of 'hard' or material capabilities. The administration started to invest in projecting Indonesia's soft power, which mainly derives from the country's political transition experience from semi-authoritarianism to a democratic civilian-led government. By expanding this soft power, Indonesia has sought to nurture what the President called 'intellectual leadership', particularly in ASEAN. According to Yudhoyono, the country sought to be a 'peacemaker, confidence-builder, problem-solver, and bridge-builder' (Yudhoyono 2005, 387). Fully aware of its identity as a country with the largest Muslim population in the world, Indonesia portrayed itself as a genuine example where 'democracy, Islam and modernity can go hand-in-hand'.

However, in the early years, Yudhoyono's first term, the country was challenged by the tsunami disaster that hit Aceh in late December 2004, causing hundreds of thousands of deaths and destroying almost all the infrastructure in the province. The government gradually returned to its foreign policy activism again after two years, which is marked by the attendance of President Yudhoyono in the Non-Aligned Movement Summit in Havana in September 2006. At the summit, he declared Indonesia's aspiration to bridge the developed and developing worlds. One year later, Indonesia was able to secure several positions in the international arena, including a stint as a non-permanent member of the UN Security Council (2007–2009), and membership in the UN's Economic and Social Council (2007–2009) and Human Rights Council (2007). The year 2006 also marked a significant increase in Indonesia's peacekeeping contribution, when it contributed a total of 1058 personnel to five UN missions, including 850 troops for UNIFIL. By 2010, Indonesia was listed as one of top 20 largest troop contributing countries to UN peacekeeping, and was ranked sixteenth in 2014.

In this context and in the area of peacebuilding, Indonesia expanded its role as a 'champion' of democracy in the region, as well as facilitator and peace observer. At the regional level, during the process to create the ASEAN Charter, Indonesia's late Foreign Minister Ali Alatas insisted that the principles of rule of law, good governance, democracy promotion, and protection of human rights to be included as the new principles of ASEAN.[1] Later on, Indonesia took a leading role in the formulation process of the ASEAN Political Security Community Blueprint, which mandated the establishment of the ASEAN Human Rights Body—later named the ASEAN Intergovernmental Commission on Human Rights and the ASEAN Institute for Peace and Reconciliation—a new institution established in 2011, which was specifically tasked to conduct research in peace and conflict resolution.

At the bilateral level, Indonesia also offered to facilitate peace processes in other countries in the region. In 2008, the government explored potential involvement in facilitating the peace process in Southern Thailand, but the Thai government eventually rejected this. Then, starting in July 2012, Indonesia also participated in the International Monitoring Team (IMT) to monitor the implementation of the peace agreement between the Government of the Philippines and the Moro Islamic Liberation Front (MILF). Indonesia earned the trust of the Philippine government to participate in IMT until 2015. At the global level, in its effort to project democratic values as the foundation to create peace, Indonesia initiated the Bali Democracy Forum (BDF) in 2008. The forum, which invites Asia-Pacific leaders, aims to promote and foster regional and international cooperation in the field of peace and democracy through dialogue, allowing leaders to share their experiences and best practices. The Institute of Peace and Democracy (IPD), which was specifically created to organize the BDF, has been successful in convening an annual meeting. The eighth meeting of the BDF took place in 2015.

Before entering into more detailed elaborations in the next few sections, one can see through the historical evolution of Indonesia's peacebuilding activities some continuities and changes. Many of the values and principles that shape Indonesia's peacebuilding have remained the same. However, some changes have also been observed, particularly in the way adherence to the non-interference principle has been interpreted and applied in conducting peacebuilding activities.

From the analysis on Indonesia's worldview and foreign policy by Paige Johnson Tan, two major aspects show continuity. The first is the way Indonesia perceives its role in the region as well as in the world. Second, it is the country's underlying attitudes toward major powers and the world system as a whole. These two aspects reflect the doctrine, present since Suharto, that Indonesia's foreign policy be 'active and independent' (Tan 2007, 157).

The first aspect indicates the 'active' element in Indonesia's foreign policy. As a large country in the region, Indonesia believes it should play a significant role in establishing a 'world order' based on 'perpetual peace', as enshrined since 1945 in the preamble to the constitution. In the New Order era, after the country's economy grew significantly in late 1980s, the Soeharto government stated its intention to re-establish its active and assertive role in the world (Tan 2007, 159–160). Indonesia re-asserted this aspiration after domestic political and economic conditions improved in the post-reformation era, as lingering internal conflicts were settled. As mentioned by President Yudhoyono in the mid-2005, '...After all, we have today an Indonesia that is capable and eager to actively engage the international community in the common task of building a better world' (Yudhoyono 2005, 397).

The second aspect is Indonesia's 'independent' policy. After the bitter experiences of colonialism, Indonesia shared with other post-colonial countries the sentiment that the global system is still operated by and for the interests of the powerful countries. Therefore, in the Indonesian leaders' view, it is very important to be neutral as a nation-state, navigating between superpowers during the Cold War, and even lead the region along a neutral path. What typifies Indonesian thinking, however, is the idea that neutrality should lead each country to 'national resilience', which will then create 'regional resilience'. It means that each country and the region should come up with their own solutions to their own problems, limiting the interference of external powers in order to maintain stability. The first Foreign Minister of the Soeharto administration, Adam Malik, elaborated on this concept in 1971:

> ...However dominant the influence of these big powers may be, I think there is and there should be scope for an indigenous Southeast Asian component in the new emerging power balance of the region. In fact, I am convinced that unless the big powers acknowledge and the Southeast Asian nations themselves assume a greater and more direct responsibility in the maintenance of security in the area, no lasting stability can ever be achieved. (Wulan and Bandoro 2007, 28)

The idea was reaffirmed during the post-reformation administration. When talking about the ASEAN Community, President Yudhoyono stated that 'we in ASEAN are taking full responsibility for our own security'(Yudhoyono 2005, 395). Indonesia's peacebuilding activities therefore value respect for the host country's sovereignty and focus on gaining confidence and trust from local stakeholders, who have the resilience to build sustainable peace.

While peacebuilding during the New Order era focused on playing a facilitator role, the Yudhoyono administration took a different route by sharing values that can contribute to creating sustainable peace, namely respect for democracy and human rights. The post-reformation government has stepped up its peacebuilding in the region, such as in Myanmar, where Indonesia assisted in implementing security sector reform to create military professionalism and separate the military from politics.

Several factors explain these different approaches. First, during the New Order era, Indonesia was governed by a military authoritarian regime, so even discussion about democracy and separation of the military from politics was unthinkable. Second, playing a facilitation role requires 'hard power', that is, economic and military strength in order to be able to influence conflicting parties to stop fighting and come to the negotiation table. Post-Soeharto governments are still struggling to rebuild that economic and military strength. As an alternative, Indonesia has developed and projected its soft power—values and wisdom gained from experiences during the political transition period.

Concepts and Terms

In Indonesia, especially among policymakers, the term 'peacebuilding' has been translated into Bahasa Indonesian as 'bina perdamaian' (which literally means peacebuilding). However, most of the existing literature on peacebuilding in Indonesia has elaborated on peacebuilding activities inside the country, since Indonesia has been—and is still in some areas—dealing with separatist and communal conflicts. No study has yet been conducted analyzing Indonesia's involvement in peacebuilding in other countries. This is not surprising, since interest in the topic is relatively novel. Therefore, the understanding of this type of 'external' peacebuilding is rather limited.

Peacebuilding in the Indonesian context, rather than viewed rigidly as a set of activities conducted after peace has been secured through peacekeeping missions, is applied more broadly as a variety of activities related to peace. Indonesia's external peacebuilding efforts can be identified in at least three areas: (1) promotion of democracy and human rights; (2) mediation/facilitation role; (3) humanitarian action, including disaster relief.

At the policy level, these external peacebuilding activities have been included in the democracy and conflict resolution program, one of the seven program priorities mentioned in the Draft Design for Indonesia's South-South Triangular Cooperation (SSTC) .[2] The SSTC viewed peacebuilding as one of Indonesia's comparative advantages, together with good governance.[3] From here, it is clear that peacebuilding is viewed as a capacity to be shared with other countries, and therefore has been put within the framework of Indonesia's development assistance, together with other capacities in economic and socio-cultural fields.

Promotion of Democracy and Human Rights

As mentioned earlier, Indonesia's experiences with peaceful democratic transition, despite some sectarian and communal conflicts as well as ethnic-based riots, are considered valuable modalities that can be shared with others that are facing similar challenges. There were fears that Indonesia, during this period of political turbulence, would be 'balkanized' into smaller regions along ethnic-religious lines. The ability to survive and maintain its unity and become a relatively 'healthy' state, in terms of its political and economic achievements, is something to value and learn about.

Indonesia's successful democratic transition is even more unique, given its status as the largest Muslim state. The fact that Indonesia has not become an Islamic state after the political reformation process, maintaining its status as a secular country, has been portrayed as evidence that Islam can go hand-in-hand with democracy. As mentioned by President Yudhoyono in 2005,

> ...We are home to the world's largest Muslim population. We are the world's third largest democracy. We are also a country where democracy, Islam, and modernity go hand-in-hand.... (Yudhoyono 2005, 390)

It is interesting to note that sharing its experience with democracy has been underlined as one of the seven program priorities in Indonesia's SSTC.[4] The intention to build Indonesia's democracy promotion capacity grew following the Arab Spring, which started in Tunisia and later Egypt. Using the one- and second-track approaches, the Indonesian government, through the IPD, organized a workshop, in Jakarta in April 2012, that brought together delegates from Egypt, Tunisia, and Indonesia to discuss several issues, such as Islam, the state, and politics; political and constitutional reforms; election laws and management; the role of political parties and civil society; the army's role in democratic society; and the participation of women in the political process (Eliraz 2014).

Indonesia's ability to share its experience with democratic transition to assist other burgeoning Muslim majority democracies has been highlighted by other international observers.[5] Australian diplomat Greg

Moriarty, for example, argued that the Indonesian democratic transition served as a good example for the 'Arab Spring' countries that Islam and democracy can be compatible (Alford 2011).

Recently, Indonesia has also shown interest in promoting democracy to its fellow ASEAN member Myanmar. When it was under authoritarian rule, the country received harsh criticism from the international community due to serious human rights violations, including political repression by the military junta, making it ASEAN's 'Achilles heel'. Indonesia, since Myanmar's political opening, has looked to create pathways to promote democracy into the country. It started with the first formal visit of President Yudhoyono to Myanmar in 2006. It continued with the Second Forum of the Joint Commission for Bilateral Cooperation (JCBC) between Indonesia and Myanmar in 2011, which took place in Yangon, in which Foreign Minister Marty Natalegawa met with his Myanmarese counterpart, U Wunna Maung Lwin, and with Aung San Suu Kyi—the symbol of Myanmar's democratic struggle. On this occasion, the Indonesian Foreign Minister expressed the country's intention to work with Myanmar's government to support capacity building in the fields of good governance, democracy, and human rights (Maulida and Adamrah 2011).

Mediation/Facilitation Role

Indonesia's role as a mediator, facilitator, and observer is nothing new. As mentioned earlier, during the Cold War era, Indonesia was praised for its active role in the Cambodian peace process, organizing the Jakarta Informal Meeting I and Jakarta Informal Meeting II.

More recently, in the early 1990s, Indonesia was actively involved in brokering peace in the Southern Philippines. Indonesia has been particularly engaged in the peace process between the Government of the Philippines (GPH) and the MNLF) at the request of the Organization of Islamic Conference (OIC) forum, while Malaysia is more involved as a third-party facilitator between the GPH and the Moro Islamic Liberation Front (MILF). As mentioned earlier, Indonesia's facilitating role culminated in the First Round of Formal Peace Talks held in Jakarta in October–November 1993, which resulted in the signing of a Memorandum of Agreement and the 1993 Interim Ceasefire Agreement. Indonesian officers then also joined as members of the OIC) Observer Team that coordinated the implementation of the ceasefire agreement. Jakarta was chosen as the host of several follow-up meetings to establish a transitional structure and mechanism for the provincial government in the autonomous region, besides New York and Jeddah. Then, a peace agreement was reached between the GPH and the MNLF in September 1996 (Sastrohandoyo 2008, 15–30). While it is understood that peace is a process, Indonesia has continued its role as part of the IMT since 2012. Until 2014, at least four teams were sent to monitor peace in this area.

Indonesian non-governmental organizations (NGOs) have also played crucial facilitation roles. Muhammadiyah, an international non-governmental organization (INGO) based in Indonesia, has participated in the International Contact Group, a hybrid mediation support initiative asked to provide support to the parties.[6]

Indonesia also attempted to act as a mediator in Southern Thailand between the Thai government and the Muslim groups residing in the southern part of the country. The Indonesian government, led by Vice President Jusuf Kalla (who now also serves as the Indonesian Vice President for the second time), managed to host a peace talk in Bogor in 2008 attended by Thai officials and representatives of insurgent groups. The effort did not produce an agreement and was later rejected by the Thai government since it insisted that the talks should be kept strictly domestic (The Jakarta Post 2010).

Humanitarian Action

While humanitarian action, including disaster relief, is normally separated from peacebuilding efforts, in the context of Indonesia, humanitarian assistance has been utilized to pave the way to conduct peacebuilding. This distinct feature has been created as a strategy to ensure that state sovereignty is respected, since humanitarian action is often considered less threatening than peacebuilding activities that can be perceived as challenging a government's capacity to deal with post-conflict situations. Furthermore, humanitarian assistance can be crucial to gaining trust from the host countries, since such efforts are often viewed as a gesture of good will. Humanitarian assistance can also be utilized to share experiences with disaster and crisis management.

Cyclone Nargis provides a good example of the usefulness of humanitarian assistance. In this context, Indonesia played a leading role in approaching the military junta in Myanmar and challenging it to open access to outside humanitarian aid to help the victims. Indonesia drew upon the experience of handling the impact of the tsunami disaster that hit Aceh in

December 2004, in which the peace negotiations between the Indonesian government and the Aceh separatist movement resumed immediately after the tragedy took place. The Indonesian government saw an opportunity for the regime in Myanmar to open up to the outside world, which became another path to spread democratic and human rights values in the country through long-term and sustained engagement with international community. As elucidated by Foreign Minister Hassan Wirajuda in the wake of Cyclone Nargis disaster,

> Based on our experience with tsunami, we want to make sure there's more after the relief phase. Reconstruction, rehabilitation and even prevention. We want to nurture that sense of wanting to open up on Myanmar's side to have a long-term engagement with the international community. (Hotland 2008)

Indonesia has also been actively involved in finding ways to help Myanmar's Rohingya minorities. Starting with the flow of Rohingya people stranded in Indonesia's territories, mostly in the northern tip of Sumatera island in 2012, the Indonesian government has been domestically pressured to help the group, which faces repression and discrimination in Myanmar. The local people, such as the Acehnese, have helped the Rohingya to get food, medication, and shelter after traveling through the Indian Ocean for months.

In September 2012, the Indonesian Red Cross (PMI) through its Chairman Jusuf Kalla, who was actively involved in the Aceh peace process while he served as Vice President, visited Myanmar and shared some best practices and suggestions based on the Indonesian experience in dealing with peace in Aceh, in a forum to discuss peaceful solutions to the civil conflict in Myanmar (Taufiqurrahman 2012b). He also signed an agreement with the Myanmar Red Cross to provide financial and technical assistance for short- and long-term programs that address the refugee crisis in the Rakhine state. Kalla stated that PMI would like to stay in the Rakhine state for the post-conflict reconstruction program (Taufiqurrahman 2012a). While PMI has received permission to conduct its activities in the country, unfortunately other humanitarian agencies, such as Médecins Sans Frontières-Holland (MSF-H), have been denied access since February 2014 to continue humanitarian activities in the country (Fan and Krebs 2014, 9–10). Despite these obstacles, the fact that PMI still has access should be seen as an opportunity for Indonesia to play a significant role in the country, especially to help resolve ethnic tensions.

Looking at Indonesia's capacities, based on its experiences dealing with its own communal conflicts, since the late 2012 President Thein Sein has asked Indonesia to assist the Myanmar government in resolving the ongoing ethnic tensions that are taking place in the Rakhine state, where most Rohingya people have been displaced (Santosa 2012).

Recently, in late December 2016, the Indonesian government has once again taken the initiative to send humanitarian aid to the Rakhine state to ease the suffering of the people, especially the Rohingyas. The tension has risen in the area as the government responded through the military measure to search for the perpetrators after the attack against the police in the Mungdaw and Rathedaung townships in early October 2016. This action has been followed by the Indonesian government proposal to the OIC during the Extraordinary Ministerial Conference in Kuala Lumpur on January 19, 2017, which basically calls for it to conduct four things: (1) to offer humanitarian aid and security advice for avoiding further clashes; (2) to work closely with the Myanmar government; (3) to cooperate with regional organizations, such as ASEAN; and (4) for the OIC member countries to assist the country through economic development, with the possibility to get assistance from the Islamic Development Bank (Antara News 2017).

Origins and Underlying Principles/Philosophy

Based on the elaborations above, we can see that peacebuilding in the Indonesian context has been viewed rather differently from traditional actors. Peacebuilding, while it certainly entails activities to rebuild core government functions to prevent lapses into conflict, also includes supporting activities to build trust in order to allow more 'direct' peacebuilding efforts to take place. This is crucial since peacebuilding has been seen as external intervention by outside actors into a country's domestic affairs, which is sometimes considered a challenge to the host government's sovereignty.

Such distinct approaches also entail a set of unique principles. There are at least two principles to highlight.

The first principle is the importance of carefully considering the 'comfort' level of the host country in accepting the offer to help with a peacebuilding process, while at the same time seeking an entry point. This is critical to gaining the trust of the partner country and eventually determines the level of success achieved in this peacebuilding effort. The host government should reach the stage where it feels the need for and is comfortable enough to open up itself to receiving other countries' assistance in the peacebuilding process.

How to achieve that comfort level? First, it is done through persuasive action. For example, representatives from the Indonesian government approached Middle East countries such as Egypt and Tunisia in the midst of the Arab Spring uprisings to share Indonesia's democratic transition experiences.[7]

Second, Indonesia provides humanitarian assistance, such as the response to the devastative Cyclone Nargis caused in Myanmar. When the Myanmarese government was condemned for its refusal to give access to international humanitarian agencies to enter the country during Cyclone Nargis and even 'threatened' to receive a UN Security Council response under the 'Responsibility to Protect' (RtoP) principle, as proposed by the French government, Indonesia immediately rejected such a proposal. Indonesian Foreign Minister Marty Natalegawa argued that by invoking the RtoP principle, 'it would jeopardize and undermine aid work, not only for Myanmar, but also future humanitarian situations', since RtoP is only applied in situations related to the four serious crimes, that is genocide, ethnic cleansing, war crimes, and crimes against humanity (Hotland 2008). Indonesia has played an influential role to consolidate support from all ASEAN member countries for Myanmar's chairmanship bid in ASEAN for 2014. Indonesia viewed that ASEAN membership would motivate the Myanmarese government to further democratize and adopt more stringent human rights values (Adamrah 2011).

Consent from the host country is a must. While Indonesia often took the initiative in engaging with other countries, it always emphasized consultation with and consent from the host country. For example, when Indonesia offered assistance in monitoring the mid-term elections in Myanmar in 2012, it patiently waited for the signal from the Myanmarese government as to whether it needed an election monitoring team (Kompas, January 2012). Also, in the case of Southern Thailand, the Indonesian Foreign Minister stated that any request for assistance from the Thai government would be welcomed, but Indonesia would not interfere preemptively (The Jakarta Post 2010). Consent fosters a sincere engagement with the host government in the peacebuilding process. This reflects Indonesia's desire for the host government to feel confident that the offer of peacebuilding assistance will not challenge its sovereign control over its internal affairs. With this so-called constructive engagement, it is expected that Indonesia, in its efforts to conduct peacebuilding in other countries, will not burn bridges, but rather maintain its relations and be able to exercise influence and persuasion with other governments.

The second principle is 'sharing'. This concept of 'sharing' has been mentioned in almost every effort to help other countries in this peacebuilding context. Based on several interviews, this concept of 'sharing' has been defined in at least two ways. First, it is to emphasize that Indonesia has no intention to dictate or impose certain lessons or values to the host countries. According to the Executive Director of the Institute for Peace and Democracy, I Ketut Erawan, this approach has been taken because Indonesia believes that each country has local modalities/capacities to start its peacebuilding process. Furthermore, there are cases, such as in Myanmar, where the local stakeholders, including the government, asked Indonesia to share its experience in managing its ethnic relations. Related to Indonesia's initiative to support Myanmar in its democratic transition, as highlighted by the former Indonesian Foreign Minister Marty Natalegawa, Indonesia has been willing to be a 'study case' for any country to learn. Moreover, Minister Natalegawa stated that, 'With the approach that we are doing, they do not feel that they are being dictated because what we try is to share our experiences and lessons that we gained before…' (Kompas, February 2012). Second, the things that are shared are based on Indonesia's own experiences with democratic consolidation, among other challenges. Indonesia has also been open to share its mistakes and setbacks with the partner countries. By doing so, Indonesia has been able to secure trust and has more credibility, since it is not dictating the path forward for host countries. Thus, Indonesia also believes that there is no 'one-size-fits-all' recipe to build peace, since each country has its own distinct characteristics and challenges. Indonesia shares not only success stories, but also its past mistakes and failures. Therefore, each host country can choose what should be adapted to its own context.

Such principles are meant to accommodate respect for state sovereignty and non-interference in others' domestic affairs. Again, it is believed that the success of peacebuilding efforts depends on the ability of the actors to work at a pace that is in line with the standards of the host country, a pace that does not threaten the control of the host government over its own domestic sphere. This may be a long process, and is often criticized as ineffective by traditional peacebuilding actors, mainly Western countries, but building trust is considered essential for the success of peacebuilding programs.

This leads to the question of whether the application of such principles actually positions external peacebuilding actors as weak vis-à-vis the host government. One senior Indonesian diplomat said that we should not forget the element of 'firmness' in any persuasive approach undertaken. This has been shown in the case when the former Foreign Minister Hassan Wirajuda approached the military junta in Myanmar to allow humanitarian aid. Wirajuda was able to put pressure on the junta by asking the Foreign Minister of Myanmar what ASEAN membership meant for Myanmar and what Myanmar's membership meant to ASEAN in terms of ASEAN's internal coherence and international profile (Widyaningsih and Roberts 2014, 108). By explaining the consequences of not allowing ASEAN to play a role in responding to the disaster, the 'persuasive' effort resulted in the opening up of the country for the flow of humanitarian assistance.

Motivations

It is a daunting task to explore the drivers behind Indonesia's peacebuilding activities abroad. In interviews conducted with various government officials, most of them immediately referred to one of the country's national objectives stated in the Preamble of the Constitution, which is 'to participate toward the establishment of a world order based on freedom, perpetual peace and social justice'. Such statements, mostly made by senior diplomats, imply that there is still a strong tendency to argue that it is inappropriate to talk about direct benefits as if the government seeks 'rewards' for the good deeds that it does for others. However, discussions with some younger diplomats reveal a growing alternative view that now is the time for the government to start thinking about what real or tangible benefits to pursue if the country wishes to maintain its active role, particularly in the peacebuilding and peacekeeping fields. They argued that while such idealism is to a certain extent still valid, it is also important to think about how Indonesia's contributions can also serve the country's national interests in a more tangible way.

CSIS's earlier study on the SSTC described these complexities. The study, in which Indonesia's peacebuilding activities were included as one of country's niche capacities to share, concludes that SSTC activities so far have not had clear objectives. There are three categories of 'benefits' that can be applied to Indonesia's peacebuilding context. First, intangible benefits such as showing Indonesia's good will and solidarity toward other developing countries are emphasized. Second, while helping others, Indonesia can also benefit by learning from the experiences that the beneficiary/host countries go through. Third, while there might be some tangible political and economic benefits, it is always necessary to avoid imposing Indonesia's interests and agenda and to be as subtle as possible when dealing with this issue. This is crucial to maintain Indonesia's reputation among developing countries (CSIS 2014).[8]

In the peacebuilding context, the second 'benefit' above has been affirmed. Through its interactions with the partner countries, Indonesia has learned many useful lessons to help develop its democracy. One example, in Indonesia's engagement with Tunisia to help the country set up its election system, policymakers learned that Tunisia's election system ensures equal opportunity for women candidates to be elected by putting the names of men and women candidates alternately in the ballot papers for national and local elections.[9]

Another motivation is the aspiration to play a role as a middle power, which has to a certain extent influenced the initiative to embark on peacebuilding activities abroad. It is particularly based on the perception of Indonesia's identity as the biggest country in Southeast Asia in terms of size and population, and also as a proponent of the first Asia-Africa Conference in 1955, the largest association of developing countries. Additionally, the country perceives itself as having a distinct capacity that may not be inherited by others. Former President Yudhoyono, in the beginning of his first term, described the country as home to the world's largest Muslim population as well as the third largest democracy. Indonesia aspires to be a model, according to him, for how democracy, Islam, and modernity go hand-in-hand. Having this special quality, Indonesia envisions itself playing an active role as a peace-maker, confidence-builder, problem-solver, or bridge-builder that connects different countries and civilizations.

CSIS's study on Indonesia's SSTC activities[10] makes a similar argument that the government tends to be subtle when discussing the tangible economic and political benefits of peacebuilding. According to the interviewees, this tone is struck to avoid the perception that Indonesia's vested interests and agenda are imposed on the recipient countries. This is important to ensuring that Indonesia's presence is accepted among host countries, so that it is perceived as an impartial/neutral actor and can continue its role as peace-maker or bridge-builder. Therefore, an important motivating factor for Indonesia's peacebuilding activities is to enhance its global presence and build its reputation as a responsible member of the international community that contributes significantly to the maintenance of international peace and security. There are three words, according to the study on Indonesia's SSTC, to describe its motivation: good will, solidarity, and presence (CSIS 2014, 84–85).

Finally, there are debates on the extent religious considerations influence the government's decisions about which countries Indonesia engages in. There has been clear and sustained pressure from Indonesia's Muslim majority public to persuade the government to assist Muslim communities that are facing discrimination and persecution in their home countries, both within the region (Southern Philippines, Southern Thailand, and currently Rohingya minorities in Myanmar) and further afield, such as in the Palestinian territories and Syria.[11] However, as mentioned by one of Indonesia's leading international relations experts, this current focus on Islam as part of the country's national identity is relatively new, beginning in the post-Soeharto era, which commenced in 1999 while emphasizing that solidarity among developing countries often prevails over solidarity among Muslim countries (Anwar 2010, 47).

Rather than simply invoking its Islamic identity, the country has a distinct aspiration to show how Islam can go hand-in-hand with democracy. This is due to what Indonesia perceives as its unique status as the world's largest Muslim population and the third largest democracy. Indonesia sees a niche in its engagement: emphasizing its Muslim identity to gain confidence from the host countries while promoting democracy as a key to sustaining peace.

Debates on Aspects of Peacebuilding

Since peacebuilding abroad is relatively new for Indonesia, there has been little debate on the subject to date. Nevertheless, from interviews conducted with government officials and peacebuilding activists in Indonesia, one important issue can be highlighted.

The most common debate centers on whether the country should actually play a role in helping other countries deal with their internal crises. While there has been a strong call from within Indonesia to play an active role to promote democracy abroad to exert its soft power, many officials possess self-awareness that the country is not in the best strategic position to play a significant role abroad due to internal political problems. Its democracy is still very much 'a work in progress' and faces many challenges (see Sukma 2012, 90 and Karim 2013). Some take the view that Indonesia's domestic challenges make it difficult to support democracy abroad.

Activities/Programs and Impact

Despite Indonesia's activism in peacebuilding, data on these activities are scattered and not well-documented in a single and centralized location. Nevertheless, some information can be gathered through the Ministry of Foreign Affairs (MoFA) and related institutions like the IPD.

In peacebuilding efforts related to the first area of democracy promotion and human rights, the government mostly conducts workshops, seminars, and trainings for the stakeholders in host countries. Two workshops appear in the online reports of the MFA's Directorate of Technical Cooperation (KST) within the period 2006–2013:

1. International Training Workshop on 'Democratization and Good Governance' held in Jakarta from October 28 to 31, 2008, organized by the Directorate of KST. The beneficiaries were participants from Timor Leste (four), Palestine (four); Cambodia (two); Lao PDR (two); Papua New Guinea (one), Viet Nam (two), and Indonesia (one).
2. International Workshop on Democracy Sharing Experiences Between Indonesia and Arab Countries held in Jakarta, Pekanbaru, and Bandung from September 13 to 20, 2013. The beneficiaries were from Jordan (five), Sudan (five), Somalia (one), Egypt (three), and Yemen (three).

Another source of Indonesia's peacebuilding activities is the Blue Book on Indonesia-Myanmar Capacity Building Partnership 2013–2015. That source reveals these activities within the peacebuilding framework (Table 3.1).

For such activities, government institutions, such as the Ministry of Foreign Affairs, Ministry of Law and Human Rights and Ministry of Defense, and other government-related institutions, such as the National Human Rights Commission, have been involved as the main actors. Among those activities, the Indonesian government has been very active in organizing the annual Bali Democracy Forum since December 2008. This Forum invites state leaders to discuss the development of democracy in the Asia-Pacific region. It is seeks to 'promote and foster regional and international cooperation in the field of peace and democracy through dialogue-based on sharing experiences and best practices that adhere to

Table 3.1 Proposed peace-related Indonesian programs/activities in Myanmar (2013–2015)

Year	*Period*	*Programs/activities*	*Organizer*
2013	October	Training on promoting national reconciliation for social welfare	• MoFA (Directorate KST)
	December	Dialogue between Indonesian and Myanmar parliaments	• IPD • MoFA (Directorate of East Asia and Pacific)
	June	Workshop and training on chairmanship in ASEAN	• IPD • MoFA (Directorate of East Asia and Pacific)
2014	March	Workshop on enhancing Supremacy of Law in the framework of protection of human rights	• MoFA (Directorate KST, Directorate of East Asia and Pacific, and Directorate of Legal Affairs) • Ministry of Law and Human Rights
	July	Discussion on strengthening election monitoring system	• Election Commission • Local (Jakarta) Election Monitoring Body • MoFA (Directorate KST and Directorate of East Asia and Pacific)
	October	Workshop on national action plan on human rights	• MoFA (Directorate KST, Directorate of East Asia and Pacific) • Indonesian Embassy in Yangon
2015	July	Training program on peace-building in the process of sustainable development in Myanmar	• MoFA (Directorate KST and Directorate of East Asia and Pacific • Ministry of Defense (MoD) • Indonesian Embassy in Yangon
	November	Workshop on enhancing capacities in democracy and human rights	• MoFA (Directorate KST, Directorate of East Asia and Pacific, and Directorate of Legal Affairs) • Ministry of Law and Human Rights

Source: Blue Book on Indonesia–Myanmar capacity building partnership 2013–2015 (Indonesian Ministry of Foreign Affairs 2013)

the principle of equality, mutual respect and understanding, with the participating countries sharing its ownership'.[12] The IPD was formed by the Ministry of Foreign Affairs with the support of Udayana University, based in Bali, to serve as the implementing agency for the Bali Democracy Forum.[13]

The mediation/facilitation/monitoring roles usually involved certain high-ranking active or ex-government officials or other prominent figures. The monitoring/observer role usually involved civil servants and military personnel, which was the composition of the Indonesian delegation that participated in the IMT in the Southern Philippines.

Finally, in the humanitarian actions area, the activities have been diverse, ranging from providing health facilities, building schools, natural disaster relief efforts to help the victims, to providing temporary shelters for the displaced Rohingya minorities.

Budget

Most of Indonesia's peacebuilding activities are funded through the national budget, but some activities receive funding or grants from external partners. Unfortunately, it is still difficult to determine the specific allocations from the national budget for Indonesia's SSTC, let alone activities related to capacity building in democracy and conflict resolution per se. While there may be some information available about the targeted countries and types of assistance, there is no specific information available about budget allocation for each program.

The activities to promote dialogues on democracy organized by IPD cost around US$67,000 (IDR 800 million) per activity, which includes preliminary visits to conduct a needs assessment, consultations and networking with local stakeholders, and workshops and trainings.[14] Since IPD is independent of the government, it seeks funding support from external partners, such as AusAID, USAID, and different foreign embassies in Indonesia, while cost-sharing has been utilized for some activities in collaboration with several ministries.[15]

Table 3.2 shows some pieces of information that can be traced from 2010 to 2014, which is related to Indonesia's peacebuilding activities abroad.

Table 3.2 Indonesia's peacebuilding assistance in selected countries (2010–2014)

Target country	*Year*	*Form*	*Amount*
Palestine	2014	Aid	USD 5,00,000 (IDR 1 billion)
	2014	Aid	USD 1 million
	2014	Capacity building	USD 1.5 million
	2012	Aid	USD 1,00,000
	2012	Fund to develop cardiac center in Gaza	USD 2.1 million (IDR 20 billion)
	2010	Aid	USD 20,000
	2010	Training for Palestinian businessman	USD 66,700 (IDR 600 million)
Myanmar	2014	Funding to build four schools	USD 1 million
(Rakhine state)	2013	Emergency relief and funding to redevelop housings	USD 1 million
South Thailand	2013	50 scholarships for college students to study at Islamic Universities in Indonesia	n/a
Syria	2014	Aid	USD 5,00,000

Source: Author's compilation from different media sources

Impact

Just as it is difficult to put together a comprehensive and systematic accounting of Indonesia's peacebuilding activities, it is also hard to measure the impact of those activities on sustaining peace. As in the case of Indonesia's overall SSTC framework, the ultimate problem is that there have been no evaluation or monitoring mechanisms to date. There has been an absence of evaluations of completed projects, which could prove useful to assess which activities work and which do not (CSIS 2014, 55).

Thus far, the main indicator of success is positive feedback from the relevant stakeholders or follow-up requests from the host countries for further engagement, such as in Indonesia's engagement with Egypt in sharing its democratic experiences.[16] Another example is the acknowledgement given by the highest leader of the Moro Islamic Liberation Front (MILF)), Al Haj Murad Ebrahim, in support of Indonesia's continuing role with the IMT in ensuring the success of the peace process in the Southern Philippines (Ladiasan 2014). In addition, Myanmar President Thein Sein asked Indonesia to assist his country in resolving ethnic tensions, particularly those involving the Rohingya people. Moreover, the Myanmar government also indicated its hope and support for Indonesian private sector investment in the Rakhine state—the area where most Rohingya people live—in order to create more jobs to ease the social and economic problems there (Santosa 2012).

In the case of ASEAN, the achievements, interestingly, have been measured in terms of the ability of some ASEAN countries to 'unite'. The Aceh Monitoring Mission (AMM) to conduct peacebuilding tasks, mainly to monitor the decommissioning of GAM (the separatist Free Aceh Movement group) weapons, redeployment of the Indonesian security forces, reintegration of ex-combatants into the society, as well as the legislative process have been deemed at least a partial success due to the participation of some ASEAN member states (Brunei, Malaysia, the Philippines, Singapore, and Thailand), including Indonesia, which made the mission impartial, without denying the significant support given by some European Union member states during the early phase of AMM. There was even a proposal to make AMM a model for future cooperation in crisis management between regional actors (Feith 2007, 1–7).

This can also be seen in the establishment of the IMT—in which Indonesia, Malaysia, and Brunei participated—to monitor the implementation of the peace agreement between the Government of the Philippines and MILF. In fact, the consent from the host country, as shown by the Indonesian and the Philippines governments, for ASEAN or some ASEAN member states, in collaboration with external partners to conduct peacebuilding activities, is by itself already an indicator of achievement.

Conclusions and Way Forward

The account above demonstrates that Indonesia views its peacebuilding role as part of its overall assistance and cooperation with other countries, particularly fellow developing countries. While some peacebuilding efforts entailed humanitarian actions, including aiding the people in host countries with some economic assistance, the government tends to separate peacebuilding efforts from 'routine' development assistance that supports economic and socio-cultural ends. In its peacebuilding efforts, Indonesia focuses more on sharing capacities in the political field, particularly by sharing its democratic and human rights values and playing a mediation or facilitation role.

Rather than having a rigid template to be brought to the host countries, Indonesia tends to approach them with a 'blank sheet'. Indonesian diplomats and analysts interviewed for this study suggest that Indonesia often takes a longer time to explore the needs of respected countries while opening up genuine communications with different local stakeholders both from government and non-governmental actors. Indonesia believes that each country has its own strengths. Indonesia's role is to support each country as it crafts its own peacebuilding process, rather than pushing it from the outside. This approach contributes to the establishment of a sense of national ownership, which is critical to ensure the success of any peacebuilding effort. Furthermore, a persuasive approach is necessary in peace efforts in order not to challenge the government's sovereignty. The demand for learning from Indonesia's experiences should come from the host countries, rather than being imposed by the Indonesian government.

Indonesia emphasizes a mutual learning process when conducting peacebuilding activities. Rather than the partner countries simply learning from Indonesia's experiences, it is always a two-way exercise in which Indonesia also learns from the other side. Since Indonesia, in its encounter with partner countries, is willing to divulge that it is also still struggling with many internal problems that threaten sustainable peace, partner countries are persuaded of the value of Indonesia's role, especially to be open in exploring and discussing their problems. This first step is crucial to the process of finding solutions.

However, Indonesia's peacebuilding role faces many challenges. The first challenge comes from within the government: a lack of coordination among different government institutions. Within the Ministry of Foreign Affairs, for example, several directorates handle peacebuilding in Myanmar. Based on geography, Myanmar is handled under the responsibility of the Directorate of ASEAN Political Affairs and Security, as well as the Directorate for East Asia and Pacific. Peacebuilding is also categorized as part of Indonesia's public diplomacy, and some activities are coordinated by the Directorate of Technical Cooperation under the Directorate-General of Public Diplomacy. Other activities involve other ministries or agencies such as the police or military institutions.

The second challenge is the lack of detailed and centralized databases containing records on peacebuilding programs and activities. Related to this is the dearth of standardized monitoring and evaluation mechanisms to measure achievements as well as mistakes in order to make improvements. So far each institution generally keeps its own notes on evaluations, if any. However, the public rarely has access to such notes and reports.

Third, while there is much research to be done, Indonesia's niche capacities and distinct approach in conducting its peacebuilding in the region, as well as in the global arena, represent a distinct contribution. Its approach reflects broader approaches of rising powers that ultimately fill gaps left by the efforts of traditional Western actors.

Rather than competing, the different approaches taken by traditional actors and rising powers complement one another. Traditional actors have provided useful guidelines that define peacebuilding and list the essential activities and principles that must be applied in order to sustain peace in the long run. Nevertheless, the distinct approaches introduced by rising powers are also important, since these actors' recent experiences with peacebuilding within their own borders provide a certain legitimacy. These approaches emphasize the need to respect the host country's sovereignty, as well as the importance of gaining confidence and trust from the very beginning of the peacebuilding process and working at a pace that is comfortable for local stakeholders.

However, rising actors still face challenges, mainly in securing funding to sustain their global and regional peacebuilding activities. Traditional actors can play a role in collaborating with the rising powers to conduct peacebuilding activities. Through the framework of triangular cooperation, traditional peacebuilding actors can provide funding for the programs initiated and designed by the rising actors. Traditional actors can also help rising powers frame their experiences more effectively. UNDP, for example, has a depth of knowledge in peacebuilding projects as well as how to monitor the implementation of those projects in a professional manner. Such knowledge is important to transform rising powers into more advanced actors in peacebuilding. However, it is important that they bring their own distinctive experiences and wisdom to their peacebuilding efforts.

Finally, consolidation of Indonesia's own material capabilities is important to sustain the expansion of its peacebuilding activities, particularly if Indonesia wishes to continue its role as peace facilitator/mediator. Using soft power is indeed important and useful, but not enough. By doing so, Indonesia can regain its leadership in the region and enhance its global role.

Notes

1. ASEAN Charter, article 2.
2. In the Draft Grand Design for Indonesia's South-South Triangular Cooperation, there are seven program priorities mentioned. The other six programs are capacity building in the field of trading and export; infrastructure and road construction program; family planning and reproductive health program; scholarship for developing countries; capacity building in macro-economy, public finance, and micro-economy; and capacity-building in the field of community empowerment. It should be noted that the Grand Design is in the form of final draft that is still awaiting the government's promulgation.
3. Similar to the Grand Design, this Blue Print also awaits the government's promulgation. The other comparative advantages are poverty reduction; agriculture and food security; infrastructure; disaster and climate change risk management: human resource development; development of science; socio-cultural development; macro-economy, economic management, and public finance; and microfinance; trading, service, and investment. Peacebuilding is listed as number 6 in the list.
4. According to the final draft of the Grand Design of Indonesia's SSTC, there are seven program priorities: (1) capacity-building in democracy and conflict resolution; (2) capacity-building in the field of trading and export; (3) infrastructure and road construction program; (4) family planning and reproductive health program; (5) scholarship for developing countries; (6) capacity-building in macro-economy, public finance, and micro-economy; and (7) capacity-building in the field of community empowerment.
5. See, for example, the transcript of interview conducted by the International Business Times with Dilshod A. Achilov, Professor of Political Science at Tennessee State University, who is an expert on the Middle East and Islam in Palash Ghosh, 'Arab nations may look to Turkey and Indonesia as models of modern Islamic states', in http://www.ibtimes.com/arab-nations-may-look-turkey-indonesia-models-modern-islamic-states-part-1-272111 and http://www.ibtimes.com/arab-nations-may-look-turkey-indonesia-models-modern-islamic-states-part-2-272119.
6. An interesting story about the prominent facilitator from Malaysia of the Southern Philippines talks, Datuk Tengku Abdul Ghaffar Tengku Mohd, can be viewed in an article by Razak Ahmad, 'Holding peace talks over a cuppa', October 21, 2012, http://www.thestar.com.my/News/Nation/2012/10/21/Holding-peace-talks-over-a-cuppa/. For more details about the roles of ICG, read Conciliation Resources, *Innovation in Mediation Support: The International Contact Group in Mindanao* at

http://www.c-r.org/resources/practice-paper-innovation-mediation-international-contact-group-mindanao and Democratic Progress Institute, *Briefing: International Contact Group for the Southern Philippines Peace Process*, 2014, at http://www.democraticprogress.org/briefing-international-contact-group-for-the-southern-philippines-peace-process/.

7. Interview with Ambassador Artauli RMP Tobing in Jakarta, June 18, 2015.
8. Centre for Strategic and International Studies, *Study on Policy Implementation and Funding Partnership Strategy of South-South and Triangular Cooperation*, August 2014. This report is part of the Capacity Development Project for South-South and Triangular Cooperation (CADEP-SSTC): a cooperation between the Government of Indonesia, through the National Coordination Team on South-South and Triangular Cooperation (NCT-SSTC), and the Government of Japan, through the JICA Indonesia Office.
9. Interview with Dr. I Ketut Erawan, Executive Director of the IPD, June 17, 2015.
10. This report is part of the CADEP-SSTC: a cooperation between the Government of Indonesia, through the NCT-SSTC, and the Government of Japan, through the JICA Indonesia Office.
11. See, for example: 'ASEAN urged to pressure Myanmar over Rohingya crisis', *The Jakarta Post*, June 3, 2015, http://www.thejakartapost.com/news/2015/06/03/asean-urged-pressure-myanmar-over-rohingya-crisis.html.
12. 'What is the Bali Democracy Forum?', http://bdf.kemlu.go.id/index.php?option=com_content&view=article&id=445&Itemid=106&lang=en.
13. IPD has just recently in the mid-2015 gained its independent legal status as a foundation that makes it no longer under the special status in connection with Udayana University.
14. Interview with Dr. I Ketut Erawan, Executive Director of IPD, June 17, 2015.
15. The supporting embassies are, for example, Embassy of Netherlands, New Zealand Embassy, Norwegian Embassy, Embassy of Japan, and Embassy of Switzerland—see http://www.ipd.or.id/about-ipd/partners-and-donors.
16. Interview with Dr. I Ketut Erawan, Executive Director of IPD, June 17, 2015.

References

Adamrah, Mustaqim. 2011. Myanmar Set to Chair ASEAN: FM. *The Jakarta Post*, November 16.

Alatas, Ali. 2001. *A Voice for a Just Peace: A Collection of Speeches by Ali Alatas*. Jakarta: PT Gramedia.

Alford, Peter. 2011. Indonesia a Model for Arab Uprisings. *The Australian*, August 27.

Antara News. 2017. Indonesia Proposes Four Actions for Rakhine. *Antara News*, January 21. Accessed January 23, 2017. http://www.antaranews.com/en/news/109037/indonesia-proposes-four-actions-for-rakhine.

Anwar, Dewi F. 2010. Foreign Policy, Islam and Democracy in Indonesia. *Journal of Indonesian Social Sciences and Humanities* 3: 37–54.

Centre for Strategic and International Studies. 2014. *Study on Policy Implementation and Funding Partnership Strategy of South-South and Triangular Cooperation*. Jakarta.

Eliraz, Giora. 2014. Indonesian Democracy Comes to Tunisia. *Australia Israel and Jewish Affairs Council (AIJAC)*, March 19. Accessed January 23, 2017. http://www.aijac.org.au/news/article/indonesian-democracy-comes-to-tunisia.

Fan, Lilianne and Hanna B. Krebs. 2014. Regional Organisations and Humanitarian Action: The Case of ASEAN. *Humanitarian Policy Group Working Paper*.

Feith, Pieter. 2007. The Aceh Peace Process: Nothing Less than Success. *United States Institute of Peace Special Report* 184:1–7. Accessed January 30, 2017. http://www.usip.org/sites/default/files/sr184.pdf.

Hotland, Tony. 2008. Indonesia Defends Stance on UN Role in Myanmar. *The Jakarta Post*, May 15.

Indonesian Ministry of Foreign Affairs. 2013. *Blue Book on Indonesia-Myanmar Capacity Building Partnership 2013–2015*.

Karim, M. Faisal. 2013. Indonesia Should Promote Democracy Globally, Starting with Egypt. *East Asia Forum*. http://www.eastasiaforum.org/2013/08/22/indonesia-should-promote-democracy-globally-starting-with-egypt/

Kompas. 2012a. Indonesia Has a Big Role in Myanmar [Indonesia Punya Peran Besar di Myanmar]. *Kompas* February 3.

———. 2012b. Myanmar: Indonesia Mungkin Ikut Pantau Pemilihan Umum [Myanmar: Indonesia May Join to Monitor Election]. *Kompas* January 5.

Ladiasan, R.T.. 2014. Chairman Murad Thanks Indonesia for Sending New Contingent with IMT. http://afrim.org.ph/newafrim/tag/international-monitoring-team-imt

Leifer, Michael. 1983. *Indonesia's Foreign Policy*. London: George Allen & Unwin.

Maulida, Erwida, and Mustaqim Adamrah. 2011. RI Set to Help Democratize Myanmar. *The Jakarta Post*, December 29.

Narine, Shaun. 1998. ASEAN and the Management of Regional Security. *Pacific Affairs* 71(2): 195–214.

Santosa, Novan I. 2012. Myanmar Asks RI to Help Settle Rohingya Problem. *The Jakarta Post*, November 21.

Sastrohandoyo, Wiryono. 2008. Indonesia and Southeast Asian Territorial Peace Process. *Asia Europe Journal* 6(1): 15–30.

Sukma, Rizal. 2012. Domestic Politics and International Posture: Constraints and Possibilities. In *Indonesia Rising: The Repositioning of Asia's Third Giant*, ed. Anthony Reid. Singapore: ISEAS.

Tan, Paige J. 2007. Navigating Turbulent Ocean: Indonesia's Worldview and Foreign Policy. *ASIAN Perspective* 31(3): 147–181.

Taufiqurrahman, M. 2012a. Kalla Pledges Aid to Myanmar Rohingya. *The Jakarta Post*, September 10.

———. 2012b. Former RI VP Joins Myanmar Peace Process. *The Jakarta Post*, September 11.

The Jakarta Post. 2010. Foreign Help not Needed in Southern Thailand: PM. *The Jakarta Post*, July 27.

Weatherbee, Donald E. 2005. Indonesian Foreign Policy: A Wounded Phoenix. *Southeast Asian Affairs* 1: 150–170.

Widyaningsih, Erlina, and Christopher B. Roberts. 2014. Indonesia in ASEAN: Mediation, Leadership, and Extra-mural Diplomacy. *National Security College Issue Brief* 13: 105–116. Accessed January 30, 2017. http://nsc.anu.edu.au/documents/Indonesia-Article13.pdf

Wulan, Alexandra R., and Bantarto Bandoro. 2007. *ASEAN's Quest for a Full-fledged Community*. Jakarta: CSIS.

Yudhoyono, Susilo B. 2005. *Transforming Indonesia: Selected International Speeches*. Jakarta: Office of Special Staff of the President for International Affairs.

Lina A. Alexandra is Senior Researcher, Centre for Strategic and International Studies (CSIS), Jakarta.

CHAPTER 4

Peacebuilding Through Development Partnership: An Indian Perspective

Lt. Gen. (ret.) P.K. Singh

Introduction

As the largest democracy to have emerged out of the bonds of colonialism, India has played an important role in providing valuable aid and assistance to newly independent and developing countries around the world since its independence. In order to fulfil its international obligation of helping countries make the difficult transition to self-reliance and development, India has contributed to building strong and peaceful countries and regions across the globe by sharing with them the benefits of its own experience as well as global best practices, along with providing valuable aid and assistance.

To put India's development assistance programme in its correct perspective, it is absolutely necessary to understand the factors shaping Indian discourse over the years. India played an important role on the global stage even before it became an independent nation on 15 August 1947. The Indian Armed Forces provided the largest volunteer armies to participate both in the First and Second World Wars, where there were hundreds of thousands of casualties and faced demobilisation immediately after the

Lt. Gen. (ret.) P.K. Singh (✉)
United Service Institution of India, New Delhi, India

C.T. Call, C. de Coning (eds.), *Rising Powers and Peacebuilding*, Rethinking Peace and Conflict Studies,
DOI 10.1007/978-3-319-60621-7_4

wars. During the First World War, the Indian Army was one of the first to face the horrors of Chemical Warfare. India was also a founding signatory of the League of Nations as well as the United Nations (UN). During 1943 India was faced with a famine in Bengal, where reportedly two to three million people died, yet the export of food grains from India to support the global war effort continued uninterruptedly.

While independence broke the shackles of British colonialism, it also partitioned the country and saw the greatest displacement of population that the world had ever known. It led to rioting and communal violence that left thousands dead. Before the nation could get to grips with this, the Pakistan Army supported by irregular forces invaded the Indian State of Jammu and Kashmir. Being a founding member of the UN and believing in its principles, India took the issue to the UN hoping for justice, but what followed was an eye-opener for India, as also a lesson on what to expect from great powers and international institutions. Insurgency, supported by foreign countries, also reared its head in the early to mid-1950s, and India's experience in successfully handling these insurgencies, where it used the security forces along with the civilian administration in addressing social-politico-economic development, shaped its outlook towards development assistance.

India also faced a major refugee problem in 1971, when over ten million people from East Pakistan flooded into India. This and other events led to a short Indo-Pakistan war in December 1971, resulting in the creation of Bangladesh. India not only pulled back its troops from Bangladesh within about three months after the hostilities, but also relocated over 92,000 Pakistani prisoners of war from Bangladesh to India, thereby ensuring their safety in consonance with the Geneva Conventions. India's contribution to the UN peacekeeping operations is well known. These factors, amongst others, need to be kept in mind while analysing India's contribution to development partnership, peacekeeping and peacebuilding.

The Peacekeeping Paradigm

India's contribution towards building the infrastructure for peace and stability in developing countries precedes and, to a large extent, anticipates, the concept of "peacebuilding" as enunciated by the UN. India's aid and assistance programmes have not only helped countries tide over the onset or aftermath of major crises, but have often come in early to forestall potential crises from destabilising a country or a region. Close partnerships in the development process have naturally led to strong contacts, and the benefits of the association have exceeded beyond the "assistance" paradigm. It is this attitude of mutual respect and goodwill between the development assistance partners that has proven more successful for India than just the quantity or amount of aid delivered per se.

However, to compare India's development aid and assistance practices with the UN's principles of "peacebuilding," it would be important to study the two concepts at the outset.

The UN Perspective

The emergence of the theory and practice of "peacebuilding" has been one of the most innovative developments in peace and conflict research over the past generation. It is believed that just as peacekeeping was the UN's most important contribution to peace and security in the first 50 years of its existence, peacebuilding could become its most important innovation in the future (Ryan 2013).

The concept of peacebuilding in the UN was introduced in 1992 by UN Secretary General Boutros Boutros-Ghali in the report "An Agenda for Peace," wherein he defined peacebuilding as "action to identify and support structures, which will tend to strengthen and solidify peace in order to avoid a relapse into conflict" (United Nations Information Centre for India and Bhutan 2006). Although the report had only a few paragraphs devoted to the concept, it acted as a catalyst for further research and evolution of the concept.

A more detailed understanding of the term was given by the UN Secretary General's Policy Committee in 2007, which described peacebuilding as "a range of measures targeted to reduce the risk of lapsing or relapsing into conflict by strengthening national capacities at all levels of conflict management, and to lay the foundation for sustainable peace and development" (United Nations Information Centre for India and Bhutan 2006). The Secretary General's Report of 2009 identified five recurring priority areas for international assistance. The first was the support to basic safety and security; the second referred to political processes; the third referred to the provision of basic services; the fourth referred to the restoration of core government functions; and the fifth identified economic revitalisation as a priority area.

Although the idea of "peacebuilding" has been well received, it has faced many challenges over the years. Thus, the Policy Committee's aforementioned statement in 2007 also enunciated the way in which peacebuilding strategies need to be developed and implemented. It states, "Peacebuilding strategies must be coherent and tailored to the specific needs of the country concerned, based on national ownership, and should comprise a carefully prioritised, sequenced, and relatively narrow set of activities aimed at achieving the above objectives."

It is noteworthy that the importance of local ownership, as is evident in the statement above, has remained a key component to the idea of peacebuilding, but it has been difficult to observe in practice. Cedric de Coning has highlighted this shortcoming in peacebuilding efforts by stating that "the notion of local ownership has become a buzzword. It is one of those words that has to be in any document about end states and exit strategies, yet no one really expects it to be meaningfully pursued" (de Coning 2013).

He points out that "external peace-builders see themselves as acting in a kind of unacknowledged guardian role, in which they act according to what they think are in the best interest of the society. Very few recognise or acknowledge the role the international community plays in undermining local ownership" (de Coning 2013).

Again, the political nature of peacebuilding is often ignored. This issue was squarely addressed by the UN Secretary General in his address to the first session of the Peacebuilding Commission on 23 June 2006, when he stated:

> "We must also remember that peacebuilding is inherently political. At times the international community has approached peacebuilding as a largely technical exercise, involving knowledge and resources. The international community must not only understand local power dynamics, but also recognize that it is itself a political actor entering a political environment". In this regard, the statement of Mr Jan Eliasson, the UN Deputy Secretary General, during the debate on post-conflict peacebuilding, wherein he said that "peacebuilding is most effective when political, security and development actors support a common, comprehensive and clear strategy for consolidating peace,"[1] merits consideration.

An Indian Perspective

India has a distinguished legacy of international peacekeeping and peacebuilding dating back to the 1950s when as a newly independent and democratic country, it reached out and helped other newly independent countries emerge from the scourge of colonialism by partnering in the establishment of state institutions and developmental activities. In essence, the foundation of later South–South Cooperation (SSC) can rightly be attributed to these partnerships, which cemented national identities with those of a later day larger South–South movement.

Right from the beginning the economic and technical assistance that India extended to other developing countries was voluntary and not an obligation, like the Overseas Development Assistance (ODA). Further unlike the ODA, India characterised its assistance as development partnership and not a donor–recipient relationship. India's basic approach to development assistance was that it was demand-driven, given without conditionalities, administered in a decentralised manner and would not constrain the sovereignty of its partners. Simply put, India's philosophy was that despite being a poor, developing country just out from the shackles of colonialism, it had an international responsibility and obligation to share its modest resources and capabilities with other developing countries.

India has clearly articulated its position on issues pertaining to peacebuilding during various debates at the UN. It has given particular emphasis to local ownership, inclusiveness and relevance rather than being imposed from above. In his statement at the UN Security Council Open debate on post- conflict peacebuilding on 12 July 2012, Mr Vinay Kumar, Charge d'Affaires, Permanent Mission of India to the UN (PMI), said, "We, therefore, think that the core institutions of governance are the key to sustainable peace. They must be rooted locally rather than being imposed from above. Their local relevance and inclusiveness will make all the difference in the governance process. It is, therefore, important for the PBC (Peacebuilding Commission) to align its objectives with national priorities and ensure that all plans and programs are implemented under national leadership and through national institutions so that gains are sustainable even if slow" (Kumar 2012).

In its statement on the Report of the Peacebuilding Commission on its 7th Session and the Report of the Secretary General on the Peacebuilding Fund on 26 March 2014, India stated that: "Peacebuilding is important. It is necessary to rebuild institutions and infrastructure in nations torn by civil war if we want to solidify peace and avoid a relapse into conflict. A certain amount of external guidance is implicit in peacebuilding, but it should not be at the cost of local ownership and agenda.... The external footprint should be light to avoid any outcomes of neo-colonialism or humanitarian intervention" (Mukerji 2014).

In his statement, at the Informal Interactive Dialogue of the General Assembly on 8 September 2014, Mr Abhishek Singh, First Secretary, PMI, stated, "Peacebuilding involves a range of measures targeted to reduce the risk of lapsing or relapsing into conflict by strengthening national capacities at all levels for conflict management, and to lay the foundations for sustainable peace and development. Peacebuilding strategies must be coherent and tailored to specific needs of the country concerned based on national ownership, and should comprise a carefully prioritized, sequenced and therefore relatively narrow set of activities aimed at achieving the above objectives. The emphasis should be building national capacities and national ownership" (Mukerji 2014).

It is therefore heartening to note that today India has provided development assistance to over 160 countries since its independence, encompassing multiple sectors, while at the same time adhering to its declared philosophy.

Philosophy and Evolution of Indian Development

Partnership Architecture

Right at the outset it needs to be understood that the "Indian Development Partnership Architecture" is a work in progress and there is no single document or White Paper that spells out the "architecture." The building blocks of this "architecture" have to be culled out from the then prevailing national/international scenario, policy statements, participation in bilateral and multilateral development organisations and so on. India's development partnership architecture could therefore be looked as an experimental model that has undergone a series of institutional innovations at different points in time.

India's foreign policy philosophy since independence in 1947 under its first Prime Minister Jawahar Lal Nehru has often been seen as one laced in an element of idealism. However, in the early years of its independence, India realised that countries in the global south that were emerging from colonialism would be affected by fragility, poverty, lack of infrastructure and possibly conflict or violence and would need development partnership right from the moment they gained independence. Although the term "South–South Cooperation" was not coined then, the seeds of its need and values can be traced to this phenomenon of helping countries in the South build a peaceful environment through development aid and partnership.

The foreign policy philosophy of India was based on the ideal of peaceful co-existence, wherein the economic development of all countries would be an obligation of the whole international community. India's development partnership was thus a commitment to internationalism, wherein all countries emerging from the scourge of colonialism and the after-effects of the Second World War would contribute to the evolution of a new and just global order. In 1947 when India became independent, it neither had any experience in the field of international aid/partnership, nor was there any substantive architecture for this available that would suit its ideas of development needs and partnership. Therefore, India's development partnership programme is an evolutionary process that takes into account its own developmental experiences and its own vision of social and economic development.

India's development partnership programme commenced in 1949 and precedes the concept of peacebuilding as we know it today. Right from the outset, India's basic philosophy towards development assistance was that any aid/assistance would be demand-driven, given without conditionalities, be administered in a decentralised manner and would not constrain the sovereignty of its partners in any way. An important point to note is that India has not made the same distinction between development assistance and peacebuilding activities that the traditional actors seem to make. Another point worth mentioning is that although never very clearly spelt out, India shares her experiences of democracy, pluralism and tolerance with the host countries, without interfering in their internal politics and social dynamics.

Some of the important milestones in the evolution of India's Development Partnership programmes that commenced in 1949 itself were the establishment of the Cultural Fellowship in the Ministry of External Affairs (MEA) and the follow-up by a special concessional loan to Burma (Myanmar) in 1949 itself to help meet its balance of payment crisis. The Colombo Plan for Cooperative Economic and Social Development in Asia and the Pacific was conceived in January 1950 and launched on 1 July 1951 as a cooperative venture by seven Commonwealth nations, including India, thereby showing that India was willing to partner multilateral organisations in addition to its bilateral developmental relationships.

In 1954, an overseas Indian Aid Mission (IAM) was launched at Kathmandu, Nepal, for coordinating and monitoring implementation of various Indian projects in Nepal. In 1964, the first agreement was signed with Nepal for periodic review of development projects. Seeing its success, a joint commission for project reviews was established in

Afghanistan in 1969. This commission, which was set up in other countries too, was tasked to also identify resources and capabilities for undertaking projects of mutual interest and also exploring possibilities for expanding trade. The IAM was renamed as the Indian Cooperation Mission (ICM) in 1966, signifying that the Indian partnership was not just about aid but was a cooperative partnership, and in 1980 the ICM was merged under the new Economic Cooperation Wing of the Indian Embassy in Kathmandu. In November 2003, India and Nepal signed a Memorandum of Understanding (MOU) for initiating the Small Development Projects (SDP) in Nepal. The SDP was based on local needs through community participation with development directly reaching the beneficiaries in a short period of time. The project costs were less than US$ 0.7 million. The implementation of the SDP was overseen by a Project Monitoring Committee, which ensured that there was no cost and time overruns. These projects are so successful in Nepal that India is now implementing SDP in Afghanistan, Sri Lanka, Bhutan and Myanmar.

Many ministries are involved in the Indian Development Partnership Programs. For instance, Ministry of Rural Development is the nodal ministry of two international organisations connected with rural development. These are as follows:

- The Afro-Asian Rural Development Organisation (AARDO). This is an inter-governmental, autonomous organisation founded in 1962 with a view to promote coordinated efforts, exchange of experiences and cooperative action for furthering the objectives of development of rural areas. It has 30 African and Asian nations, including India, as its members. Earlier, AARDO was known as the Afro-Asian Rural Reconstruction Organisation. The AARDO has its permanent headquarters at New Delhi.
- Centre for Integrated Rural Development of Asia and the Pacific (CIRDAP). India is a member of the inter-governmental CIRDAP, which was established in July 1979 at the initiative of the countries of the Asia-Pacific Region and the FAO of the UN with support from several other UN bodies. It has 15 member countries, including Afghanistan, Bangladesh (host country), India, Myanmar and Vietnam. It came into being to meet the needs of various developing countries of that time. It was mandated to facilitate the provision of services that will influence policy formations and programme actions towards rural development and poverty alleviation (CIRDAP 2017).

Indian Technical and Economic Cooperation Programme (ITEC)—Realising the importance of capacity building and skills development, India launched the ITEC in 1964 under its MEA to share knowledge and skills with fellow developing countries. The ITEC programme, which is fully government funded, is essentially bilateral in nature and is in line with its stated objective of respecting sovereignty and fostering a cooperative approach. It is demand-driven and does not impose any conditionalities. It furthers national development priorities of India's partners and has national ownership at its core. Under the ITEC and its sister programme, SCAAP (Special Commonwealth African Assistance Programme), a total of 161 countries in Asia, Africa, East Europe, Latin America, the Caribbean as well as Pacific and Small Island countries are invited to share in the Indian developmental experience acquired over six decades. For civilian training programmes, a total of 8280 slots were allotted to ITEC/SCAAP partner countries during 2013–14, for which approximately US$ 23 million was budgeted. Similarly about 1500 vacancies for security training were allotted to ITEC partners for nominating their personnel for training in the field of Security and Strategic Studies, Defense Management, Marine and Aeronautical Engineering, Logistics and Management and so on. Although ITEC was initially conceived as a programme at the bilateral level, in recent years, ITEC programmes have also been used for cooperation activities conceived in regional and inter-regional contexts such as Economic Commission for Africa, Industrial Development Unit of Commonwealth Secretariat, UNIDO, Group of 77 and G-15. It has also been associated with regional and multilateral organisations such as the Association of Southeast Asian Nations (ASEAN), African Union (AU), Bay of Bengal Initiative for Multi-Sectoral Technical and Economic Cooperation (BIMSTEC), Afro-Asian Rural Development Organisation (AARDO), Caribbean Community (CARICOM), World Trade Organization (WTO), Pan-African Parliament, Indian Ocean Rim—Association for Regional Cooperation (IOR-ARC) and India-Africa Forum Summit. ITEC is the flagship programme for India's capacity-building effort, not only because of its magnitude and wide geographical coverage, but also for innovative forms of technical cooperation. Approximately US$ 3 billion has been spent by India on the programme since its launch in 1964.

Pan-African e-Network—With the growth of the economy and the technology, especially in the IT and health care sector, India embarked on an ambitious and visionary project in 2009, known as the "Pan-African e-Network," to provide educational and medical support to 54 participating African countries, remotely via satellite technology through a grant of US$ 125 million. The network is equipped to support e-governance, e-commerce, remote mapping and meteorological data sharing. Over a dozen super-specialty hospitals in India have been connected to African hospitals where tele-consultations and continuing medical education sessions are conducted. Simultaneously about 50 learning centres in Africa were connected to five Indian universities, thereby providing education facilities to thousands of students.

Alongside the processes mentioned above, the MEA itself continues to evolve, learning not just from its own experiences but also from best practices in the development architecture globally. In 1961 the Economic and Coordination Division was established in the MEA to coordinate technological cooperation, and in 1964 the ITEC programme was launched as a part of this Economic Division. With the success of the ITEC programme and the consequent increase in workload, the ITEC Division was established in the MEA in 1995. In 2004, the India Development and Economic Assistance Scheme (IDEAS) was launched to provide lines of credit (LOC) by the EXIM Bank, and in 2005 a new division called the Development Partnership Division was created in the MEA for better delivery of development projects. During the budget speech of 2007, the Union Finance Minister had proposed the setting up of the India International Development Cooperation Agency for Coordinating all projects, lines of credit, technical cooperation, deputation of experts and training of foreign nationals in India. However, this agency was never set up and instead a new division called the "Development Partnership Administration (DPA)" was set up in 2012 for coordinating all aspects of India's Development Assistance.

As regards financial support, while the capacity-building ITEC programme was totally Government funded, loans and grants were also provided. To increase the amount of funding available for development activities, since 2003, LOC covering 63 countries totalling almost US$ 12 billion have been extended, with Africa receiving almost 60% of this. Similarly, the DPA is implementing a number of grant assistance programmes, which include construction of 50,000 houses for internally displaced persons in Sri Lanka, construction of the Salma Dam and power sub-station in Doshi and Charikar, and the Parliament building in Afghanistan. The EXIM Bank (2012) data on operative LOC for financial year 2011–12 provides the following detail (Table 4.1).

Table 4.1 EXIM Bank Operative Lines of Credit (2011–12, US$ million)

1. Asia	–	3458
2. Africa	–	4313
3. Americas	–	191
4. Europe and CIS	–	148
5. Total	–	8160

Diversity and Magnitude of Development Partnership

To get a good understanding of the diversity and magnitude of India's development partnership, one needs to just look at the India–Africa and India–Afghanistan development programmes.

India–Africa Programmes

India's links with Africa stretch back centuries, cutting across social, economic, political and diplomatic issues. The shared experience of colonialism leading to economic deprivation, fight for independence, partnership in the Non-Aligned Movement, the urge to promote SSC all come together, and it is difficult to separate one from the other. The fact that Indian peacekeepers under the UN flag have been participating in all UN missions in Africa also adds to this unique relationship between India and Africa. Therefore, examining India–Africa relations in silos may not bring out the true picture. Table 4.2 highlights the framework for Africa–India cooperation (Kragelund 2010).

Building on the foundations of the partnership laid through the ITEC programme amongst others, India launched the Focus Africa Programme in 2002 and was followed in 2005 by the Conclave of India-Africa Project Partnership, and in the next eight years there had been 22 Indo-African business conclaves. Buoyed by the healthy all-round economic and trade linkages, India hosted the first India–Africa Forum Summit in 2008 and the next summit meeting was held in 2011.

India–Afghanistan Programmes

A striking example of India's development assistance programmes that are in consonance with UN peacebuilding principles and the stated needs, requirements and involvement of the recipient country in promoting its

Table 4.2 Africa–India framework for cooperation

Areas	*Sub areas*	*Focus*	*Forms*	*Concrete initiatives*
Economic cooperation	Agriculture, trade, industry and FDI, SMEs, finance, regional integration	Food security, market access, exports to world markets and joint ventures	Cooperation, capacity-building, experience-sharing and TA	Financial support to African Union over mutually agreed programmes of continental importance
Political cooperation	Peace and security, civil society and governance	Governance structures, civil society, peacekeeping operations	TA, capacity building and cross fertilization of ideas	Joint Platform for Discussion of Global Issues (South–South basis)
Science technology and research	Science and technology, ICT	Technology transfer, quality standards and ICT regulation	Experience sharing, cooperation	Roll out the Pan-African E-Network project
Social development	Education, health, water and sanitation, culture and sports, poverty eradication	MDGs, HRD, access to health care	Experience sharing, cooperation	Increase ITEC scholarships
Terrorism		Regulation and governance	Partnerships	–
Infrastructure, energy and environment	–	PPP and creation of enabling environment	Cooperation	–
Media and communications	–	South–South communication	Cooperation	–

development and capacity building can be gleaned from the large-scale multisectoral assistance India has provided for the reconstruction and developmental programmes in Afghanistan. This development partnership dates back to the years shortly after Indian independence and continued during the civil war that followed the Soviet withdrawal in 1989, despite significant internal economic pressures. India provided Afghanistan with millions of US dollars in grants and humanitarian assistance through the UN during the 1990s. Since 2002, India has played an active role in the reconstruction of Afghanistan, with its programmes following priorities of the Afghan government and people.

The "Afghanistan National Development Strategy-Executive Summary 2008–2013—A Strategy for Security, Governance, Economic Growth and Poverty Reduction" (Afghanistan 2013) lists eight pillars for their national development: security; good governance; infrastructure and proper utilisation of natural resources; education and culture; health and nutrition; agriculture and rural development; social protection; and economic governance and private sector development. It is noteworthy that India's development assistance programmes to Afghanistan have substantially contributed to almost all of the pillars of national development enlisted by the Afghanistan National Development Strategy. Thus, India's reconstruction and developmental programmes in Afghanistan are tailored to the specific needs and ownership of the Afghan government and its people, as is enshrined in the values of the UN ideals of peacebuilding.

India has played a significant role in the reconstruction and rehabilitation of Afghanistan. India's extensive developmental assistance programme, which now stands at around US$ 2 billion, is a strong signal of its abiding commitment to peace, stability and prosperity in Afghanistan during this critical period of security and governance transition. This makes India one of the leading donor nations to Afghanistan, and by far the largest in the region.

The government of India has taken on several medium and large infrastructure projects in its assistance programme in Afghanistan. Some of these include construction of a 218 km road from Zaranj to Delaram for facilitating movement of goods and services to the Iranian border; construction of a 220KV DC transmission line from Pul-e-Khumri to Kabul and a 220/110/20 KV sub-station at Chimtala; upgrading of telephone exchanges in 11 provinces; expansion of national TV network by providing an uplink from Kabul and downlinks in all 34 provincial capitals for greater integration of the country; and three airbus aircraft to Ariana Airlines and construction of the new Afghan Parliament building. In the area of skill development, the Indian government offers training to Afghan officials/nationals in diverse fields through 500 ITEC slots allocated annually to Afghanistan; special ITEC courses for Afghan government officials; 614 ICAR scholarships under the India–Afghanistan Fellowship Program during 2012–13 to 2020–21; training via tele-education at the Afghan National Agriculture Sciences and Technology University, Kandahar, and at the Indira Gandhi Institute of Child Health, Kabul; and ICCR scholarships to 1000 Afghans every year to pursue under graduate courses in various Indian universities in major cities across India.

Major on-going Indian projects in Afghanistan include Salma Dam, Doshi and Charikar power substations; restoration of the Store Palace; and wheat assistance to Afghanistan to the tune of 1.1 million MT, out of which 7,11,882 tonnes of wheat has already been supplied. India has also decided to donate 1000 more buses to Afghanistan along with improving related infrastructure.

A significant addition to India's development portfolio in Afghanistan is the Small Development Projects (SDP) scheme for developing infrastructure in the fields of agriculture, rural development, education, health and so on. Announced during Prime Minister Manmohan Singh's visit to Afghanistan in 2005 initially with an amount of US$ 20 million, the scheme was further enhanced with additional provision of US$ 100 million in November 2012.

India is contributing to the security sector by providing equipment and training to the Afghan National Army and the Afghan Police. To help promote rule of law, India has trained Afghan judges and lawyers at the Indian Law Institute. As part of support to democracy, India has trained staff members of the National Assembly Secretariat at the Bureau of Parliamentary Study and Training on various aspects of parliamentary functions. Training was also imparted to journalists and news agency officials.

Development Partnership Administration (DPA)

From relatively modest beginnings, India has become an important player in the area of international development cooperation. Over the past few years, India's development assistance has started to cover a large number of countries, and, consequently, the projects being implemented by the MEA have increased substantially. Recognising this, the DPA was created in the MEA in January 2012 to effectively handle India's aid projects through the stages of concept, launch, execution and completion.

India's development partnership is based on the needs identified by the partner countries, and the effort of the MEA is geared toward accommodating as many of the requests received from partner countries as is technically and financially possible. DPA has started to create in-house, specialised technical, legal and financial skills in order to fast-track all stages of project implementation. DPA has three divisions. Currently,

DPA I deals with project appraisal and LOC; DPA II deals with capacity-building schemes, disaster relief and the Indian Technical and Economic Cooperation Program; and DPA III deals with project implementation. As the DAP in the MEA is gearing towards meeting its mandate, it is expected that effective and efficient handling of all aid projects from the stages of concept, launch, execution and completion would result in efficient implementation of projects, in close cooperation and facilitation of the partner countries.

While the lead agency in India's development partnership strategy will continue to be the MEA, it needs to be reiterated that other ministries in the government will continue to have an important role. MEA will therefore continue to advise the Ministry of Finance regarding assistance packages and priorities; coordinate with the Ministry of Commerce in relation to LOC; coordinate with the Ministry of Water Resources for hydroelectric projects; and coordinate with the Ministry of Defense for overseas projects to be undertaken by the Border Roads Organisation or for humanitarian assistance and disaster relief by the armed forces. The DPA while not formulating development assistance policy will deal with its implementation by focusing on greater synergy and coordination, streamlining the delivery mechanism and improving the effectiveness of the total development assistance/aid provided.

Emerging Powers and the Dynamics of South–South Cooperation (SSC)

During the last two decades, there has been a major shift in geopolitics with the emergence of new economic and military powers on the global stage. Many of these countries have the capacity to take on the role of peacebuilding because like the big industrialised nations of the past they have the finances, capacities and expertise to provide effective support in peacebuilding missions around the world. Underscoring the importance of emerging powers in maintaining and promoting peace at the global level, Benjamin de Carvalho and Cedric de Coning have noted:

> what distinguishes emerging powers from merely regional ones is that they are often responded to by others on the basis of system-level calculations about the present and near future distribution of power. Consequently, emerging powers can be said to be emerging from their regions onto the global scene, and they possess a certain set of attributes, or serious potential,

> to bid for great power status—i.e. taking on even greater responsibility for co-managing the global order in the short to medium term. (de Carvalho and de Coning 2013, 2)

They further state that:

> the rising powers are committed to the reform of the global order, and that they are pursuing a multilateral rule-based global architecture that can provide the legal and political framework necessary to ensure a more equitable, enforceable and stable global order, in which it would be impossible for any one country, or bloc of countries to dominate the system. (Ibid, 6)

These new emerging powers, particularly countries like India, China and South Africa, are becoming very important players in the development cooperation arena too. The emergence of these countries as development partners is very visible in Africa, where they have significantly expanded their presence through foreign direct investment, trade and knowledge transfer. Their achievements in addressing their own development challenges through innovative approaches make them more attractive as development partners, and have eroded the North's exclusive hold on matters of international development.

Debate over Role of South–South Cooperation (SSC)

Conceptually, SSC refers to the sharing of knowledge and resources between developing countries with the aim of identifying the most effective steps towards the eradication of their developmental challenges. It is strongly based on the notion of development through equitable access to trade, investment and technology and takes place at bilateral as well as inter/intra- regional levels. The emerging powers are offering the developing countries a choice, thereby introducing some form of competitive challenge in the existing development aid system and possibly this causes some tension in the North–South debate. This notwithstanding, it must be reiterated that SSC must be seen as a complement to and not a replacement of North–South Cooperation (NSC).

In the framework of SSC, there is no distinction between the partner countries. All the countries engaged have something to offer and take from each other. The key values of the SSC are respect for national sovereignty, national ownership and independence, equality, non-conditionality, non-interference in domestic affairs and mutual benefit. However, there are conceptual differences between the NSC and SSC, which are highlighted in Table 4.3 (Chaturvedi 2014).

Table 4.3 Comparison between North–South and South–South development partnership

Indicators	*Aid programme (North–South)*	*Development partnership (South–South)*
Nature and purpose of support	ODA. Stated to be altruistic in nature	Mutual benefits and growth
Philosophical perspective	Framework approach	Ingredient approach
Participants	At least one participant has very high per capita income	Both partners may have very low per-capita income
Level of development	Large differences in stages of economic development between donors and recipients	Both partners almost at the same stage of economic development
Role of participants	Donors and recipient of ODA	Relationship of equality, both may contribute to the process
Conditionality	"Top-down" with policy conditionality and no predictability	Request-driven and generally free from conditionality of any kind, so largely within timelines
Flexibility	Multilayered time-consuming bureaucratic structures, hence added transaction cost	Highly decentralised and relatively fast with a few implications for transaction cost
Priority sectors	Grant assistance and budget support for social sectors	Economic and technical cooperation largely confined to projects in infrastructure and productive sector investment
Adherence to global governance framework like Paris Declaration	Donors use guidelines of Paris Declaration, which they evolve as an instrument for effectiveness	Providers are out of the purview of any global arrangement such as Paris Declaration, in which they are not involved. Hinges on mutual trust of partner countries
Data, monitoring and evaluation	Peer-reviewed by DAC-OECD. Data are compiled and periodically released by the national governments and DAC-OECD	No monitoring mechanisms beyond occasional reports of data and anecdotal details
Role of NGOs	Extensive	Limited
Role of Private Sector	Limited	Extensive

The above notwithstanding, the fact is that as of now the South–South countries somewhat lack the requisite structural and organisational capacity to effectively pursue their aims. This contrasts sharply with the developed North that has well- funded institutions and mechanisms that coordinate their interests. Perhaps to overcome these challenges we see trilateral groupings such as the India–Brazil–South Africa dialogue forum or the multilateral groupings such as BRICS, spanning many continents (Ugwuja et al. 2014).

The growing role played by India and other developing countries in the area of development assistance seems to be causing anxiety in the West as they are apprehensive of losing influence in a field that they dominated. India has reservations about the Busan process, which is viewed as an attempt to standardise the delivery of assistance/aid on the norms and principles of the West. India is also generally cautious of some of the premises underlying the post MDG development agenda. India would not like to see that it becomes a means for the West to pass on a greater burden to developing countries. It needs reiteration that whereas North–South aid is a historical responsibility, SSC is a voluntary undertaking. The development assistance provided by the emerging developing countries should be viewed as different from the North–South commitments. It is neither a substitute for North–South aid nor should it be used as an excuse for developed countries to reduce their aid programmes.

Challenges and Opportunities

India's Development Partnership, while contributing to peacebuilding, is very different from economic intervention in support of counter-insurgency or counter-terrorism operations, such as those waged by ISAF in Afghanistan. It needs to be understood that economic assistance/partnership in the same country at the same period of time may have two totally differing aims as well as outcomes. India's development partnership assistance in Afghanistan since 2002 and that of other donors who also were supporting military operations there would therefore be quite different in conception and implementation, although they may both support peacebuilding. Thus, the peacebuilding situation addressed by India and others could have different but possibly complementary outcomes, which need to be understood. Further, foreign powers that intervene in local conflicts often seek to end the fighting and "restore stability" possibly within the duration of the intervention or immediately after it. So their economic activities for "restoring stability" are likely to be quite different from economic activities that are part of India's development partnership, which is a long-term strategic partnership. These pose challenges but can be overcome by greater transparency, coordination and synergy between the host country and aid providers.

The challenge posed to the safety of foreign citizens working in development partnership programmes as also of the investment made by the government and private entities in conflict-affected countries is a matter of serious concern. Providing security to men, material and investment is a serious challenge, which has to be factored in. India has provided security for its diplomatic mission and projects in Afghanistan in close cooperation with the government of Afghanistan.

A question that is sometimes asked is about development intervention aggravating conflict situation in the host country. While there has been no reported case of Indian development partnership programmes aggravating the conflict situation, this issue needs to be constantly kept in mind. This could best be done by following India's fundamental principles of aid/assistance being inclusive and demand-driven with local ownership, given without conditionalities and would not constrain the sovereignty of the host country in any way.

India is neither part of the Organisation for Economic Cooperation and Development (OECD) and its Development Assistance Committee (DAC) nor does it report its development assistance to DAC. However, India has taken part in the OECD-led international dialogue on development. While this dialogue contributed to mutual understanding regarding aid and development cooperation, India did convey its concerns on some of the premises underlying the OECD led dialogue. Although it is early to say, but the possibility of an alternative to the OECD definition of aid could emerge. India and other rising powers could consider doing so by putting out a draft vision of development aid, which would encompass the key features of SSC, including trade, investment, technology transfer and so on.

The challenges of bringing in greater transparency, creating a level field for public and private sectors, and promoting a greater role for non-governmental organisations and academia have often been discussed over the years as has been the fact that one could learn from the best practices of the international community and also share the lessons/experiences of India. The DPA is addressing these issues and one hopes to see movement on these fronts. The DPA could also consider bringing out a "White

Paper" on India's Development Partnership programmes. Many internal and external challenges that India faces come up during closed-door discussions. Some of these pertains to project conceptualisation; appraisal, monitoring, political sensitivities and vested interests in the partner countries and so on. The DPA is aware and has started to tackle these challenges, and we should see new guidelines, greater transparency and public outreach in the near future.[2]

International development aid given by any country would be linked to their national interests and foreign policy strategy. Although not stated in so many words, can India's development assistance/partnership programmes be any different? While there is no doubt that India's development partnership activities must conform to its guiding principles, it must also be closely linked to its commercial, strategic and foreign policy interests. This is a challenge which the MEA has negotiated very successfully in the past and must continue to do so in the future too.

Conclusion

The defining characteristic of India's development assistance programmes has been to share its experience in poverty alleviation and economic development. India's policymakers strongly believe that given the aid and assistance through effective development partnership, unstable and underdeveloped countries can emerge as healthy and strong constituents of the international community. This can establish the prerequisites of progress and harmony that can then propel the engines of growth and development and yield ever appreciating returns. India's own emergence from its colonial past into a vibrant democratic and global economic power has made it both a role model and major player in the realm of peacebuilding and development partnership.

As stated in this chapter, India's contribution towards building the infrastructure for peace and stability in developing countries not only precedes the concept of peacebuilding as enunciated by the UN, but also conforms to the way in which "peacebuilding strategies must be coherent and tailored to the specific needs of the country concerned, based on national ownership, and should comprise a carefully prioritised, sequenced, and relatively narrow set of activities aimed at achieving the above objectives."

India has not made any major distinction between development assistance and peacebuilding activities as many Western actors seem to do. One Indian official characterised these discussions as "academic hair-splitting," a view that many others seem to share. The UN Secretary General's Policy Committee in 2007 itself described peacebuilding as "a range of measures targeted to reduce the risk of lapsing or relapsing into conflict by strengthening national capacities at all levels of conflict management, and to lay the foundation for sustainable peace and development." Further, India's basic philosophy towards development assistance has been that any aid/assistance would be demand-driven, locally owned, given without conditionalities and void of any constraints on the sovereignty of its partners. These principles have stood India in good stead and need to be preserved.

Although deliberate, well-conceived and integral to India's foreign policy since independence, the development assistance programmes were pursued more as an important convention rather than as part of clearly articulated and declared policy as perhaps India was incrementally evolving this dimension to its foreign relations, based on its careful study of various international initiatives, in the field of international development aid. India's assistance to its neighbours in 1948 followed by the Colombo Plan of 1950 and later the ITEC programme and now the DPA underscore the country's proactive albeit incremental steps in this regard. However, there is no denying that India has not been able to leverage its development aid as it has never been promulgated in a coherent manner and so it has not been researched on the basis of contemporary standards. Still, there has been a growing realisation of this aspect, which has led to the formation of the DPA in the MEA. It is a step in the right direction, although one does not see a completely centralised form of development assistance being pursued in the near future.

The chapter also shows that India's development assistance programmes have been global in reach, covering every continent of the world. India's development assistance in Africa and Afghanistan, amongst others, not only indicates the wide spectrum of activities of their assistance, but also their large time horizon. Most of this assistance is not well known and has not been widely disseminated. It is hoped that the chapter would initiate the process of bringing out all aspects of India's development assistance, and analysing it comprehensively by researchers and think tanks.

As stated earlier, from a modest beginning in 1948, today India has become an important player in the area of global development cooperation. This, coupled with its significant role in UN peacekeeping/peacebuilding operations, will only help its stature grow. Hopefully, India and the other rising powers will solidify their rightful place in the global security and development architectures.

Notes

1. Report of the Security Council on Post-Conflict Peacebuilding at its 7359th meeting on 14 January 2015, S/PV. 7359.
2. At a Roundtable held in March 2013 at the Observer Research Foundation, New Delhi, Ambassador P.S. Raghavan, who was then heading the DPA, had highlighted some of these issues in his keynote address.

References

Centre for Integrated Rural Development for Asia and the Pacific (CIRDAP). 2017. http://cirdap.org/

Chaturvedi, Sachin. 2014. Features of South-South Cooperation and Global Dynamics. *Forum of India Development Cooperation (FICD) Policy Brief No 1. Research and Information System for Developing Countries (RIS).* http://fidc.ris.org.in/?p=43

de Carvalho, Benjamin, and Cedric de Coning. 2013. Rising Powers and the Future of Peacekeeping and Peacebuilding. *Norwegian Centre for Conflict Resolution (NOREF) Report.* http://noref.no/Themes/Emerging-powers/Publications/Rising-powers-and-the-future-of-peacekeeping-and-peacebuilding/(language)/eng-US

de Coning, Cedric. 2013. Understanding Peacebuilding as Essentially Local Stability. *Stability* 2(1): 1–6. http://www.stabilityjournal.org/articles/10.5334/sta.as/.

Export Import Bank of India (EXIM Bank). 2012. Catalysing India's Foreign Trade. *2011–2012 30th Annual Report.* Mumbai: EXIM Bank. http://www.eximbankindia.in/Assets/Dynamic/PDF/Publication-Resources/AnnualReports/8file.pdf

Kragelund, Peter. 2010. The Potential Role of Non-Traditional Donor's Aid in Africa. *ICTSD Programme on Competitiveness and Sustainable Development, Issue Paper No. 11.* International Centre for Trade and Sustainable Development: Geneva. http://www.ictsd.org/downloads/2011/03/the-potential-role-of-non-traditional-donorse28099-aid-in-africa.pdf

Kumar, Vinay. 2012. Statement by Mr. Vinay Kumar, Charge D'Affaires, Permanent Mission of India to the United Nations at the UN Security Council Open Debate on Post-Conflict Peacebuilding. New York. http://www.unic.org.in/display.php?E=12395&K=

Mukerji, Ashoke. 2014. Statement by India on the Report of the PeaceBuilding Commission on its 7th Session and the Report of the Secretary General on the Peace Building Fund on March 26, 2014.

Ryan, Stephen. 2013. The Evolution of Peacebuilding. In *Routledge Handbook of Peacebuilding*, ed. Roger MacGinty, 25–35. New York: Routledge.

Ugwuja, Alex A., Kelechi C. Ubaku, Nwachukwu J. Obiakor, and Bruno Ibekilo. 2014. South—South Cooperation and The Prospects of a New International Economic Order: An Insight Into The India Brazil-South Africa (IBSA) Dialogue Forum. *International Journal of Humanities, Social Science and Education* 1(8): 171–182.

United Nations Information Centre for India and Bhutan. 2006. Secretary-General's Address to the First Session of the Peacebuilding Commission. http://www.unic.org.in/display.php?E=566&K=UN_Peacekeepers

P.K. Singh Lt. Gen. (ret.) is Director, United Service Institution of India, New Delhi.

CHAPTER 5

Breaking with Convention: Turkey's New Approach to Peacebuilding

Onur Sazak and Auveen Elizabeth Woods

Introduction

Turkey owes its status as a rising power to the steady political and economic development that it enjoyed in the initial years of the twenty-first century and to the weakening of the Western, rule-based liberal order. This has enabled regional actors with relative economic stability and security to assume certain responsibilities that traditionally fell to the Great Powers in the Cold War era. Like most BRICS countries and other rising powers, Turkey has ridden the tailwinds of this global opening. Turkey also shares with some other rising powers the experience of rapid economic growth, relative stability, and an ongoing political transition and reform. As the world shifts to a more multipolar system, Turkey has been using its religious, ethnic, and cultural ties to try to consolidate its soft power, both regionally and further afield. During this period, Turkey has

O. Sazak (✉)
Support to Life, Sabancı University, Istanbul, Turkey

A.E. Woods
Istanbul Policy Center, Sabancı University, Istanbul, Turkey

C.T. Call, C. de Coning (eds.), *Rising Powers and Peacebuilding*, Rethinking Peace and Conflict Studies,
DOI 10.1007/978-3-319-60621-7_5

raised its profile as a regional actor and an emerging power, especially as the Arab Spring produced opportunities, crisis, and warfare on its borders.

These lessons, as well as the country's status as a European Union candidate, a committed NATO ally, and a buffer state for the West, heighten Turkey's role in the facilitation of peace in the region and reinforce its image as a bridge between geographical and cultural divides.

As a Western-oriented, secular state with a majority Muslim population, Turkey is increasingly regarded as a pivot in effectively addressing both humanitarian and security aspects of the entrenched conflicts in Syria and the greater Levant. Turkey hosts approximately 2.8 million Syrian refugees (UNHCR, February 2017). At the same time it provides support for opposition forces in Syria and allowed members of the anti-IS (Islamic State) coalition, such as the USA to use its airbases. For much of its history, however, Turkey has been plagued by rampant insecurity and economic and political instability. It has experienced four military coups and a 30-year armed insurgency. As such, Turkey's recent activities may be supported by economic and international shifts in power, but its conceptualization and approach to peacebuilding is very much informed by the country's experiences of insecurity.[1]

The Emergence of Turkish Peacebuilding

Security and stability are two central issues that have guided Turkey's strategic considerations. In the wake of World War I and the fall of the Ottoman Empire, modernization through alignment and membership of Western institutions was seen as crucial to preserving the security and stability that had been lost in the preceding years. It is also in this context that some of the traditional principles of Turkey's foreign policy have emerged, such as non-interference and respect for sovereignty. Turkey's domestic and foreign policies have also been significantly influenced by the founder of the Republic, Mustafa Kemal Atatürk. A number of his speeches, particularly the phrase "Peace at home, peace in the world" have been used to frame Turkey's international engagement, from its first forays into peacekeeping in the 1990s to recent peacebuilding activities. Former Prime Minister Ahmet Davutoğlu had also reiterated this principle stating that Turkey has tried to build a proactive foreign policy based on peace and stability at home (2012). This ideal, however, has come under significant strain since the Arab Spring spread to the Levant, and its transformation into a violent civil war in Syria and rampant insecurity in Iraq. These issues have directly affected Turkey's own security and stability. The suicide attacks since the June 7, 2015 general elections that have hit major towns in the southeast, the Turkish capital Ankara, and the country's largest city Istanbul, are nearly all traced to IS cells that infiltrated the porous borders in the South. This has been accompanied by renewed clashes between Turkish security forces and the PKK (The Kurdistan Workers' Party), which are equally detrimental to Turkey's stability and its image as a "peacemaker." In an additional blow to Turkey's security, it endured a coup attempt on July 15, 2016, which led to the purging of thousands from the military, education institutions, and judicial and state agencies.

For much of Turkey's history, security, and stability were conceived in military terms and in relation to territorial integrity. Turkey's first and only international intervention during the Cold War was its mediation between Iran and Iraq in the 1980s. This can be seen from a traditional security perspective, given the proximity of both countries to Turkey's eastern flank. Following the loosening of the Cold War strictures, the Turkish International Cooperation and Development Agency (TIKA) was established in 1992 with the objective of expanding Turkish relations with the newly independent Turkic States of Central Asia. TIKA was conceived as a mechanism of Turkish soft power through cooperation in the economic, cultural, and humanitarian fields (Murphy and Sazak 2012). For much of this period, however, TIKA was left to languish as an agency due to internal instability and a focus on a harder, security-driven concept of military engagement. Turkey's first foray into peacebuilding during this time was in the Balkans in the 1990s, contributing troops to multilateral peacebuilding and peace enforcement missions with the United Nations (UN) and North Atlantic Treaty Organization (NATO).

The shift from such hard security-based peacebuilding to the civilian participation and technical assistance that characterizes Turkey's activities in recent years was facilitated by a change in domestic dynamics. Over the last decade, the Turkish Armed Forces has been losing its influence in foreign policy matters, which are now primarily determined by civilians in government. This was accompanied by expanded civilian and police participation in peace operations, increased engagement in multilateral organizations, and a revival of TIKA activities. Facilitated by a period of relative political and economic stability and internal reforms that eased restrictions in political, religious, and social spheres, Turkey began to expand its official development. Although retaining a strong military was a necessity due to the instability of the surrounding region, under the

Justice and Development Party (AKP) civic and economic power was promoted as a more sustainable method of foreign engagement (Murphy and Woods 2014).

Domestic changes were accompanied by a restructuring of Turkish foreign policies priorities and goals under the AKP. This has served to both promote the prestige of a more internationally active Turkey and to reinforce the success of the country's leadership to a domestic audience (Achilles et al. 2015). Guided by then-Prime Minister Ahmet Davutoğlu (key adviser and later foreign minister from 2009–2014), a multilateral foreign policy emerged that sought a balance between proactive engagement and crisis management. Turkish leaders have emphasized the need for preventive diplomacy that should be intricately linked to any conflict management strategies, whether it is peacekeeping or peacebuilding activities. Identifying mediation and dialogue as essential tools in this preventative diplomacy, officials have stated that "peace mediation and facilitation efforts are the most cost-effective and efficient way of preventing and resolving conflicts" (United Nations Security Council 2011). Reflecting this position, Turkey has headed a number of initiatives. In 2005 the Alliance of Civilizations, which promotes interreligious and intercultural dialogue, was launched by the Prime Ministers of Spain and Turkey. In 2010, Turkey and Finland created a "Group of Friends of Mediation" consisting of 41 countries that support efforts by the UN and regional organizations in the area of mediation. And in May 2016, Turkey hosted the first World Humanitarian Summit, in Istanbul. These are diverse and cross-cultural examples that Turkish officials have identified as reflecting the country's approach to peacebuilding (Davutoğlu 2014). Through these initiatives Turkey has sought to promote flexibility, trust, and cooperation as the basis of successful mediation. In parallel to these efforts, Turkey launched a process on peacebuilding during its time on the Security Council from 2009–2010, which included these initiatives and brought together the Council for thematic meetings in Istanbul from 2010 to 2013 (Turkish Ministry of Foreign Affairs 2016).

Issues around "hard security" are still a strategic priority for Turkey's foreign policy, as seen in the country's engagement in Syria. But conceptualizations of security have broadened. As Davutoğlu stated, "stability cannot be built on the basis of force alone," (Davutoğlu 2012). Referencing the decade of reforms inside Turkey, Turkish officials have sought to find a balance between freedom and security in order to achieve stability (Murphy and Sazak 2012). Over the years, the concept of "security" has become more multidimensional, focusing on human needs through good governance and economic stability. This is evident in Turkey's rhetorical embrace of "humanitarian diplomacy," an ambiguous concept that Turkish officials have increasingly used to frame its repositioning in the aftermath of the Arab Spring. Humanitarian diplomacy as a concept claims to reject state-centric realpolitik and external interference in domestic affairs. Highlighting the importance of acknowledging "local values" and local ownership, it instead emphasizes the need to put human dignity and human security at the forefront of policy considerations (Keyman and Sazak 2014). There are of course limits to such aspirations, which can be seen Turkey's strategic engagement to the crises in Iraq and Syria.

The Tools of Turkish Peacebuilding

There is no concept paper that explicitly describes Turkey's definition of peacebuilding. It can, however, be understood through bilateral and regional activities, norms, and discussions, such as those already mentioned, that have emerged among the country's representatives over the last decade. Most Turkish officials discuss the term peacebuilding within the context of development and reconstruction of a conflict-affected country. Turkey's approach to peacebuilding can be characterized as a twofold process, encompassing both statebuilding and peacemaking within society. Reflecting a structural approach to peacebuilding, Turkish officials emphasize the centrality of good governance, strong responsive institutions, and rule of law for building an effective state and, therefore, in their view, a stable and peaceful society.[2] Activities related to these goals by officials include infrastructure projects, technical assistance, and capacity-building programs for state institutions and personnel. This kind of structural peacebuilding must also be accompanied by an inclusive peacemaking process at all levels. Turkish officials feel that this is only possible through national ownership of goals and culturally sensitive engagement with all stakeholders, including civil society, professional associations, and women. This is particularly important with regard to political institutions and inclusive economic recovery, which Turkish officials say are essential for a peaceful society. Activities associated with societal peacebuilding include mediation efforts, education programs, religious support, and inclusive economic development.

Like other rising powers, economic interests are intricately linked to Turkey's foreign policy and its peacebuilding activities. Such interests have not only led to financial dividends for Turkey in the past but also promoted peace in some cases. Notably, the historically tumultuous relationship between Turkey and its Kurdish neighbors in Iraq has greatly improved with ongoing military cooperation between the administrations in Ankara and Erbil. The expansion of economic and diplomatic relations with Iraqi Kurdistan not only helped to improve relations, but was also a lucrative partnership (Hacaoğlu 2014). At the time, exports to Iraq in 2013 reached $12 billion, with $8 billion going to the Kurdish Regional Government, becoming one of Turkey's largest export markets (Çağaptay et al. 2015). There are also some links between Turkey's economic interests and its aid practices in general. In Afghanistan, Turkish companies ranked fifth in terms of total number of foreign investors, with 140 registered in the country in 2013 (Çolakoğlu and Yegin 2014). Turkey's bilateral trade with Somalia was $72 million by 2015. Officials have also been frank about their interest in expanding economic relations with Somalia, one of the most prominent countries in Turkey's development activities.[3] While not a specific policy, a pattern has emerged in which the establishment of a diplomatic presence in a new country is often soon followed by investment from Turkish companies and new flight links through Turkish Airlines.

Turkish diplomats are firm in their conviction that trade is better than aid for development.[4] Many Turkish officials regard economic development, ideally through the diverse participation of the society as an essential component of peacebuilding, with one diplomat stating "[W]e don't think that peacebuilding could achieve its goals if there is no economic recovery and participation of the whole part of the society in the program."[5] Officials believe economic investment provides alternative financial opportunities to criminality and extremist narratives, and supports national ownership of development.

Many of the initiatives that Turkish officials consider as peacebuilding activities are funneled through Turkish development aid. In 2014, Turkey's Official Development Assistance (ODA) was $3.6 billion (TIKA 2016). This represents nearly a 30 percent increase between 2012 and 2014 alone (see Fig. 5.1).[6] Despite Turkey's participation in a number of multilateral initiatives, the vast majority of this aid is provided in bilateral assistance. For example, in 2013, only $151 million of $3.3 billion of ODA was provided through multilateral contributions (TIKA 2016, 8). In 2014, this was $88 million (TIKA 2016, 9). This illustrates Turkey's preference for bilateral engagement.

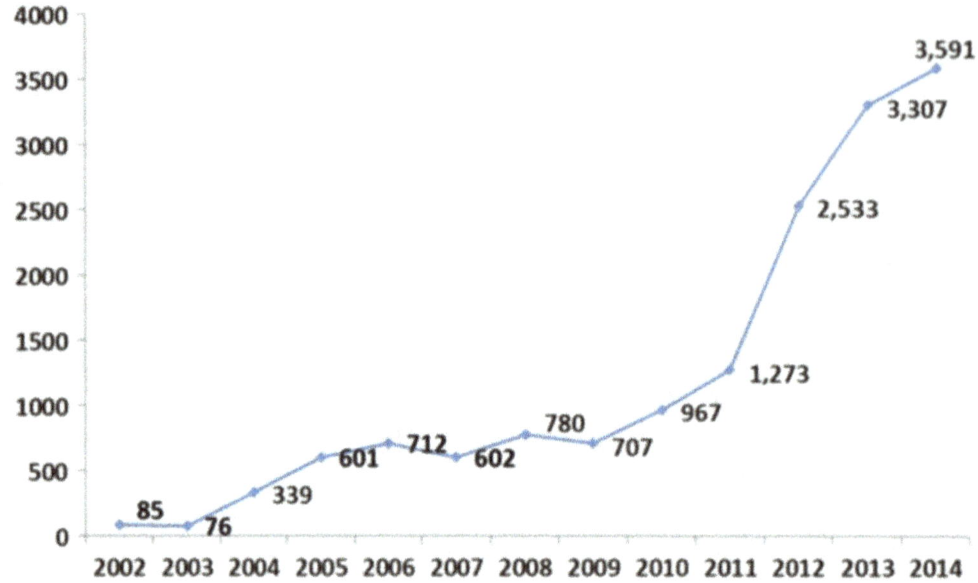

Fig. 5.1 Turkey's development assistance 2002–2014 ($US millions)

Turkey has expanded its activities to some of the world's most entrenched conflicts. From 2011 until 2014, Syria, Somalia and Afghanistan were among the top five largest recipients of Turkish ODA (TIKA 2012; 2013; 2014a, b; 2016). While Turkey does provide support to non-Muslim countries such as Ukraine, Macedonia, and Kenya, to name just a few, the bulk of the State's activities appear to be carried out in Muslim majority states. Many of these countries would also be on the list of least developed or fragile states. Examples of both the structural and social peacebuilding approaches of Turkey are evident in its activities in conflict-affected countries like Afghanistan, Somalia, and Balkan countries such as Bosnia and Herzegovina and Kosovo.

Much of what can be defined as Turkey's structural peacebuilding activities consist of technical capacity programs, infrastructure projects, and the provision of basic services that are focused on the recipient state institutions. Technical assistance, or cooperation as it is alternatively called, is broadly defined by Turkey as "strengthening capacities and effectiveness of individuals, organizations and institutions through transfer of ideas, technologies, knowledge and skills" (TIKA 2014b, 25). This can include a wide range of activities from the state to the local level such as trainings and scholarships to the provisions of equipment and materials. Additionally, a strong understanding of constructive development is common to both Turkish state agencies and non-state actors has strong historical roots.

Since the Ottoman Empire, privately funded philanthropic development has focused on the construction of buildings and infrastructure, as well as the funding of services such as schools, hospitals, and mosques (Bikmen 2008). Examples of infrastructure projects include renovating state buildings such or building schools and roads are common across all the countries in which Turkey is engaged.

Many infrastructure and technical cooperation programs appear to focus on improving the provision of basic services such as medical and judicial standards. For example, Turkey provides a range of trainings from judges and prosecutors in Kosovo to medical staff in Somalia (TIKA 2014a, b). Turkish officials have said that they feel capacity-building programs directly support statebuilding by legitimizing the state's authority and making services more effective. From this perspective, a legitimate and effective state is a form of peacebuilding that offers alternatives to non-governmental organizations such as militant or secession groups. However, Turkish officials are quick to emphasize that their support must be seen as apolitical in nature, stating: "We can only offer them certain technical expertise without any strict recipe. It is after all the requirements of the host country to determine how they will proceed."[7]

Technical assistance and capacity-building programs are also a characteristic of Turkey's social peacebuilding, given their broad definition and aims. Most of capacity-building programs include training and technical assistance to support economic empowerment and appear to be focused at the local level through municipalities and communities. Technical equipment assistance has been provided, for example, to the Governorship of Sar-e Pol in Afghanistan for vocational training programs for women, and the Agricultural Development Project in East Bosnia was established to support the return of families from the 1992–1995 war (TIKA 2014a, b). These are just some of the local projects aimed at economically empowering communities. Technical assistance is also a part of other social peacebuilding activities in the education field, such as providing technical equipment for high schools and universities.

Education initiatives have been one of the more widely known areas associated with Turkey's peacebuilding activities. This is due in part to the publicity around its extensive scholarship programs in Somalia. State scholarships have been provided by, among others, Diyanet (the Ministry of Religious Affairs) and the Education Ministry to students from Central Asia, Africa, the Middle East and Eastern Europe (Türkiye Bursları). Most education programs in the past had been run by third sector organizations such as Hizmet or Gülen-linked schools. In many countries programs associated with this group have since been closed. The Turkish state tends to run smaller education-orientated programs, such as providing school materials and equipment, funding and renovating buildings, and promoting Turkish language and cultural courses. Education initiatives such as these are not only a method of expanding Turkish soft power, but are also felt to contribute to social peacemaking through intercultural dialogue. Both officials and third state actors believe that education is a key peacebuilding tool that can counter the narrative of extremism and provide opportunities for the future.

Finally, Turkey's social peacebuilding activities are also characterized by an emphasis on mediation and religiously sensitive programs. Officials have stated the importance of mediation, not only at an inter-state level but also at the local level, through everyday activities and engagement with locals. This may range from consulting with communities to discussions with political authorities on bilateral projects. Turkish officials feel that mediation and consultation are mechanisms that support their own espoused principles of national ownership. These principles can perhaps also be seen to guide the concept of cultural and religiously sensitive programs. These range from sponsoring intercultural activities such as visits to Turkey or football tournaments to providing Qurans or circumcision ceremonies for boys for example, in countries such as Afghanistan and Niger (TIKA 2014a, b; 2016). The building of mosques or events during Islamic festivals such as book fairs or Iftar have been staged from Afghanistan to Mogadishu and Pakistan. Given the scope of these programs globally, religious sensitivity is clearly a central aspect of Turkey's activities. Such programs are not only pragmatic but they also add legitimacy to Turkish activities in the eyes of locals. In Afghanistan, reports noted that Turkish projects were more acceptable to communities than others because of their perceived sensitivity to local Afghan culture (Murphy and Sazak 2012).

Impact and Conclusions

Over the last decade, Turkey's approach to peacebuilding has transformed from the strategic state-centric security engagement of the 1990s to a more multifaceted conceptualization that encompasses both statebuilding and social peacemaking. This has been facilitated by a change in civil-military power dynamics since 2000 and a broader understanding of security that considers the issue of human needs. Peacebuilding activities in recent years range from technical assistance for state services to education and religious programs. This has been developed in parallel with new foreign policy activities that emphasize both mediation and enhanced economic ties as potential peacebuilding strategies that are of mutual benefit to both Turkey and recipient states.

In spite of Turkey's good intentions to promote peace and stability in its region and the rest of the world, Ankara's capacity to execute this vision has some shortcomings. An estimated 2.8 million Syrian refugees, the resurgence of war with the PKK, IS' penetration deep into the country's urban centers, the continuing political volatility in the aftermath of the July 15 coup attempt and a receding economy constitute serious obstacles to the sustainability of Turkey's peacebuilding operations. In addition, for the last several years Turkey's ambitious foreign policy goals and determination to project its soft power have alienated various supporters. Counting on African support to win another term on the UN Security Council in 2016, Turkey only received the votes of 60 countries out of 193 (Sassounian 2014).

Turkey's struggle against the Gülen network over the last few years, which is accused of orchestrating the July 15 coup attempt in addition to undermining the government of the AKP, has also affected the country's relations with developing countries. Ironically, Gülenist charity organizations had been among the most visible non-governmental organization (NGOs) in providing humanitarian assistance to sub-Saharan Africa (Sassounian 2014). Viewed in light of Turkey's false predictions about the longevity of the Assad regime in Syria, Ankara's recognition of the depth of the crises that it is trying to help resolve both domestically and internationally, and its influence over the respective parties is challenging. In other words, the rhetoric-capacity mismatch in Turkish foreign policy risks moving Turkey farther away from "zero problems with neighbors" toward the dangerous territory of "zero neighbors without problems" (Sassounian 2014).

A number of basic organizational challenges have also hindered the Turkish state from realizing its potential to increase the quality and range of its peacebuilding initiatives. The most persistent of these impediments is coordination problems. First identified in a 2012 report a lack of effective interagency cooperation has been the most visible problem in Turkish peacebuilding activities (Sassounian 2014). The most vital ministries and government agencies that are involved in peacebuilding operations, such as the Foreign Ministry, Health Ministry, Development Ministry, and TIKA, were not informed about each other's activities both at the higher echelons of decision making or in the field. Recent research indicates that very little progress has been made in this area in recent years at both the state and third sector levels (Achilles et al. 2015). One representative of an international organization based in Ankara volunteered that most TIKA bureaucrats in charge of coordination are not even familiar with the basic UN procedures and terms.[8] The lack of institutional training and knowledge of procedures within organizations like TIKA also complicates communication and coordination between the field offices and Ankara. In such situations, the quality and effectiveness of the country programs often depends on the individual in the field office. If the person assigned to a country office is in fact interested in the mission, TIKA operations in that particular country often provide more substantive results for the beneficiaries.[9]

This lack of consistency in coordination and consistent implementation of principles and goals also affects the development and monitoring of programs. There is a disparity between the prestige and rhetoric around Turkey's engagement and the actual effectiveness of the activities implemented. While TIKA publically provides data on the number of participants or equipment involved in technical assistance programs, greater analysis on how these programs are determined or their impact is not made available. There have been reports in the past of peacebuilding programs such as infrastructure projects or trainings being implemented without consultation with local authorities or research on other aid groups working in the area (Larson 2015; Deloffre 2015; Gloyd 2015). These problems appeared to have occurred in countries that TIKA had become newly active in, such as Somalia, Senegal, or Uganda.[10] This also indicates an important vacuum in the pre-deployment analyses and monitoring activities for state operations in the field. Such patterns can, however, exacerbate overcrowding, duplication, and waste.

These internal capacity issues that the Turkey has grappled with have undoubtedly been exacerbated by the post-coup purges that have ravaged state institutions, agencies, and civil society organizations. In addition to these problems is the equally detrimental challenge of financing international operations. The influx of Syrian refugees, for instance, has cost the state an estimated $12 billion (BirGün 2016) and led to nearly $2 billion worth of resources being rechanneled from foreign operations. This has diverted significant Turkish resources from high profile activities in fragile countries such as Somalia (Achilles et al. 2015). In addition, the volatility of the Turkish lira against hard currencies, as well as ongoing political uncertainty, has taken a toll on the economic stability that is necessary to sustain the funds for Turkey's peacebuilding initiatives.

Notes

1. Interview with a Turkish Diplomat, June 2015, and Foreign Ministry Official, March 2015.
2. Telephonic interview with a Turkish Foreign Ministry Official, March 2015, Ankara.
3. Interview with Turkish Foreign Ministry Officials, August 2015.
4. Interview with a Turkish Diplomat, February 2014.
5. Telephonic interview with a Turkish Foreign Ministry Official, June 2015, Ankara.
6. This graph is the authors' compilation based on official statistics from the Turkish Cooperation and Coordination Agency.
7. Interview with a Turkish Diplomat, 2015.
8. Interview with a UNDP-TIKA Coordinator, 2015.
9. Ibid.
10. Ibid.

References

Achilles, Kathryn, Onur Sazak, Thomas Wheeler, and Auveen Elizabeth Woods. 2015. Turkish Aid Agencies in Somalia: Risks and Opportunities for Building Peace. March 2015 Report. Saferworld and Istanbul Policy Center. Available at https://www.files.ethz.ch/isn/189390/turkish-aid-agencies-in-somalia.pdf

Bikmen, Filiz. 2008. The Rich History of Philanthropy in Turkey: A Paradox of Tradition and Modernity. In *Philanthropy in Europe: A Rich Past, a Promising Future*, ed. N. MacDonald and L. Tayart de Borms, 223–234. London: Alliance Publishing Trust.

BirGün. 2016. umhurbaşkanı Erdoğan, Alman ARD televizyonuna konuştu. *BirGün*, July 26. Accessed August 1, 2016. http://www.birgun.net/haber-detay/cumhurbaskani-erdogan-alman-ard-televizyonuna-konustu-121521.html

Çağaptay, Soner, Christina Bache Fidan, and Ege Cansu Saçıkara. 2015. Turkey and the KRG Signs of Booming Economic Ties. *The Washington Institute for Near East Policy*. Accessed February 12, 2017. http://www.washingtoninstitute.org/policy-analysis/view/turkey-and-the-krg-signs-of-booming-economic-ties-infographic

Çolakoğlu, Selçuk, and Mehmet Yegin. 2014. *The Future of Afghanistan and Turkey's Contributions*. Istanbul: International Strategic Research Organization (USAK).

Davutoğlu, Ahmet. 2012. Principles of Turkish Foreign Policy and Regional Political Structuring. *Center for Strategic Research* 3. http://sam.gov.tr/wp-content/uploads/2012/04/vision_paper_TFP2.pdf

———. 2014. Republic of Turkey Ministry of Foreign Affairs. Speech at the Ministerial Conference of the Non-Aligned Movement, Algeria, May 28. http://www.mfa.gov.tr/speech-delivered-by-h_e_-mr_-ahmet-davuto%C4%9Flu-at-the-ministerial-conference-of-the-non_aligned-movement_-28-may-2014_-algeria.en.mfa

Deloffre, Maryam. 2015. International NGO Behavior and Interactions with States. Presentation at the IPC-TİKA workshop on International Humanitarian NGOs and Health Aid, Istanbul, March 27.

Gloyd, Stephen. 2015. Sustainability of Health Aids. Presentation at the IPC-TİKA Workshop on International Humanitarian NGOs and Health Aid, Istanbul, March 27. Group of Friends of Mediation. *United Nations*. Accessed February 1, 2016. http://peacemaker.un.org/friendsofmediation

Hacaoğlu, Selcan. 2014. Turkey Embracing Iraq's Kurds as Trade Erodes Old Enmity. *Bloomberg Business*, July 11. Accessed February 12, 2017. http://www.bloomberg.com/news/articles/2014-07-10/turkey-s-embrace-of-iraqi-kurds-shows-trade-eroding-old-enmity

Keyman, Fuat, and Onur Sazak. 2014. Turkey as a Humanitarian State. *Project on the Middle East and Arab Spring Paper* 2.

Larson, Paul. 2015. Logistics of Health Aids. Presentation at the IPC-TİKA workshop on International Humanitarian NGOs and Health Aid, Istanbul, March 27.

Murphy, Teri, and Onur Sazak. 2012. Turkey's Civilian Capacity in Post-Conflict Reconstruction. Istanbul: Istanbul Policy Center. https://research.sabanciuniv.edu/21550/1/IPM-Turkish-CivCap.pdf

Murphy, Teri, and Auveen Woods. 2014. Turkey's International Development Framework Case Study: Somalia. *IPC-MERCATOR Policy Brief.* Istanbul: Istanbul Policy Center. http://ipc.sabanciuniv.edu/wp-content/uploads/2014/02/SOMALIISBN11.pdf

Sassounian, Harut. 2014. Why the UN Rejected Turkey's Bid for a Security Council Seat. *The Huffington Post*, October 28. Accessed October 26, 2015. http://www.huffingtonpost.com/harut-sassounian/why-the-un-rejected-turke_b_6036878.html

Turkish Cooperation and Coordination Agency. 2012. *Turkish Cooperation and Coordination Agency Annual Report 2011.* Ankara.

———. 2013. *Turkish Cooperation and Coordination Agency Annual Report 2012.* Ankara.

———. 2014a. *Turkish Cooperation and Coordination Agency Annual Report 2013.* Ankara.

———. 2014b. *Turkish Development Assistance 2013.* 2014b. Ankara.

———. 2016. Turkish Development Assistance: From Turkey to the World—2014 Report. Ankara. http://www.tika.gov.tr/upload/2016/INGILIZCE%20SITE%20ESERLER/KALKINMA%20RAPORLARI/DA%20Report%202014.pdf

Turkish Ministry of Foreign Affairs. 2016. Candidacy of the Republic of Turkey to the United Nations Security Council for the period 2015–2016. Accessed January 30, 2017. http://www.mfa.gov.tr/candidacy-of-the-republic-of-turkey-to-the-united-nations-security-council-for-the-period-2015-2016.en.mfa

Turkiye Bursları. n.d. Türkiye Bursları Scholarships. Accessed January 30, 2017. http://www.turkiyeburslari.gov.tr/index.php/en/

United Nations Security Council. 2011. United Nations Security Council, 6472nd Meeting. New York. Accessed June 20, 2015. http://www.securitycouncilreport.org/atf/cf/%7B65BFCF9B-6D27-4E9C-8CD3-CF6E4FF96FF9%7D/TL%20S%20PV%206472.pdf

United Nations High Commissioner on Refugees. 2017. Syrian Regional Refugee Response: Inter-agency Information Sharing Portal. Accessed February 12, 2017. http://data.unhcr.org/syrianrefugees/regional.php

Onur Sazak is Advocacy and Coordination Manager at Support to Life, and Ph.D. candidate in Political Science at Sabancı University, Istanbul.

Auveen Elizabeth Woods is Researcher, Istanbul Policy Center, Sabancı University, Istanbul.

CHAPTER 6

South African Peacebuilding Approaches: Evolution and Lessons

Charles Nyuykonge and Siphamandla Zondi

Introduction

Following the demise of apartheid, South Africa has made considerable strides in advancing itself as a global player and champion of African interests within the continent and globally. This has been most manifest in its role in peace and security. With its dual membership as a non-permanent member of the United Nations Security Council (UNSC) in 2006–7 and 2009–10, its membership in the G20 from 2009 and its role in the United Nations Peacebuilding Council, South Africa has positioned itself as a key player in the new efforts at international and African peace and security. As one of the architects of the African Peace and Security Architecture (APSA) and the recently developed African Capacity for Immediate Response to Crises (ACIRC), designed to rapidly deploy in response to threats to peace and security, South Africa has positioned itself as a crucial

C. Nyuykonge (✉)
The African Centre for the Constructive Resolution of Disputes (ACCORD), Durban, South Africa

S. Zondi
Head of the Department of Politics, University of Pretoria, Pretoria, South Africa

C.T. Call, C. de Coning (eds.), *Rising Powers and Peacebuilding*, Rethinking Peace and Conflict Studies,
DOI 10.1007/978-3-319-60621-7_6

role player in efforts to manage security threats in Africa. South Africa has also contributed resources to peacebuilding endeavors, including the recent pledges and donations of

- over US$1 million to support the Central African Republic's (CAR) recovery efforts under the leadership of the Economic Community of Central African States (ECCAS) and the African-led International Support Mission to the Central African Republic (MISCA);
- about US$10 million to curb violence in Mali;
- over US$8 million toward assisting the then-Transitional Federal Government of Somalia;
- the first AU peace support operation in Burundi (Lucey and Gida 2014) and the special United Nations Force Intervention Brigade (FIB), endorsed by the AU to support the Democratic Republic of Congo's (DRC) national army (FARDC) in defeating the M23 rebellion operating in the Eastern region of the DRC.

Additionally, one of the first things the ANC did when it assumed power was to write off the debts of Swaziland, Mozambique, and Namibia, each valued at about ZAR1 billion (about $60 million) (Besharati 2013). Today, South Africa is transforming its aid and development cooperation activities from the African Renaissance Fund to the South African Development Partnership Agency (SADPA). The SADPA)is projected to operate an annual budget of R500 million (approximately US$50 million) (Besharati 2013). Although the size of its budget and its technical resources are much smaller than those of many traditional donors, through the SADPA, South Africa strives to achieve impact on the African continent.

South Africa's peacebuilding approach has been modeled on its own post-conflict reconstruction program called the Reconstruction and Development Program (RDP). The RDP includes a socioeconomic policy framework that was designed to address the immense socioeconomic problems brought about by the long years of the apartheid regime. Specifically, it set its sights on alleviating poverty and addressing the massive shortfalls in social services across the country by relying upon a stronger macroeconomic environment. Unlike traditional peacebuilding, this framework was need-driven and offered houses, built roads to marginalized communities, and made health care and other social services affordable to victims of apartheid. In addition, the RDP attempted to combine measures to boost the economy such as contain fiscal spending, lower taxes, reduce government debt, and foster trade liberalization with infrastructural projects. Consequently, the policy adopted both socialist and neo-liberal elements whose implementation across Africa has drawn a number of criticisms, particularly because in its engagements South Africa has not been consistent on its assistance and outreach to states in need. This inconsistency casts a shade of doubt on the credibility of South Africa as an actor not much different from the interest-driven traditional peacebuilding actors from the global north. For instance, some have questioned its involvement in regions outside Southern Africa such as its mediation roles in Cote d'Ivoire and Burundi (Nibishaka 2011). Even in Southern Africa, its motives and interests have been a subject of debate about whether it is advancing its power/hegemonic interests under the pretext of regional common good (Kagwanja 2009). It has been accused of imposing its own model of transition featuring government of national unity and truth commissions in situations where this model might not be applicable. It has also been criticized for showing inconsistent ambition for Africa's peace, showing energy in some cases and pulling back in others, such as Somalia. It has been accused of using its peace diplomacy to open markets for its multinationals, which exploit other Africans. The spike of violence against African migrants and refugees in South Africa has also shamed the country (Fayomi et al. 2015). Of course, South Africa has sought to assure fellow Africans that its interests are genuine and motives are grandiose. It has adjusted its approaches and sought to consult more now than before. It has sought to communicate a bit more clearly and to intervene only after careful consultations with other African countries. As a result, over time, its interventions have been limited to those that are done under a multilateral mandate such as the SADC mandate for Zimbabwe's peace facilitation, the UN-mandated intervention in the DRC, and the AU–UN mandate in Darfur, among others (Zondi 2012). More recently, it is voting patterns in the United Nations Security Council, especially on Resolution 1973, which in the guise of imposing a No Flight Zone was converting into a mission to overthrow and unseat Gaddafi. By voting for the Resolution which other African heads of states criticized South Africa's integrity has been put on the spotlight and a constant reminder that it has turned its back from Africa is evidenced by the recurrent xenophobic incidences that have been sporadic across the country since 2008.

The above notwithstanding, some analysts have emphasized the importance of South Africa's military capability in supporting Peace Support Operations (Heitman 2013). Some have underlined the need for South

Africa to lend more support to the African Union's African Solidarity Initiative (ASI) and the Post Conflict Reconstruction and Development (PCRD) initiative in a multilateral platform, which is in sync with the AU's and REC's positions (Lucey and Gida 2014). They have argued for continued role in capacity building, implementation support, economic development, and information sharing programs, which can strengthen African states' recovery from crisis (Hendricks and Lucey 2013a, b). Some analysts have made the case for South Africa's involvement in promoting civil society engagement and the Livingstone Formula, which states that "Civil Society Organizations (CSOs) may provide technical support to the AU by undertaking early warning reporting, and situation analysis, which feeds information into the decision making processes of the PSC" (Lucey and Gida 2014).

Central to all this is the contested understanding of the concept of peacebuilding. For policy makers as well as experts in African conflict management frameworks, the concept has remained fluid and seems to generically encompass prevention, mediation, peace support operations, and post-conflict reconstruction, thereby begging for an appreciation of what exactly South Africa's interventions have constituted in countries where they have invested human and financial capital. Using the examples of Burundi and the DRC, this sub-section does not just identify the nature of South African interventions with the view of appraising the distinction between such interventions and those previously undertaken or concurrently undertaken by traditional peacebuilding actors. This distinction is further critical in relation to various platforms and instruments used by South Africa to implement their peacebuilding engagements, and is presented in two main sections with the first focusing on what peacebuilding is conceived to be in South African policy circles and the motivation for intervention and the second identifying the tangibles of peacebuilding.

Motivation for Interventions

Admittedly, peacebuilding is a broad concept that cuts across a number of zones, including matters of economy, development, law, humanitarianism, and security. Understanding the nature of support that South Africa provides to struggling, fragile, or post-conflict states is key in determining the country's definition of peacebuilding. Part of the problem is that the country's involvement in post-conflict development and reconstruction is under-reported and scarcely discussed (Hendricks and Lucey 2013a, b).

South Africa's efforts suggest an unwritten peacebuilding and reconstruction framework with emphasis on building national infrastructure and the provision of affordable essential services like health care, housing, economic and social grants, and communications infrastructure. The practice is that interventions are in many cases driven by demand, such as where South Africa is requested by multilateral organizations such the AU and SADC, certain cases such as in Zimbabwe, Madagascar, and Lesotho (Motsamai 2014). Yet, the difficulty in ending the crisis early has often led to accusations that South Africa was acting malevolently or unilaterally (Polzer 2008).

There have been occasions where, motivated by the doctrine of preventive diplomacy as expounded by the late UN Secretary-General Boutros-Boutros Ghali, South Africa has acted proactively to intervene in developing conflict such as in Lesotho in the late 1990s. On such occasion, there were accusations of unilateralism on its part though the intervention was mandated by the Southern African Development Community (SADC). Given the travails of a South African economy that has continued to grow without generating significant employment creation and given the impact of the global financial crisis on it, South Africa has found mandated interventions crucial for it to help stabilize regions on which it depends for investment without generating political problems for itself. South Africa is home to the largest pool of asylum seekers and refugees from the rest of Africa, imposing upon it the burden to respond the reasons for this migration while being sensitive to migrants' needs.

Another important fact in this approach to peace diplomacy is South Africa's anti-imperialist outlook on international affairs, being watchful for signs that western powers use difficulties in African countries to engineer regime changes and impose puppet governments. This is the policy stance that leads to South Africa intervening even at great costs to eliminate the conditions that lead to such eventualities. Recent comments by former President Thabo Mbeki in an open letter on Zimbabwe policy suggest that South Africa was fearful that the UK and the USA would intervene militarily in Zimbabwe to remove Mugabe and his government and install a government of their choice, taking advantage of the deep governance crisis accelerated by the ZANU-PF one-party state agenda and violations of the rights of citizens that opposed it. Similarly, its 2011 intervention through the AU committee in Libya, trying to mediate between parties and hoping for a political solution in conflict between the Qaddafi government and rebels, was motivated by the AU policy to prevent unconstitutional changes of government and a wish to see Africa take the lead in solutions to African problems. Indeed, NATO-led forces brought down the Qaddafi government and in the process Qaddafi was killed. The result was a power vacuum that left a train of anarchy in that country, and that has destabilized large parts of the Sahel region. South Africa voted in favor of UN Security Council Resolution 1973, which authorized the NATO-led intervention in Libya, is still hotly debated in South Africa's foreign policy circles.

However, in the last decade, the demand for South African assistance in Africa's troubled hotspots has increased exponentially. These demands have found themselves competing with domestic pressures and citizenry demands for jobs, improved wages, and most recently "free education" across the board. According to Hendricks and Lucey (2013a, b), in certain cases, despite these domestic pressures, there is an "expectation … [within the continent] … that South Africa will not just be another donor, but a partner with a vested interest in the development of the continent." Maqungo goes further to say that, although demands come from everywhere, South Africa's peacebuilding activities have been directly focused on the African continent safe for when supporting a project within a larger multilateral arrangement such as within the UN Peacebuilding Commission, BRICS or IBSA.[1] When supported a peacebuilding project as part of a conglomeration of states, South Africa cannot lay claim to a different approach but the prevailing national sense is that, South African support "is not massive" but it is a demonstration of solidarity.

According to Kwezi Mngqibisa, post-apartheid South African interventions are justified by the feeling of a moral obligation to support Africa, as Africa did for her during the century long apartheid dispensation.[2] And so to the African states seeking assistance from South Africa, there is the expectation that unlike development aid from traditional peacebuilding actors that piles on their national debt, South Africa's aid is different and designed to trigger economic growth. In emphasizing the distinction, Maqungo contends that while traditional peacebuilding actors such as the UN have specific mandates to prevent conflicts, South Africa's interventions are driven by interests that she exemplifies as geographical, security, humanitarian, and furtherance of personal and political party relationships by wielders of power and drivers of state policy at a particular time. To Maqungo, geographical interests are seen in cases such as Zimbabwe and Lesotho, where because of the geographical proximity, if South Africa does not intervene early enough to avert a crisis, it would be directly affected by the spillover of such crisis. Pertaining to humanitarianism as a motivation for South African interventions, Maqungo cited interventions such as Mandela's mediation in Burundi and said, South Africa had no direct interest or stakes in the Burundi process, but because the death of Nyerere left a vacuum that prompted the continent to solicit the moral authority of Mandela to intervene, the country got drawn into it (at great cost). But interestingly, personal friendships such as that between President Bozize (Central African Republic's present) and Thabo Mbeki (SA) also drive deployments, such as the security sector reform mission to Central Africa before the overthrow of Bozize. Maqungo also suggested that experience sharing such as between liberation movements like South Africa's African National Congress (ANC) and the Sudan People's Liberation Movement (SPLM) can motivate interventions.

The Essence of South African Peacebuilding Support

It should be stated from the onset that unlike some development partners who sharply differentiate between mediation, peacekeeping, peacebuilding, and humanitarian assistance, South Africa's broad spectrum approach is fluid and utilizes the concept of Post-Conflict Reconstruction and Development (PCRD) to refer to funding for humanitarian and development assistance; and with cases such as Somalia, such funding can be used for capacity building trainings, policy development, inter-government exchange of ideas and electoral support, which all gear toward building a strong and resilient state.

More broadly, in terms of peacebuilding support, South Africa has provided states with substantial assistance in the areas of good governance, dialogue and reconciliation, security sector reform, human resource and infrastructure development, policy implementation, economic development and trade, information sharing and exchange visits among South African dignitaries, as well as humanitarian assistance. Key examples that can be cited are training and restructuring advice provided by South Africa to the DRC national army (FARDC) and police, police in South Sudan, military in the Central African Republic and the Disarmament, demobilization and reintegration (DDR) process in Cote d'Ivoire. In such capacities, South African expertise and resources have been essential in the development of key policy reforms, institutionalization of accountability frameworks, and support for electoral processes in recipient countries. Furthermore, South Africa has fostered dialogue and reconciliation in many instances through financing negotiations, facilitating mediations, and channeling international buy-in of the process.

Moreover, human resource and infrastructure development assistance committed by Pretoria has ensured training, capacity-building workshops, professional exchange visits for key sectors of government and civil society organizations, as well as the building of new roads, hospitals, airports, schools, and water and irrigation schemes in conflict-affected countries. In addition, South Africa's commitment and know-how have also been essential for the implementation of nationally identified priorities such as DDR, fund raising and sponsorship programs to procure key state capacities such as public safety, data administration, and asset management in beneficiary countries. In the same vein, South Africa's support and export of technical knowledge in the areas of economic development and trade have helped many nations like the Democratic Republic of the Congo (DRC) to increase their national incomes by increasing the utility of national endowments such as mines and water reserves.

A good illustration is South Africa's technical assistance and skills training for Congolese to build a hydroelectric plant in the Bas Congo Corridor and facilitation of the business communication through regular flights and the setting up of leading South African businesses. Concomitantly, South Africa has provided information sharing and exchange visits, combined with humanitarian assistance, manifest vital support for CSOs immersed in democratization, gender mainstreaming, peacebuilding, dialogue, security sector reform, and transitional justice. By the same token, the South African non-governmental organization Gift of the Givers (GOTG) is the largest African humanitarian NGO and the South African government often donates funds to the GOTG as it has a proven track record of delivering humanitarian assistance in Africa and beyond, including in Afghanistan and Pakistan.[3] During the 2011 famine crisis that hit Somalia, an estimated 11 chartered "flights carrying 175 tons of supplies and … another 132 containers carrying 2640 tons of aid on several ships … [t]ogether with the medical support [to] … four hospitals" were sent from South Africa into Somalia (GOTG 2012). It is estimated that this cost approximately ZAR80 million (approximately US$10 million) over a one-year period.[4] This provided food security to about 126,000 people among whom 7000 were and several hundred physically challenged families (GOTG 2012).

The above examples from the DRC, South Sudan, Burundi, and Somalia offer tangible evidence of South Africa's peacebuilding support. When one talks about peacebuilding and South Africa, the above come to mind first.

The Categories of Interventions

Following from the above, South Africa's approaches to peacebuilding are strongly informed not just by its own recent history, but a strong national interest that benefits from peaceful resolution of seemingly intractable conflicts. This, according to its policy documents, compels South Africa to participate in peace missions to alleviate the plight of other peoples who are struggling to resolve similar conflicts (Department of Foreign Affairs 1999). Specifically, the 1999 White Paper on South African participation in international peace missions contemplates that civilian assistance, armed forces, and police officers are essential tools for peace, and their work in promoting the respect for human rights, good governance, and institution building is critical to reconstructing sustainable peace as opposed to the use of force which was previously characteristic of military interventions (Department of Foreign Affairs 1999). South Africa therefore committed through this document to work with the UN, the AU, SADC, and other multilateral agencies such as BRICs and IBSA to make appropriate contribution to international peace missions. South Africa's potential contributions include the services of a diverse group of civilians with expertise and experience in areas that may be fundamental to the success of a peace mission (conflict resolution, election monitoring, medical care, demining, telecommunications, etc.). Consequently, whether in South Sudan, the DRC, Burundi, or Somalia, the principles that have defined South Africa's intervention and peace support have been the same and have adopted a more nuanced terminology of peace missions as opposed to the traditional peacekeeping or peacebuilding mandates. The difference is that, from inception, a government decision to support a fragile country or one in conflict is seen as a peace mission, and all support such as below seeks to transform the ailing configuration of conflict and restore durable peace by putting in place resilient institutions and infrastructure (see Tables 6.1 and 6.2).

The tables above demonstrate the width of South African support to South Sudan and to the DRC and in a sense provide a snapshot of how peacebuilding support is channeled and funded. How different then are

Table 6.1 South African peacebuilding support in South Sudan (Hendricks and Lucey 2013a, b, 3)

Governance	Development of the Child Act (University of Cape Town) Observing the referendum (35-member team consisting of members of the parliament, government officials, and analysis unit (PRAU))
Capacity building	Training of diplomats by the Department of Foreign Relations and Cooperation's (DIRCO), Policy Research and Analysis Unit (PRAU) Regional Capacity Building Project for Civil Service by the Public Administration Leadership and Management Academy (PALAMA) Capacity building of top- and middle-level government managers by the University of South Africa (UNISA) and the Nelson Mandela Metropolitan University (NMMU) Training of South Sudan Police Service (SSPS) by the South African Police Service (SAPS) on operational training and senior management, crime prevention, sexual harassment, community policing, cybercrime, and crowd management Training of key security personnel and institution building by the South African National Defence Force (SANDF) Exchange between the universities of Juba and Fort Hare (Higher Education Department) and the University of the Western Cape (Law department)
Implementation support	Mediation between Sudan and South Sudan (Mbeki as Chair of AUHIP) Support with electoral materials for election in 2010 As part of UN Police (UNPOL) under the UN Mission in South Sudan (UNMISS) Securing airspace during independence day celebrations (SANDF) Demining (Mechem—Subsidiary of Denel) Refurbishing government buildings (KV3)
Economic Development & Trade	Arms (Denel), beer (SAB Miller), and mining exploration (New Kush Exploration), agribusiness (Joint Aid Management), cellular network (MTN), cement (Afrisam), and banking (Stanbic) MoU with Council of Geoscience to map minerals
Other	NGOs engaged in conflict resolution and capacity building, namely IJR, ACCORD, ISS, SAWID, IGD, AISA, and the SA Council of Churches. There are also South Africans working in other organizations in South Sudan in their individual capacities

Table 6.2 South African peacebuilding support in the DRC (Hendricks and Lucey 2013a, b, 4)

Governance	Assistance with the development of a master plan for the reform of the armed forces Needs assessment for the army, navy, air force and military health (proposed) SA Police Services (SAPS) development of a five-year plan (not fully implemented) Interpol (SA representative stationed at National Congolese Police (PNC) to assist with planning) Development of an organic law for decentralization of government and public administration, and vision and strategy document for the public service Anti-corruption legislative and institutional framework Establishment of the diplomatic academy Supporting the legislative drafting and development of a legal and constitutional framework Trade policy formulation; quality control; competition policy; intellectual property; and micro-finance Deployment of election observers
Human resource development	Training of army (three battalions; rapid detection force; new recruits) Training of PNC to police elections; VIP protection training; professionalization of PNC; office administration training/human resource and project management for police; arms control proliferation training Training of civil society for engagement in community policing forums and SSR Training of prosecutors, investigators, auditors, civil society & business to develop and implement integrity initiatives Training of immigration officials Training of senior DRC public servants and public management Training of diplomats; foreign language training Training on conflict resolution and negotiation, SA foreign policy, management and leadership and mission administration; training on anti-corruption Training of DRC magistrates Building capacity for infrastructure development (i.e. job inspection, licensing of civil construction agents, setting up of information, financing, infrastructure development) Administrative assistance for CENI Training of DRC revenue authorities

(*continued*)

Table 6.2 (continued)

Infrastructure development	Rehabilitation of the Mura base; rehabilitation of the Maluku police training center; renovation of ENA (school of public administration); refurbishment of foreign ministry building to set up diplomatic academy
	Bas Congo corridor (deep-water port at Banana, rehabilitation of Matadi Port, rehabilitation of the railway line, Matadi to Kinshasa); Zambia Copper Belt spatial initiative
	ACSA undertook financial needs assessment (airport construction)
Implementation support	DDR; identification and registration of FARDC personnel; destroyed illegal and redundant weapons and ammunition
	Security patrols
	Transportation of ballot papers for elections; air support for elections; deployment of SAPS members for elections; donation of 4×4 vehicles, communication equipment and desks, tents, and computers
	Institutional development of national ministries, provincial legislature, and municipal local councils
	Census of public service personnel; pilot project—asset register for immovable assets in relation to infrastructure sector
	Feasibility study for Bas Congo Corridor and Zambia Copper Belt; technical expertise by Telkom to Congolese telecoms network; Eskom feasibility study for electrification of Kimbanseke area; financial needs assessment of state-owned enterprises
	Preparation of funding applications; organizing investor conferences to raise funds for PCRD projects
Economic development and trade	Support for the development of trade and industry in DRC
	Mining of bauxite, aluminum smelter, hydro-electricity (as part of the Bas Congo Corridor)
	SAA flights, retail sector (Shoprite), telecommunications (MTN, Vodacom), Western Power Corridor Project; Standard Bank
Information sharing	Workshops by, e.g. IDASA (democratization and establishment of sustainable policing in the DRC); SAWID (gender mainstreaming); ACCORD (workshops in peacebuilding); IGD (dialogue on PCRD and elections); ISS (gender mainstreaming in the security sector); IJR (information sharing on transitional justice)
	Information sharing between provincial and local councils in SA and DRC
Humanitarian	Gift of the Givers—humanitarian assistance

South African peacebuilding support interventions from those of Western and established actors? One obvious difference is that South Africa's support is quite small in size and quantity compared to Western established donors, owing to the fact that South Africa is an emerging actor in this field and still having to address critical development challenges domestically. For this reason, over time, Pretoria has provided development assistance through a variety of different institutions and not been directly involved as in the first decade of its post-apartheid democracy.

South Africa's efforts listed above demonstrate the breadth of assistance including conflict prevention, mediation, peace support and post-conflict reconstruction as vehicles for peacebuilding, which makes South Africa's approach to this assistance comprehensive. The modalities for delivery of this assistance are clearly distinct from Western and established actors in this field, namely South Africa's engagements are through the African Renaissance Fund as well as a host of national departments individually, whereas with established actors the assistance is coordinated by a single agency. Some of the South Africa actions were funded by Western donors, through so-called triangular North–South–South Cooperation arrangements. For instance Norway funded the training of South Sudanese police by the SAPS and the Netherlands funded the building of brassage centers for the FARDC by the SANDF. Similarly, the South African NGO actions listed in the tables above were also largely funded by Western donors. Another area of difference is that South Africa, like other emerging and Southern actors, does not feel obliged to push the ideology of human rights and democracy in their assistance. As a result its pre-conditions have little to do with conforming to certain political cultures preferred by South Africa, as contrasts with established donors.

Lessons Learned

There is no gainsaying that in its international engagements South Africa has taken a clear South orientation, endeavoring to be the "voice of Africa" in aid negotiations. It has been vocal about global-aid effectiveness. Although development support has remained a tiny quotient of its support to countries such as Burundi, the DRC, and South Sudan, the competition for this aid has increased and exposed a much decentralized and internally competing South African public system. This is largely because in the 20-year-old democratic dispensation, the ANC has tried to transform the image of South Africa in Africa as a driver of growth, human capacity, and freedom on the continent while also trying to right the wrongs of apartheid.

At the same time, recent efforts have raised questions about South Africa's commitment to deliver on its ambitious peace support agenda.

Somalia offers one example. In February 2012, during the International Contact Group of Somalia conference in the UK, South Africa committed R100 million (US$7.5 million) toward assisting the Transitional Federal Government achieve its priorities objectives before the end of its term in September 2015. South Africa has insisted that the assistance be informed by government to government relations. Somali administrations have been adamant that the assistance should be directed toward building national government structures that would later engage in relations with their South African counterparts. Regardless of different expectations, considerable progress was made with Somalia with the opening an embassy in Pretoria and the recognition of Somali consular instruments by South African immigration authorities.

Despite this progress, little movement has been recorded thus far in South African efforts to get accredited in Mogadishu. Differences have also hampered spending the pledged assistance. The South African government supported the ACCORD-managed South Africa–Somalia Assistance (SASA) Project, also known as the "Somalia Initiative." The Somalia Initiative, working with the peacebuilding priorities identified by Somali local and national stakeholders, aimed to reverse the potency of a relapse. The government, however, argued that it, rather than a broader group of stakeholders, should direct the expenditures since the allocation for SASA is part of pledged funding.

Such ambiguity has been at the core of contestations as to whether South Africa is really doing anything in Somalia, whether there is even the will by Pretoria to live up to the foreign policy pledges and pace previously set in Burundi, the DRC, and South Sudan. As a result, the perceptions about South Africa are varied. And justifiably so, because South Africa's track record as demonstrated in the case of the DRC and South Sudan has been visibly large and impressive—thus begging the question why a change in the case of Somalia. Is it resource scarcity? Is it an absence of geo-strategic importance? These notwithstanding, when asked to identify specific activities that South Africa has supported, an interviewee stated that "South Africa gives seminars and gives some money but it is not enough."[5] Another view was that "South Africa's support has been through the Gift of the Givers and partnerships with educational institutions."[6] But the recurrent sense of more was expected from South Africa seemed like the country had set its commitment to the continent higher than it could respond to. In spite of this, there is a strong African desire to strengthen ties with South Africa and to develop a mutually beneficial relationship.

Another cause for concern about South Africa's continued peace efforts on the continent was its decision to draw down its troops from Sudan in April 2016. Whereas this decision was part of a broader austerity measure to respond to domestic economic challenges, it also exposed an often under-valued precondition for peacebuilding: the indispensability of resources. The existence of political will and policies are not enough to drive peace support operations. There is a fundamental need for resource availability, a stable domestic economy and a politically stable and mature democracy which sees value in humanitarianism and global peace endeavors for peace support to flow. It may seem that South Africa, itself 20 years into a process of post-conflict recovery and democratization, overcommitted itself and started experiencing fault-lines that in other states have triggered relapse.

Before now, South Africa's support to other states has been sourced from its African Renaissance Fund (ARF). The dispensing of development assistance through the ARF almost created the unintended contemplation that South Africa had graduated from a developing country and joined the ranks of developed countries. But recent economic challenges, widening inequality, and soaring unemployment were stark reminders of the need for South Africa to reconfigure its intervention framework. Against this backdrop, the South African Development Partnership Agency (SADPA) was conceived to address the shortcomings in the management and implementation of development projects experienced with the ARF. SADPA would use development cooperation as a tool to advance South Africa's foreign policy goals, while the newly created South African Council of International Relations (SACOIR) decide on foreign policy priorities as indicated by the National Development Plan. The SACOIR and SADPA are therefore two new organs designed to balance national interest and foreign policy. While the SACOIR underscores and promotes practical opportunities for cooperation, to tackle the problems of poverty, inequality, and unemployment, SADPA would offer development assistance where the opportunity for South Africa's interest are not undermined to the detriment of its people.

Conclusion

As South Africa continues to consider the future of its involvement in seeking solutions and stability in the complex and old crisis in Somalia and finding finality to the drawn-out assistance to the never-ending crisis in the DRC, three issues come up sharply in respect of the country's post-conflict interventions. The first is the fact that all interventions derive their success or failure from the objective conditions in the crises which South Africa responds. Where the situation is ripe for mediation and stabilization, the country's approach succeeds in a limited time. But where the intervention occurs in an ongoing conflict with no conditions for subsiding, as in Somalia and the DRC, it gets drawn out. The second is that South Africa's interventions are generally framed by the broad thrust of South Africa's foreign policy and worldview. Thus, its commitment to stabilizing Africa and enable a renaissance that will benefit South Africa's diverse economy underpins its decisions on interventions. Thirdly, South Africa is laden with the responsibility of playing a lead role among other countries in achieving the shared goals of the continent on account of its own benefits from African solidarity during the anti-colonial, anti-apartheid struggle and on account of its relative capacities.

Among the lessons evident from engagements like the DRC and Burundi is the fluidity of the concepts of mediation, peacekeeping, and peacebuilding as South Africa applies them. South African peacekeepers and the domestic mission support team which includes civilians play divergent roles in helping the state to recover. These roles are often not just military but a blend of military, civilian and police.

South Africa's peacebuilding initiatives in Africa highlights important novel approaches promoted, while offering vital lessons for all stakeholders to improve upon. Among the lessons learned are the need to avoid adopting a narrow security prism to interventions in complex conflicts and refrain from attaching conditions to aid. It is also the need to avoid the use of many middle men in such interventions as some major actors do in order to avert security risks. It is important to engage local partners, inquiring from them about the conditions and solutions as well as directly responding to their needs. It is also wise not to overcrowd or the host country's vital bureaucracy, but have interventions that can be done in partnership with assisted countries within their capacity.

The case Somalia affirmed that there is still room for improvement in the sense that the bilateral engagement with NGOs like ACCORD, without taking cognizance of the Somali government priorities or allowing the latter to control the funds and define what they should be used for seemed like funds with strings can generate negative perceptions about using own institutions and exporting solutions. This single example suggests that South Africa is more successful in those cases where it was directly involved from the conceptualization of the peace process like mediation. This in part could explain the heavy investments in the DRC and Burundi processes. In these two cases, South Africa demonstrated high-level political commitment, familiarity with the issues, and felt sufficiently involved as part of the key stakeholders to the process, which is in contrast to Darfur and Somalia, where its involvement is in solidarity with the international community and thus a posture in engagement of actors, and less political commitment.

Today, with the South African Council of International Relations put in place to lead on discourses around foreign policy, there is lieu and time to broaden this discussion and work with the government toward addressing its challenges in policy implementation evidenced in the case of Somalia where a neat balance needs to be struck between meeting foreign policy objectives and responding to domestic challenges in manners where intervention is appreciated externally and its dividends well received by the South African populace.

Notes

1. Telephonic interview with Mr. Sivu Maqungo, Deputy Permanent Representative of the Republic of South Africa to the United Nations.
2. Interview with Kwezi Mngqibisa, Coordinator of SA-Somalia Project, ACCORD South Africa, July 15, 2015.
3. Gift of the Givers (GOTG) is the largest NGO operational in Mogadishu presently. Next in line are the Iranian and Turkish Red Crescent.
4. Ibid. Also note that the exchange rate as of 2012 was about 1 rand = 0.122 US$. Thus, ZAR80 million = $US10 million. In this text, exchange rates generally approximate the USD values when the pledge or aid was disbursed.
5. Interview with an official at the Office for Diaspora Affairs, Mogadishu, August 23, 2015.
6. Interview with a Somali Civil Society Activist, Mogadishu, August 25, 2015.

References

Besharati, Neissan Alessandro. 2013. South African Development Partnership Agency (SADPA): Strategic Aid or Development Packages for Africa? *Economic Diplomacy Program Research Report* 12. Accessed March 15, 2016. http://www.saiia.org.za/doc_view/347-south-african-development-partnership-agency-sadpa-strategic-aid-or-development-packages-for-africa

Fayomi, Oluyemi, Felix Chidozie, and Charles Ayo. 2015. A Retrospective Study of the Effects of Xenophobia on South Africa-Nigeria Relations. Accessed March 8, 2016. http://eprints.covenantuniversity.edu.ng/4666/1/Xenophobia%20andx%20Nigeria-South%20Africa%20%20revised%20version%20for%20submission%202015.pdf

Gift of the Givers Foundation. (2012). Somalia Starvation Crisis. Accessed December 13, 2015. http://www.giftofthegivers.org/disaster-relief/somalia/366-somalia-starvation-crisis

Heitman, Helmoed. 2013. Peace Support Intervention Operations: South African Capability is Inadequate. Presentation at the Institute for Strategic Studies' Seminar on *Peace Interventions in Africa: Can we do it?* Pretoria. https://issafrica.s3.amazonaws.com/site/uploads/Helmoed-Heitman-InterventionOps.pdf

Hendricks, Cheryl, and Amanda Lucey. 2013a. South Africa and South Sudan Lessons for Post-Conflict Development and Peacebuilding Partnerships. *Institute for Strategic Studies Briefing Paper*. http://dspace.africaportal.org/jspui/bitstream/123456789/34142/1/PolBrief49.pdf?1

———. 2013b. SA's Post-Conflict Development and Peacebuilding Experiences in the DRC: Lessons Learnt. *Institute for Strategic Studies Briefing Paper*. http://dspace.africaportal.org/jspui/bitstream/123456789/34052/1/PolBrief47_9Oct2013.pdf?1

Kagwanja, Peter. 2009. An Encumbered Regional Power? The Capacity Gap in South Africa's Peace Diplomacy in Africa. *Democracy and Governance Research Program Occasional Paper* 6.

Lucey, Amanda, and Sibongile Gida. 2014. Enhancing South Africa's Post-Conflict Development Role in the African Union. *Institute for Strategic Studies Paper* 256. http://dspace.africaportal.org/jspui/bitstream/123456789/34354/1/Paper256.pdf?1

Motsamai, Dimpho. 2014. SADC 2014–2015: Are South Africa and Zimbabwe Shaping the Organization? *Institute for Strategic Studies Policy Brief* 70. https://issafrica.s3.amazonaws.com/site/uploads/PolBrief70.pdf

Nibishaka, Emmanuel. 2011. South Africa's Peacekeeping Role in Africa: Motives and Challenges of Peacekeeping. *Rosa Luxemburg Stiftung International Politics* 2. http://www.rosalux.co.za/wp-content/files_mf/1297156628_21_1_1_9_pub_upload.pdf

Polzer, Tara. 2008. South African Government and Civil Society Responses to Zimbabwean Migration. *South African Migration Project Policy Brief* 22. http://dspace.africaportal.org/jspui/bitstream/123456789/32995/1/brief22.pdf?1

South African Department of Foreign Affairs. 1999. *White Paper on South African Participation in International Peace Missions*. Accessed March 28, 2017. http://www.gov.za/sites/www.gov.za/files/peacemissions_1.pdf

Zondi, Siphamandla. 2012. South Africa in Southern Africa: A Perspective. *Friedrich Ebert Stiftung Peace and Security Series.* http://library.fes.de/pdf-files/bueros/mosambik/09403-no-8.pdf

Charles Nyuykonge is Senior Researcher at The African Centre for the Constructive Resolution of Disputes (ACCORD), Durban, South Africa.

Siphamandla Zondi is Head of the Department of Politics, University of Pretoria, South Africa.

PART II

Case Studies

CHAPTER 7

Rising Powers and Peacebuilding: India's Role in Afghanistan

Shakti Sinha

Introduction

The gradual shift in the economic and political gravity towards the Global South, particularly the Indo-Pacific, is also reflected in the increased role of these rising powers in stabilising countries emerging from conflict. While in terms of amounts of financial resources deployed by them, aside from China whose assistance figures are ambiguous, may not appear very large, the question to be addressed is whether these new actors have brought a different approach to issues of peacebuilding, more especially with reference to projects being demand-driven and owned by recipient societies.

China, and to a lesser extent India, is accused of tailoring its assistance to take advantages of natural resources available in African countries. This criticism is further buttressed by the conviction that such flows from 'emerging donors might increase the recipients' debt levels, ignore environmental and social impacts, and focus on extracting resources … resulting in an erosion of the progress that has been made in the traditional aid community in these areas' (Dornsife 2013). On the other hand, these rising powers do not see themselves as donors but as development partners;

S. Sinha (✉)
Nehru Memorial Museum and Library, New Delhi, India

C.T. Call, C. de Coning (eds.), *Rising Powers and Peacebuilding*, Rethinking Peace and Conflict Studies,
DOI 10.1007/978-3-319-60621-7_7

their assistance may be tied but has no policy conditionalities attached to them, are demand-driven and are premised on non-interference in the affairs of recipient countries (Dornsife 2013; Roopanaraine 2013).

Going deeper, what are the strategic goals and interests of these rising powers? What motivates them to extend assistance to other, developing countries? And are these motivations different from that of traditional donors? Do they differentiate between 'normal' development and peacebuilding? Does peacebuilding imply a sequenced approach with securing peace as the first priority, followed by state-building and then development? And are the projects taken by these rising powers perceived to be successful by the governments and people of the recipient countries?

The emerging powers generally, and India specifically, because they see themselves as partners and not donors, are driven by a different set of motivations. Having suffered from colonialism which involved not just pauperisation but also loss of political agency, the emerging powers focused on the need to become economically self-sustaining, though in the age of globalisation this is a more nuanced view. Sharing experience and technology was seen as the best way to overcome the lack of capital. A primacy to national sovereignty and hence non-interference in the internal affairs of each other meant that the concept of conditionality was not accepted though tied aid was—both to overcome the need to import from the developed countries and in the spirit of mutual gain. Like traditional donors, political and strategic considerations cannot be ignored, even if the approach is context-specific.

A critical look at India's role in Afghanistan would be used to examine these sets of questions dealing with the role, innovations and effectiveness of the rising powers in building peace. India has been the fifth largest bilateral donor in Afghanistan, and the largest outside the developed countries. This offers a unique opportunity to study the performance of a non-traditional donor in a conflict-affected country; it can be no one's case anymore that Afghanistan is a country that is 'actually' emerging from conflict, and yet the country over the past 14 years has made tremendous strides in many fields, for example, school education, health coverage, communications, role of civil society, growth of a free media and holding regular elections including a peaceful transition of power.

The format of the chapter is that, after a brief introductory section, the second section will trace India's emergence as a donor, examining its driving principles and the evolution of its instruments. This too needs substantial elaboration since there is general lack of knowledge, as well as misconceptions, about the size of India's development assistance as well as misgivings about India's presence in this field, hitherto the preserve of donors from developed countries. The third section will look at India's role in Afghanistan, its development initiatives, the strategic factors driving its Afghan policy and will briefly compare India's development interventions with that of the United States. The fourth section will look at how India's development partnership is perceived in Afghanistan and whether it contributes to peacebuilding, or is divisive and exclusionary. The concluding section will attempt to draw lessons from India's development engagement with Afghanistan with a view to strengthening peacebuilding efforts in countries emerging from conflict.

India as Donor[1]

Contrary to general perception, bolstered by the fact that India is the largest borrower from the World Bank (WB) and the Asian Development Bank (ADB), India has been involved in bilateral, and multilateral, development partnership since the early days of its independence. In 1949, the newly independent Burma (now Myanmar) faced a serious crisis in its balance of payment. Prime Minister Nehru organised a meeting of Commonwealth countries that raised six million pound sterling on concessional terms for Burma; India's own contribution was one million pounds. In addition, India extended a bilateral special concessional loan of Rupees five million to Burma to buy rice from India.[2]

India was an active participant in the setting up of the Colombo Plan for Cooperative Economic Development in South and Southeast Asia during 1950–51. Though the Colombo Plan was initially designed within the traditional developed country donor-developing country recipient framework, it soon evolved as the pioneer instrument of South–South cooperation centred on 'technical cooperation and sharing of development experience.' During these early years, India extended technical cooperation partnership under Colombo Plan as well as extended financial assistance to its neighbours, for example, 'loans of around 200 million rupees to Myanmar and 100 million rupees to Nepal' in the 1950s (Chanana 2009).

From the outset, India's approach was quite different from that of the traditional donors (developed countries). For India the driving force was development partnership, and it did not see itself as a donor even when it extended concessional loans, advances in Indian budgetary parlance. India saw itself as a part, albeit leading one, of the group of developing countries emerging from decolonisation with under-developed economies. The common history of colonisation and emphasis on economic growth bound these countries together. Anti-colonialism meant that egalitarianism and partnership, not aid, should be the focus. What further made India adopt its own path was the Cold War that threatened to divide the world into two, opposing camps. Loath to lose their independence and freedom of action that they interpreted joining either camp meant, India and the others sought their space. The adoption of Panchsheel, or five points, at the Bandung Afro-Asian summit in 1955 was the result, to be followed in 1961 with the launch of the non-aligned movement. Panchsheel committed these countries to respect each others' sovereignty and not interfere in the internal affairs of other countries.

While recognising the political cause of their under-development (colonialism), in the circumstances India felt it necessary to work with its partners on addressing the economic cause of such under-development through technical cooperation and the sharing of experiences. The driving principles of India's development partnership with other developing countries were expanded to include egalitarianism, country ownership, demand-driven and lack of conditionalities (even where there was tied financing). The latter is significant as mutual respect for sovereignty ruled out imposing any conditions as lenders do. However, the lack of hard currency and desire for self-sufficiency meant that tying aid to purchases from lending country was accepted. Separately this refusal to join either camp enabled India and others to access financial and technical assistance from both camps and from multilaterals.

India did not set up a dedicated agency for external development partnership; instead it was run and coordinated by the Ministry of External Affairs (MEA) which drew on expertise of the relevant line ministries. India formalised its technical assistance efforts by establishing the India Technical and Economic Cooperation programme (ITEC), again located in MEA. ITEC has six main channels:

1. Training of workers from state-owned enterprises, bureaucrats and policy makers nominated by the partner countries;
2. Feasibility and consultancy services related to specific development projects;
3. The sending of Indian experts to the requesting country;
4. Study tours in India for individuals and groups suggested by partner countries;

5. Donation of hardware to partner countries; and
6. Humanitarian aid for disaster relief (Indian Technical and Economic Cooperation 2013).

For government of India, ITEC was about partnership and learning from each other, quite different from traditional aid. To quote MEA (2012), ITEC's basic proposition is that '…cooperative efforts of the developing countries were as important as assistance from developed countries and international organizations.' The training component has grown very substantially, and in 2012, it covered 200 different training programmes, of varying durations, at forty training institutions with a total of 5000 training slots (Ministry of External Affairs 2012) ITEC Program has evolved and grown over the years and MEA (2012) reports that ITEC and its sister programme, Special Commonwealth African Assistance Programme (SCAAP) has covered 161 countries in Asia, Africa, East Europe, Latin America, Caribbean as well as Pacific and Small Island countries, and is funded by government of India. It is estimated that by 2010, there were 'more than 40,000 alumni of the ITEC program around the world' (Ramachandran 2010).

India's development partnership programmes in general, including ITEC, are dollar-for-dollar of much greater value since these are overwhelmingly incurred within India and its developing partner countries adjusting for purchasing power parity. In other words, India's external development budget of US$1.3 billion for 2013–14 would actually translate into effectively 4/5 times larger amount for a developed donor country.[3]

India's development assistance has also been increasing at a reasonably fast pace, particularly since 2000, 'increasing seven-fold between 2000 and 2014. In 2014, Indian development assistance stands at about $1.3 billion' (ICRC 2014). This amount may be a slight underestimation as there are other items not fully caught in the budget documents. ITEC is the single largest component, US$589 million out of this amount. Figure 7.1 tracks the growth in India's development assistance in recent years. The Indian government also makes sizeable contributions to multilateral organisations, including the World Food programme, U.N. Development Program and the World Health Organization.

In fact, this tripling over five years is unprecedented, but even at the lower 2012–13 levels, India's development assistance budget 'was comparable to Austria's foreign aid budget for the same year and higher

Fig. 7.1 India's development assistance, 2009–2014
Source: *Indian Government*
Note: *Excludes line of credit*

than the foreign assistance of four of the 23 DAC countries in 2011' (OECD 2012). India's development assistance budget for the year 2015–16 includes a grant element of US$878 million and US$180 million earmarked for capacity development (including formal university education in India). There is also a target for extending Letters of Credit (LOCs), US$2 billion for Africa and US$500 million for other countries.[4]

Earlier, Indian financial assistance was limited to its immediate neighbourhood but that has since changed, though the former still dominates the flow of funds. In fact, but for developments in Afghanistan, discussed later, and the opening up of Myanmar which made these two countries receive larger and larger amounts of assistance, the share of the neighbourhood would have been considerably less. Myanmar received US$83 million in 2013–14, a steep jump from just US$10 million four years earlier. Significantly, India's aid to Africa has grown at a compound annual growth rate of 22% over the past ten years (Ramachandran 2010). The top three aid recipients of India's development cooperation are Bhutan (49%), Afghanistan (9%) and Nepal (6%).[5]

Realising that the government would be unable to meet from its budget the increased call from its development partners for assistance, India shifted gears over the years 2003–4, spanning two different governments. First, India would be discontinuing the system of offering concessional loans, learning from the HPIC experience where it had to write off advances to Guyana and others, it shifted to outright grants, and also introduced a new instrument, LOCs administered by India's Exim Bank with government picking up a major part of the interest charges, allowing partner countries to pick up highly concessional loans for investments in areas of their choice. This has allowed India to expand its development partnership portfolio considerably without a concomitant charge on its budget, with government's own commitment limited to the interest subvention charges. Exim Bank raises its capital from international bond markets since it needs hard currency for its borrowers. LOCs are tied instruments and as a rule, a minimum of 75% of goods and services procured under the LOC (with a relaxation of up to 10%) must be sourced from Indian companies. However, there is a very substantial grant element, varying from 56.4% for HPICs, 37.3% for low-income countries/LDCs and 34.4% for middle income countries (Arora and Mullen 2017).

The process starts with request received from borrower countries for specific projects. MEA's Standing Committee decides whether to move ahead, and if so, the amount of exposure and recommends the case to the finance ministry. The finance ministry checks availability of budgetary resources and finalises the terms and conditions, based on the borrowing country's income classification. The LOC is operated through EXIM bank, but the procurement process followed is that of the borrowing country. There is no oversight of this by India at all, respecting their sovereignty.

LOCs have become extremely popular and high-level diplomatic visit to such partner countries most often result in announcement of new/enhanced LOCs. Exim Bank has now in place 226 Lines of Credit, covering 63 countries in Africa, Asia, Latin America, Oceania and the CIS, with credit commitments of US$16.9 billion; the total amount of contract approvals is US$7.18 billion, and amount disbursed, US$5.77 billion (Mathew 2015). Annex I has an illustrative listing of projects.

Doubts have been raised whether these credits should even be thought of as development assistance since LOCs are seen to be promoting the exports of Indian goods and services. However, the level of tied credit, at 75% of these loans is 'comparable to the de facto tied aid given for example by the US Agency for International Development. Also, the Organization for Economic Cooperation and Development (OECD) guidelines on what is to be considered as 'soft loans' categorises such concessional Government of India-backed and Exim-bank distributed LOCs as development assistance.[6]

Africa has become the largest user of Indian LOCs, 52% of actual disbursals and 45% of amount committed (Mathew 2015). At the recent India–Africa summit (Oct 26–30, 2015), attended by 41 heads of State/government out of 54, 'India promised $10 billion in new credit and $600 million in grant aid to African countries, over five years' (Gupta 2015). India–Africa Development Fund would get an infusion of $100 million and India–Africa Health Fund of $10 million. The grant would also include 50,000 scholarships in India over the next five years.

Utilising its strength in the IT and IT enabled services (ITES) sector, India would spend a total US$125 million in setting up the Pan-African e-Network project. It is meant to assist Africa in capacity building by way of imparting quality education to 10,000 students in Africa over a five-year period in various disciplines from some of the best Indian Universities/Educational Institutions. Besides, this would provide Tele-Medicine services by way of on line medical consultation to the medical practitioners at the Patient End Location in Africa by Indian Medical specialists in various disciplines/specialties. India would cover the cost of supply, installation, testing and commissioning of hardware and software, end-to-end connectivity, satellite bandwidth, O&M support, and providing the tele-education and tele-medicine services to 53 African countries for five years.

Forty seven countries have signed up for it. The first phase of the Pan-African e-Network Project, inaugurated in February 2009, covered 11 countries, namely Benin, Burkina Faso, Gabon, The Gambia, Ghana, Ethiopia, Mauritius, Nigeria, Rwanda, Senegal and Seychelles. The twelve countries launched in 2010 included Botswana, Burundi, Cote d'Ivoire, Djibouti, Egypt, Eritrea, Libya, Malawi, Mozambique, Somalia, Uganda and Zambia.

Regular Tele-Medicine and Tele-Education services have already been started on this network. The Tele-Medicine consultations are regularly being conducted from Super-Specialty Hospitals from India to the African countries on need basis. In addition, regular Continued Medical Education (CME) sessions have started (2009) from 11 Indian Super-Specialty Hospitals. Regarding Tele-Education services from India, more than 2000 students from Africa have enrolled in five different top-ranking universities in India in various disciplines (Pan-African 2016). India has also contributed US$200 million to NEPAD and is involved in other African-led initiatives.

India's guiding principles, though not formally articulated at one place, is reflected in its approach to development partnership generally. That India's development assistance flows primarily to countries in its neighbourhood should not be a surprise. The subcontinent continues to have the largest numbers of poor people in the world, though not in percentage terms. State formation in many of these countries, or parts within, is still challenged by insurgencies, terrorist violence and weak capacities. As India seeks to emerge as a global power, its own economic achievements and military capability would not compensate for any disarray or state failure in its immediate neighbourhood. Therefore, in addition to seeing others as similarly placed on account of historical reasons and consequently as partners in economic development, India has to sufficiently invest in its neighbourhood to ensure that they too are able to grow economically. This is seen as an important factor in successful State-building. Politically, India cannot be seen to be located in a troubled region. This adds strength to India's basic ethical approach to development partnership. An analysis of Indian development assistance to Afghanistan will show whether or not it is driven by these general principles.

India's Development Partnership with Afghanistan

India's Prime Minister Narendra Modi was in Kabul on December 25, 2015, to jointly inaugurate with Afghan President Ashraf Ghani the parliament building built by the Indian government. His visit was a big hit in the Afghan media, especially the social media. The government of Afghanistan decided to name one of the blocks of the building after former Indian Prime Minister Atal Bihari Vajpayee, who had offered to build this powerful symbol of democracy as a sign of Afghanistan–India friendship and partnership. It was in his time that India re-engaged with Afghanistan in the aftermath of the US intervention that dislodged the Taliban in late 2001. The pace of engagement accelerated almost immediately, and despite fatal attacks on Indian targets including diplomats, development staff and projects, has maintained its momentum.

That India has emerged as major development partner, arguably the fifth largest bilateral donor over the 14-year period, to Afghanistan should not have come as a surprise to analysts who have worked on Afghanistan

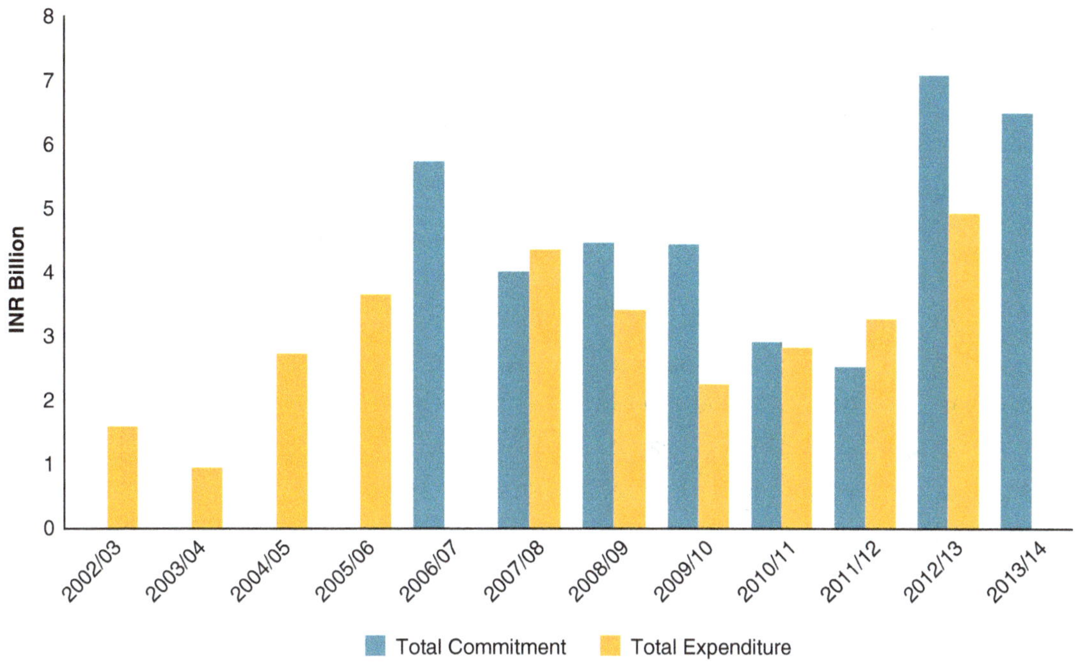

Fig. 7.2 India's development cooperation with Afghanistan: commitments and expenditures, 2002/03–2013/14
Source: Rani Mullen.2014
"IDCR Report: The State of Indian Development Cooperation."
New Delhi: Indian Development Cooperation Research, (Spring)

on the ground. India's development partnership with Afghanistan goes back to the 1950s, and till transit trade through Pakistan was not an issue, was Afghanistan's largest export market for dry fruits. The civil war (1992–96) and subsequent Taliban rule caused a break, though India did extend humanitarian assistance through UN agencies (Mullen 2013) (Fig. 7.2).

India's total commitment for the reconstruction of Afghanistan is US$2 billion, with more than half disbursed. It has funded/co-funded three very important infrastructure projects, the construction of the 218 km road from Delaram to Zaranj which gives Afghanistan access to an alternate port, Chahbahar in Iran; it has reconstructed and expanded the Salma Dam which would produce 42 MW of power and irrigate 75,000 hectares of land when fully commissioned by mid-2016; it has co-funded and built transmission towers over the Hindu Kush as part of the Northern Electric Power System (NEPS) that has brought electricity to Kabul and other areas. Some of the key Indian projects are the following:

- Food assistance to primary school children and construction and rehabilitation of schools ($321 million disbursed),
- Supply of 250,000 tonnes of wheat,
- Construction of a power line from Pul-i-Khumri to Kabul ($120 million),
- Annual scholarships to study in India—higher education (initially 500 per year, increased to 675 and then to 1000),
- Construction of Delaram-Zaranj road ($150 million),
- Construction of the Salma Dam Power Project (US$200 million),
- Construction of the parliament building ($27 million disbursed; budget $178 million), and
- Small Development Projects, initially in the South East, and then extended all over the country.

(Annex II has a comprehensive listing of all Indian development and humanitarian initiatives in Afghanistan.)

It would be useful to look at a few of these initiatives to better understand what India brings, and does not bring, to the table of State-building/peacebuilding before comparing the Indian approach with that of traditional donors.

India's biggest humanitarian intervention in Afghanistan, supply of 1 million tonnes of wheat in the form of High Energy Biscuits (HEB) distributed to 2 million school children across Afghanistan, also has a strong development impact. Midday meals are shown to be strong motivational factors in increasing enrolment. The World Food Program (WFP), a UN agency is the implementing partner. This supply to Afghanistan was done despite the logistical hurdles posed by Pakistan which had to be overcome. Similar hurdles had to be overcome to deliver 250,000 tonnes of wheat as humanitarian assistance, by technically making delivery to Afghanistan at an Indian port, so that it could travel overland from the Pakistani port of Karachi to Afghanistan.

While the reconstruction and renovation, and subsequent further upgradation of Afghanistan's only children hospital, the Indira Gandhi Institute of Child Health, initially built with Indian assistance about 4 decades back, was a visible intervention in the health sector, what earned the Indian government considerable goodwill all over the country was the stationing of Indian medical missions in cities of Kabul, Jalalabad, Kandahar, Mazar and Herat. However, after attacks on Indian doctors in Kabul leading to fatalities, most had to be shut down. In the decade that they operated, they treated hundreds of thousands of patients every year. India is also involved in upgrading medical training and diagnostics facilities. India also accepted the Afghan request to support the Afghan Red Crescent Society (ARCS) to treat Afghan children suffering from Congenital Heart Disease (CHD). Financial assistance of US$5 million would be given to ARCS over a period of five years beginning 2015, with the first tranche of US$1 million already released. Financial assistance provided by India will be utilised for the ongoing treatment by ARCS of Afghan Children at Artemis, Max and Fortis Hospitals in New Delhi. These hospitals have also offered special concessional rates for treatment of these children.

In order to increase the 'visual' presence of the government all over Afghanistan, India supported the expansion of the national TV network by providing uplink from Kabul and downlink in all the 34 provincial capitals, a force multiplier for national integration. Similar consideration drove the upgradation of telephone exchanges in 11 provinces.

Recognising that the Afghan government's lack of capacity could seriously constrain its ability to deliver services to its citizens, a key requirement for building peace, India initially offered 500 short-term training annually slots under ITEC, a figure since increased to 675. At the request of President Karzai for deployment of Indian civil servants as mentors in Afghan ministries, India tied up with UNDP's Capacity for Afghan Public Administration (CAP) programme and deputed 30 Indian civil servants who were placed in different ministries. This was a rare occasion where government of India partnered with another bilateral/multilateral agency in the actual implementation of any development partnership programme; in this case, there were other bilateral funding programme too. This was continued when CAP was modified and became the National Institutional Building programme.

However, capacity building exercises like training and deputing experts as mentors have their limitations. Afghanistan, as a war ravaged country has serious issues with higher education. India, initially offered 500 annual long-term university scholarships for undergraduate and post graduate degrees. This was increased to 675 scholarships in 2009, and to 1000 in 2012–13. And since 2014, 20 of these scholarships are also offered for pursuing PhD programmes in different subjects. The entire selection process is done by the Afghan government, in line with India's policy of no conditionality. It has been estimated that since 2001, 'more than 10,000 Afghan students have studied in India on ICCR scholarships, with some

7,000 returning home armed with an education and technical skills, which they are using to drive Afghanistan's stabilization and development.' In addition, 'some 8,000 Afghan students are pursuing self-financed degrees in different fields across India' (Haidari 2015). During his recent visit, Prime Minister Modi announced 500 long-term scholarships for children of security personnel who have lost their lives on duty.

India has also accepted the Afghan government's request to set up a full-fledged agriculture university at Kandahar, a priority for a country where the majority of their labour force is in agriculture, but where due to war, productivity levels are a fraction of what they were pre-1979. Separately, India has made available 614 Agriculture scholarships (BSc, MSc and PhD). India has also involved its private sector for running vocational training in Kabul, and funded a reputed Indian NGO, Self Employed Women's Association (SEWA) to train 1000 Afghan women in different skills and vocations.

After many stops and starts caused by insecurity and supply bottlenecks, the Indian assisted reconstruction of the Salma dam in Chishti district of Herat province is almost completely commissioned. The dam work and its supply lines were frequently attacked, allegedly at Iran's instance as the power generated by the dam (42 MW) would eliminate Herat's dependence on Iranian supply, as well as by the Taliban (*Plot to* 2013). At the height of the construction work, there were more than 2000 workers in three shifts, including around 700 Indians.[7] The total cost of the reconstruction is US$200 million.

As referred to earlier, India partnered with other bilateral and multilateral donors to bring electricity to Kabul, and many other areas in planning and executing NEPS. This is one of the largest, and definitely the most technologically challenging infrastructure projects ever undertaken in Afghanistan. Besides India, the other partners were the ADB, the United States, Germany, Japan, WB and Islamic Development Bank, a rare instance of so many internationals working in a coordinated manner led by the government of Afghanistan. Over four years, more than 1300 massive pylons were erected to hold transmission lines stretching from the Uzbekistan border to Kabul. The most difficult stretch was over the perennially snow-bound, avalanche-prone Hindu Kush Mountains, towering more than 3800 metres above sea level, was planned and executed by India. Further, an Indian company was the common contractor installing the transmission towers and lines. To add to the complication, the company manufactured most of its materials in India, but due to transit issues, the entire material 'had to be shipped from India to Iran, and then driven through Turkmenistan, into Uzbekistan, and finally into Afghanistan at Hairatan, in the north' (Asian Development Bank 2009). India has also set up three substations and is setting up one more. India's share of the project cost is US$120 million.

India was able to demonstrate both its technical expertise as well as the ability to deal with, and work together, with multilateral agencies and bilateral agencies notorious for working alone. The project not only earned the government of Afghanistan much goodwill by providing electricity to upward of 4 million people but suddenly improved their quality of life, a huge gain for government's credibility. Paradoxically, though USID was an integral part of NEPS, it separately executed many redundant (in view of NEPS) and non-viable power projects including generating stations that had no fuel linkage or would produce expensive power (McCloskey et al. 2015).

In a rare departure from its practice of directly executing its projects, though taken up at the request of the host government, India has partnered with the government of Afghanistan (Ministry of Economy) in implementing the community-based Small Development Projects (SDP). It would also be useful to compare the SDP with Afghanistan government's flagship National Solidarity Program (NSP), which is also community-based.

The SDP was launched in 2006 initially covering seven insecure, underdeveloped border provinces in 2006, with a view to allowing local communities to invest in their priority needs and in the process better connecting with the Afghan government.[8] It has since been expanded to all provinces. Government of India initially allocated US$10 million in phase one, which was supplemented by US$20 million in phase two. The third phase signed in November 2012 when President Karzai visited India substantially hiked the allocation to US$100 million, to be utilised by 2016. SDP's priority is to target the most vulnerable but as these are mostly in insecure areas, implementation becomes an issue. The Ministry of Economy (MoE) is the nodal ministry at the national level and its provincial directorates act as nodal points in their respective provinces. The steering committee has representatives from all concerned line ministries as well as the President's office. Specific proposals from communities are endorsed by the Governor and the Provincial Development Council (PDC) and sent to the MoE, which in turn then sends them for vetting to the concerned line ministries, on whose budgets these proposals are borne. Till the time of writing, the Embassy of India had approved 124 proposals, with another 185 proposals in different stages in the pipeline. Some of these approved projects have been completed, while others are in different stages of implementation, which is difficult in insecure areas. The health sector dominates with 67 approved projects followed by small, rural development projects (21) and education (17).

Review meetings are held every two weeks and the Council of Ministers is briefed every two months. Based on difficulties faced in implementation, more powers are being given to provincial governors. Presently all procurement decisions are taken by the line ministries and often small mistakes by provincial staff leads proposals being returned for rectifications or fresh processing. MoE is working on improving capacities at local/provincial level. There is a high local ownership from the community up to the ministers' level. The Afghan government convened a national conference on SDPs in end-2012, attended by 400 participants from across the country, representing civil society, provinces, ministries and so on. The conference laid down the criteria for allocation of funds to provinces keeping in mind the need for balanced growth. The intensive consultative nature of SDP policy formulation and implementation does slow down the process but ensures ownership.

It is worth comparing the SDP to another flagship project of the government, the National Solidarity Program (NSP).)The latter was far bigger, comprehensive in its coverage and in operation for much longer than the SDP. The NSP is a community-based recovery programme created to help in the recovery from decades of conflict, initially through rebuilding rural infrastructure, inspired by the success of Indonesia's Kecamatan Development Program. The actual choice of the project in NSP is left to the community. A community development cluster (CDCs) of around 25 households is established through secret ballot (mixed and single sex) by the facilitating partner (FP), often an NGO. The Government releases block grants to each CDC whose representatives in discussion with their facilitating/implementing partners chooses the specific intervention that is of the highest priority to them. NSP has since covered most of the country and is funded from the general development budget of the country, which in turn receives budgetary support from donors, both multilateral and bilateral. Within the government, the Ministry of Rural Rehabilitation (MRRD) runs the programme. The programme was considered very successful as it contributed to improving rural connectivity and agricultural productivity. MRRD's capacity was also strengthened, and it is regarded one of the star performers of the government.

Both the NSP and the SDP have their strengths and weaknesses. While NSP is quite participative at the community level, and creates the basic units of democratic choice, though doubts have been expressed about it in practice in different parts of the country, it operates outside the government system. The facilitating/implementing partner gets the credit, not the government as a whole. Its biggest lacuna is the complete absence of ownership outside MRRD, quite unlike SDP. At the same time, NSP has created considerable local, economic assets that are very useful to the community. However, leading from this, its second basic problem is inability to scale up and create projects that bring about sustainable, favourable economic outcomes. Third, what happens to the CDC once the project is over or when the NSP winds down? The resulting frustration could produce cynicism and reversion to more atomised behaviour patterns.

The SDP could do well to replicate CDC-like consultative mechanism. It would also do well to look at additional resources, including by diverting from non-productive programmes and by attracting other donors. Better tracking would improve accountability and lead to better outcomes.

Both the SDP and the NSP emblemise a different approach to peacebuilding and development than that exhibited by many traditional donors in Afghanistan. Reflecting the belief that 'State-building and peacebuilding are primarily internal processes,' (DFID 2010) then-finance minister Ashraf Ghani 'demanded that assistance was to be channelled through the ministries, and aligned with national plans and priorities' (Strand 2014). Many donors including the USAID, Japan and most UN agencies, preferred to execute projects themselves, often without even coordination with the government. The international military in particular with their Provincial Reconstruction Teams (PRTs) and the Commanders' Emergency Response Program (CERP) spent very substantial sums of money, for example, US$80 million in three quarters of 2005, aimed at 'winning hearts and minds' (Karp 2006). Unfortunately, tactical considerations such as rewarding friendly individuals and groups, or the need to 'deliver development' drove such investment decisions. This was true at both the battalion as well at national levels. In the bargain, basic 'principles for assistance were set aside for military and political objectives, leading to nepotism and corruption as the Kabul Bank scandal illustrates' (Strand 2014). The ISAF and PRT approach, though called 'winning hearts and minds,' was a top-down process that did not address an imbalance between areas receiving lots of resources and others that received little or none. They also reflected 'quick fixes' that were less effective than longer-term development approaches. Ghani's position recognised that peacebuilding and state-building are intrinsically linked and must be internally driven.

Indian development partnership is highly valued in Afghanistan, even though the total amount committed and disbursed is miniscule compared with that of the traditional donors. This is because it is in response to felt demands articulated by the Afghan government and as response to them shows in line with the needs of the people, is value for money and appropriate to the local conditions. It compares very favourably with the performance of a donor like the United States (USAID, military, Department of Agriculture etc.), as detailed in Table 7.1 (compiled mainly from analysis in McCloskey et al. 2015).

Table 7.1 Appraisal of US aid to Afghanistan

'In just six years, the IG has tallied at least $17 billion in questionable spending. This includes $3.6 billion in outright waste, projects teetering on the brink of waste, or projects that can't—or won't—be sustained by the Afghans, as well as an additional $13.5 billion that the average taxpayer might easily judge to be waste'

Afghanistan SIGAR has only examined a small percentage of the $110 billion effort to rebuild and remodel

'Super colonial' attitude ... the American military dismissed a local NGO in Kunar as unimportant because it was 'just Afghans working there'

- $8.4 billion was spent on counter-narcotics programmes that were so ineffective that Afghanistan has produced record levels of heroin—more than it did before the war started
- In 2008, the Pentagon bought 20 refurbished cargo planes for the Afghan Air Force at a cost of US$486 million, but there were no spare parts and it was 'a death trap,' according to the Special Inspector General for Afghanistan Reconstruction. Sixteen of the planes were sold as scrap for the grand sum of $32,000
- $335 million power plant in Kabul, rush job, ended up $181 million over budget, diesel-powered plant is so expensive to run ($ 245 million per year), the Afghans are only using about 1% of its capacity, intermittent use is actually harming the equipment and putting it on the path to 'catastrophic failure'
- State Department spent $106 million into refurbishing a compound in Mazar-e-Sharif to be a consulate but which cannot be used as it is deemed unsafe
- $25 million blown on a fancy military headquarters nobody used
- $14.7 million spent on a storage facility the military never used
- $34.4 million programme to push Afghan farmers to produce soybeans. However, the crop doesn't grow well in northern Afghanistan and Afghans weren't particularly interested in eating it
- USAID spent nearly $8 million on tree planting and sapling programme after being told by Afghan government and its own staff that it would fail

Before concluding this section, it is important to point out that India's development partnership extends beyond funding and implementing projects in Afghanistan, and is guided by specific, regional factors, namely peace and stability in its neighbourhood. In the past, the development of jihadism as a strategic instrument to confront the Soviet occupation of Afghanistan had negative consequences for India once the Soviets went home. The jihadis were simply diverted to India, especially to Jammu & Kashmir, which saw a raging insurgency that soon degenerated to terrorism. The collapse of the Afghan State allowed the sponsors of such jihadi groups to run training camps in Afghanistan for such groups, allowing them both the space to do so and the scope to deny any role in supporting terrorist groups. India simply cannot see a failed State in its neighbourhood or a State under the control of jihadi terrorists. India 'recognises that social and economic development of Afghanistan is vital to regional security' (Price 2013). Consequently, India was instrumental in pushing for Afghanistan's membership of the South Asian Association for Regional Cooperation (SAARC). Its membership was approved at the 13th SAARC summit in Dhaka (2005), and Afghanistan formally joined at the 14th Summit in New Delhi (2007) (Al-Madani 2005). The price India had to pay for this was the admission of China as Observer, along with Japan, the United States, South Korea and the European Union. This emphasis on regional cooperation has two implications. One is that India wants much greater economic ties between countries in the region, leading to mutual interdependence. Two, recognising that it is overwhelmingly the biggest economy in the region, India realises its responsibility to achieve this; hence India's active role in Afghanistan. As a result, the total value of trade between the two countries reached US$280 million in 2010, from just US$80 million in 2001. India 'represents Afghanistan's fifth largest source of imports, and India accounts for 20 per cent of total Afghan exports' (Al-Madani 2005).

As demonstration of India's motivations, at the '2012 Kabul 'Heart of Asia' conference, India offered to lead two confidence—building measures, intended to support Afghanistan and integrate it into the regional economy.' This included linking chambers of commerce, recognising that trade and investment was about private entrepreneurs taking the initiative. Within India there is confidence that it can 'take a lead in facilitating trade and commercial opportunities for Afghanistan and the region' (Sachdeva 2012).

With this is mind, government of India facilitated the hosting of an Investment Summit on Afghanistan in New Delhi (June 2012). The Indian foreign minister highlighted certain emerging sectors as being potentially very productive, namely 'mining, infrastructure, telecommunications, agro-based and small-scale industries, health, pharmaceuticals, education and information technology' (Price 2013).

Development partnership and peacebuilding can never be divorced from politics, but to be sustainable must be mutually beneficial, which the India–Afghanistan partnership has shown to be. It would, therefore, be correct to say that 'India has been an important economic assistance partner for Afghanistan, and can help in other fields to prevent destabilization' (Ayres 2015).

Afghan Perception of India's Development Partnership

Discussions with a cross-section of decision makers, civil society representatives, strategic community in Kabul, Mazar-i-Sharif and Herat, surveys conducted from time to time by different agencies as well as articles in the Afghan media all lead to the unambiguous conclusion that India is the most liked country, that Indian projects are favourably looked upon and that these are seen as contributing to peace building since they meet the 'felt-needs' of the Afghan people and society. As a respondent commented—any project that contributes to upgrading the economy automatically contributes to peace building. He added 'Indian projects are unique and varied.' On peacebuilding, another respondent said that 'helping our economy and facilitating daily lives of the people through better roads, communications, the Salma Dam and humanitarian assistance has contributed to peace building in its own way.'

Specifically, responding to local pressure from the Herat region, the government of Afghanistan has renamed the Salma Dam as the India–Afghanistan Friendship Dam. This project is seen as hugely liberating western Afghanistan from dependence on foreign supply, will ensure reliable and consistent electric supply and has the potential to economically transform the region.

Similarly, the naming of one of the blocks of the new parliament building as Atal block in honour of former Indian prime minister is symbolic in a country where symbols are very important. A photo tweet showing the parliament building as India's gift and another photo showing the destroyed Dar-ul-Aman palace in Kabul as Pakistan's gift went viral in the Afghan social media.[9] The present writer has worked in Afghanistan for years with the United Nations Assistance Mission (UNAMA), later as a consultant for UNDP, was frequently told by Afghans across the country and classes how they appreciate India's development assistance as it was primarily targeted at education, health and in establishing democratic institutions. And in responding to local needs. As former Deputy Minister of Energy Ahmad Wali Shairzay said 'The government wanted to import power, but they needed investment. That's when ADB and the Government of India came in' (Asian Development Bank 2009).

India is seen as a model partner in terms of dollar value and Indian projects were not seen as divisive. A respondent who has had a lot of experience dealing with donors compared NATO/ISAF assistance unfavourably with India's. According to him, the former constructed roads to meet their needs of supplies and to avoid attacks on their camps. He was particularly critical of their quick impact projects (QIPs) and CERP as these were tactically driven, including to be seen as 'rewarding' local commanders or strongmen, which has been divisive. Indian aid has not been divisive. Respondents reminded that Indian development partnership began in the 1950s, and post 2001, India is the largest regional development partner, by contrast China's support till date has been only US$125 million. Many respondents pointed that India has not indicated any priorities and left it to the government. SDP was seen by a few who mentioned it as better than NSP, which was not sustainable. India's higher education scholarship was much appreciated since human development is an Afghan priority. One respondent was critical of the choice of subjects; according to him, Afghanistan needed graduates in mining, engineering, IT, MBBS, and not so many political scientists or sociologists. Capacity building, particularly in technical fields was seen to have benefitted from ITEC. Ministry of Energy and Water officials rating it very useful and pointed out that a number of their staff had gone to India for masters' degree. In the course of implementing NEPS, the Indian state-owned enterprise, Power Grid Corporation had trained their Afghan counterparts, which was much appreciated. And the government of India in the Salma Dam contract, has made the contractor responsible for running the plant for one year, handholding the take-over process so that at the end of the year, Afghan staff would be in a position to take over.

Regarding cooperation and coordination with international development partners, the Afghans pointed out that the WB and ADB route their support through the budget and there is good coordination. Regarding India and KFW (Germany), the support is off-budget but coordination is good. The USAID support is off-budget and the coordination is not so good. In the selection of projects, the European Union selects and implements on its own but they coordinate with the government. Branch offices of line ministries in provinces are involved. However, they operate in the safe areas in the north. WB and ADB support projects selected, and designed by the government. Both institutions fund such mutually agreed projects but monitor them rigorously. In the case of KFW, the government proposes but they have own priority; procurement is by them, but there is close coordination with the government. The government proposes projects to India, which then implements it.

Afghanistan has seen high, if fluctuating, growth rates since 2001. This has created jobs in the service sector. However, necessary skills are at a premium, so there are limitations to growth being driven by it. This is particularly so since external agencies and external financial support is being retrenched. Since literacy rates are still very low, only agriculture and related activities like food processing, dairy and so on can drive growth. A number of respondents suggested that India should step up its support for this sector. With China's recent decision to gift Afghanistan a few hundred tractors, one respondent wanted joint India–China support for agricultural development.

Many specifically referred to India as Afghanistan's 'best friend' and the general expectation of respondents that it should do more, specifically 'just keep helping us in every possible way.' Besides the general comments were some specific examples and suggestions that could be used both to influence India's approach to development assistance specifically as well help evolve global consensus on facilitating peacebuilding and State-building.

India's record in executing big projects, other than NEPS, was seen as something that needs improvement, even accounting for the insecure areas where Indian projects were (eastern Herat, Farah, etc.) and problems of transit through Pakistan. The reliance on Indian state-owned enterprises was identified as the reason for this unsatisfactory state of affairs. Lack of supervision and monitoring along with lack of discretionary decision-making with the Indian Embassy in Kabul were also issues, for example, once Delhi tightened the screws and accepted greater local discretion both the Salma dam and the parliament building project picked up momentum and finished far faster than what its progress till date had shown possible.

The Indian performance in executing the difficult task of laying transmission towers over the Hindu Kush has been much appreciated by both Afghans and international partners. This was a technically complicated project, made more difficult by the fact that though it is an integrated one, its different components were executed by different agencies using different decision-making processes, different funding routes, different reporting norms, different monitoring and so on, and yet it worked well. And yet, other than NEPS and a few other projects, India prefers to act alone, and it simply refuses to pool money together with other donors. While it does extend budgetary support to Nepal and Bhutan, these are for historical reasons and an exception. This has two disadvantages that actually militate against India's approach to development partnership. One, it deprives countries like Afghanistan the benefit of large projects which require multi-donor support, particularly where Indian technology and approach would be most appropriate and cost-effective, for example, the Indian contractor who built the transmission line from the Uzbek border to Kabul could only come in because an Indian entity was tasked with part of the work. Absent the Indian presence, work funded by the other donors could conceivably have been executed but more expensively. Two, if more untied funds were extended to the Afghan government, it would be able to be seen as exercising more sovereign functions and also directly meet more of its citizens requirements. This point, however, cannot be over-stressed since India would not in the near future have the economic wherewithal to really contribute by way of 'cash' support.

The present writer can speak from personal experience that quite often India is seen as a role model in Afghanistan, both for firmly establishing democracy and for its economic achievements. As part of developing their national development strategy, the government and donors had jointly established broad sectoral consultative groups and narrower, subject-wise, working groups. Having attended many such meetings across sectors and subjects, the common feature that was clear was the desire to learn from India. The request would be to speak from the Indian experience, and not as a representative of the UN, as it was felt that such experience was more relevant to the local context. In a similar vein, the present writer underwent driving lessons in the United States with an Ethiopian lady as the instructor. She remembered and named her Indian school teachers (Mr Gupta and Mr Sharma) and said that her superior, another Ethiopian who was a senior academic in his country, also had Indian school teachers. A former Indian ambassador to Ethiopia mentioned that during the call on, the then President (Meles Zenawi) remembered his school teacher, an Indian named Mr Nair. There is a lesson in this for both India and for major donors. India effectively discontinued sending school teachers to developing countries, particularly low-income, and now restricts ITEC to technically qualified personnel. Similarly major donors could think in terms of collaborating with India to send such, relatively lower technically skilled personnel to low-income countries. This would be major costs savings with much better development outcomes. In Afghanistan, the USAID and a few others did use Indian training institutions for capacity building of Afghans for the same reasons, but this could be expanded.

Similarly, while supporting institution building, instead of trying to superimpose models of mature, high income democracies, donors could look at relevant experience from not just India, but Indonesia, Malaysia, Brazil, South Africa, Nigeria and so on. This would have greater resonance and lead to more sustainable outcomes. Development partnership should be more broad based to be effective.

This section cannot be complete without referring to an issue of major disappointment among many Afghan respondents, and that was in India's diffidence in supporting the Afghan national security forces (ANSF). A number of respondents expressed frustrations about India's refusal to step in a big way in supporting ANSF beyond a few training slots, and supply of relative less defensive equipment.[10] There was visible disappointment that 'India's response to our request for supply of arms and equipment has not been what we expected' despite the fact that the 2011 India–Afghanistan Strategic Partnership does include security cooperation.' As a result, Afghanistan was 'forced to look elsewhere.' A number of respondents were emphatic that 'India must do much more in forcing Pakistan to curb down its terrorism ... India has a good dialogue with the United States and should use that opportunity to leverage the US to put pressure on Pakistan.' Another respondent was clear in his prescription that 'India should not look at Afghanistan through the prism of Pakistan.'

This is a subject where it would be difficult to find agreement. On the one hand, India was the earliest to point the finger at Pakistan for using terrorism as an instrument of State policy, well before the rest of the world would even consider it. Logically, as an Afghan respondent told us that since both India and Afghanistan have suffered from Pakistan-sponsored terrorism, India should more actively support Afghanistan's efforts to combat terrorism. On the other hand, there is the view that though India 'can do more, but New Delhi's concerns about poking a Pakistani hornets' nest have limited the security partnership' (Ayres 2015). The jury is still out whether India's more active security support to Afghanistan would have helped the process of stabilisation in that country, and the region, or made it worse.

Afghan interlocutors were also asked about their perception of China as a stakeholder in Afghanistan, and not just as a development partner. There was general acceptance that China was a powerful neighbour and had played an active role in training and arming the Mujahideen against the Soviets. They had established contacts with various leaders, groups, tribes and so on and these were kept alive even after the withdrawal of the Soviets.

China's principal interest in Afghanistan was perceived to prevent the destabilisation of Xinjiang province and that it would participate in economic reconstruction only where it advances its own economic interests. There was general agreement that China was not interested in domestic economic and social issues affecting the Afghans and would not mind Taliban coming to power or sharing power. And that it would stay away from direct military involvement. On Aynak where a Chinese firm won a global tender to develop the world's largest copper deposits, a respondent predicted that China would not begin work in Aynak Copper mines till 2019, and that 'nobody knows that they will do so even after that date.'

India's role in Afghanistan was seen as a security threat both by China and Pakistan. Respondents were in agreement that 'there is no comparison between the development assistance provided by India and China. Nobody would write about what happened to the various projects undertaken by China after 2002.' There was a specific reference to the highways built that were of poor quality and required resurfacing within no time. Consequently, the Chinese companies concerned had to leave because of widespread criticism. There was another reference to the hospitals in Kabul which were repaired and opened had to be closed the following day, due to the scale of construction defects. Not one patient was treated there. In support, the respondent gave a news item (Smith 2012). Afghans also mentioned that even Chinese brothels had to close down and that 'every Afghan knows about it and it was in the media too.'

A respondent was apprehensive that while China was powerful by itself but when combined with Pakistan, 'it was awesome and the Afghans know what it means to be at the receiving end of this combination.' Many suggested that both, China and Pakistan have been in touch with the

Taliban—together as well as independently. It was stated that after the ouster of Taliban from Afghanistan, the Chinese met the Taliban in the gold mines being developed by China in Balochistan (they could not provide any specific details on this.) As regards arming the Taliban, they were emphatic in saying that the Chinese provided not just small arms but also HN-5 anti-aircraft missiles, mines, components for IEDs and how to fabricate them, and rocket-propelled grenades. As per the Afghans the Americans were aware of this and had even raised the issue with the Chinese. But when it came to arming the ANSF, the Chinese are hesitant to provide anything other than some token small arms.

Conclusion

India's emergence as a donor is yet to impact on the global development assistance framework and systems. However, India's impact in Afghanistan, and other neighbouring countries as well as the creeping presence in Africa can potentially lead to making the system more accountable and ensure more cost-effective delivery. At this moment of time, India and the traditional donors are on parallel tracks and as in monetary terms, India's contribution is miniscule even compared to China's, and it really does not matter. Fears about China's and India's takeover of Africa are grossly exaggerated in so far as India is concerned. Its present LOC exposure in Africa plus the targeted US$10 billion over the next five years would still be under US$18 billion. Its importance lies in its local impact that helps technologically upgrade the local industry and unleash agricultural potential, cost-effective and value for money. But in the larger interest of peacebuilding, both India and the traditional donors can learn from the other, and in some ways, seem to be doing so.

India has just overhauled its LOC guidelines, moving closer to the western model of development assistance but still respecting such partnership as being demand-driven. A number of weaknesses came up after a detailed review of past projects funded by LOCs (Mathew 2015)

- Weak project conceptualisation and lack of project synchronisation
- Change in scope and nature of LOCs by borrowing country
- Over-reliance by partner countries on a few Indian companies for project proposals and implementation
- Effects of political cycles/security issues and so on.

The new approach provides for evaluation of long-term economic benefits, highest standards for ethics, Integrity Clauses in loan agreements, inspection of all documents, wide publicity of all procurement, system of pre-qualification of contractors/consultants, vetting of contract documents (milestone-linked payments, performance guarantee, retention money, penalty for delay, ethics and integrity clauses). Country classification would also follow IMF norms, and repayment schedules and element of concession have been further liberalised. Additionally, if there is a joint venture with an Indian entity, the borrowing country could use the concessional loan as its equity in the project, allowing both for Public Private Partnerships (PPPs) and large infrastructure projects. For African countries, the requirement to use Indian goods and services has been brought down to 60%. However, there is no requirement to use anything but the borrowing countries' own systems, so respect for sovereignty remains.

The international community is also moving towards greater flexibility, value for money and respect for national systems. Following SEWA's successful skilling project for Afghan women, USAID gave it funds to run similar programmes for Afghan women, and USAID's use of Indian training institutions increased. Similarly, the WB has changed its conditionality on using its own procurement policy if it is satisfied that the borrower's processes are robust, for example, it has declared India's Power Grid as one such entity, so henceforth if Power Grid were to be the recipient of any WB loan, it can use its own processes.

The international community must also accept that India would primarily be involved in its own neighbourhood. In terms of LOCs, the order of exposure is Bangladesh, Sri Lanka, Nepal, Ethiopia, Mauritius, Myanmar, Sudan and Mozambique. The two largest single loans are to Bangladesh and Sri Lanka but since both are recent, and being transport focussed, have long gestation periods, disbursements are still relatively less. But India is sensitive to its neighbourhood and readily adopts flexible approaches, for example, 'in 2010, India extended a US$ 1 billion LOC to Bangladesh for transport infrastructure, requiring that 85% of procurement of goods and services be from India. This was modified in 2012, bringing down Indian content to 30%. And US$ 200 was converted into 'non-conditional grant.'[11] Similarly it extends financial support to Sri Lanka, both for building 50,000 houses for IDPs affected by the civil war as well as for the rehabilitation/reconstruction of three main rail lines.

The way forward for India would be to increase its engagement with OECD's Development Assistance Committee (DAC). It does take part in some dialogue but not enough. It neither follows DAC's development assistance classifications nor does it report its assistance figures to DAC. It must give up its fears about being swamped by big, traditional donors and display greater confidence. India has much relevant experience to offer, and to learn. Similarly, the insular world of traditional donors must walk the talk on country ownership and demand-driven assistance. The road to effective peacebuilding would continue to challenge all involved and constant learning is the minimum required.

Annex I: Illustrative List of Projects Funded by Letters of Credit

- Supply of railway locomotives and coaches to Angola—rail is a cheaper mode of transport than road, farmers are able to seek better markets, facilitated exploration of Kassinga Mines
- Supply of buses (single and double decker) to Bangladesh—improved public transport availability, eased traffic congestion and air pollution, generated employment for women and men
- Tractor assembly plant constructed in Benin, leading to increased supply of tractors—substantial improvement in cultivation of 40,000 hectares benefitting 1 million people
- Cement Plant constructed in Djibouti—reduced dependence on imports, but problems due to many partners
- Three sugar factories constructed in Ethiopia—delayed due to logistics but two running very well, third one still in problems due to complexity of operation including working with farmers
- Construction of national Assembly building in Gambia
- Tractor assembly line in Gambia—higher agricultural productivity
- Construction of cricket stadium in Guyana—needed for World Cup, foreign exchange earner
- Tractor assembly plant constructed in Mali—farm mechanisation has led to 30% increase in agricultural productivity, reduced dependence on imports for tractors
- High Voltage transmission line erected between Mali and Cote d'Ivoire—stable, affordable power supply to Mali
- IT Park in Mozambique—500 students trained, new ventures established by local entrepreneurs
- Manufacturing plant/assembly line for Tata Tractors in Myanmar

- Constructed Nyabarongo Hydropower project in Rwanda—country's biggest, once fully commissioned, would supply 25% needs of country
- 350 public buses supplied to Senegal—as part of NEPAD
- Supply of water pumps to Senegal—country's irrigation cover has doubled, rice production up by 177%
- Railway coaches and locomotives to Senegal—improved, and faster, public transport
- Improvement of railway infrastructure in Senegal
- Rehabilitation/reconstruction of three trunk rail lines in Sri Lanka—improved transport, peace dividend post-end of civil war
- Construction of Um Dabakir Power Plant (4×125 MW) in Sudan—will contribute to one-sixth of Sudan's total power demand
- Supply of police vehicles to Zambia—improved reach of police
- Supply of tractors to Tanzania—higher agricultural productivity and improved food security
- Assisted craft exchange programme with artists from India and Zimbabwe—knowledge sharing, adoption of better techniques, higher productivity

Annex II: India–Afghanistan Development Partnership

(List and figures taken from the Embassy of India website http://eoi.gov.in/kabul/?0707?000.)

Cumulative level of Indian assistance in Afghanistan amounts to US$2 billion—a very significant amount for a developing country, largest for any neighbouring country, and the fifth largest bilateral donor.

It has been India's endeavour to act in conformity with the best aid-effectiveness principles, taking fully into account the local government priorities, in coordination with other donors, using local sub-contractors and materials as far as practical, and with minuscule proportion of budget on security and salaries. These 'overhead costs' are significantly lower in case of Indian projects than in those undertaken by other donors.

Four areas of support.

- Large infrastructure projects
- Humanitarian assistance
- Capacity building initiatives, and
- 'Small Development projects'

a. *Large and medium infrastructure projects*, for example

- *Construction of a 218 km road from Zaranj to Delaram* for facilitating movement of goods and services to the Iranian border (the project has been completed and handed over to Government of Afghanistan);
- *Construction of 220 kV DC transmission line from Pul-e-Khumri to Kabul and a 220/110/20 kV sub-station at Chimtala*, completed and handed over; two more sub-stations are being constructed at Doshi and Charikar for which material, brought by air from New Delhi is being transported to the project sites.
- *Construction of Salma Dam* in Herat province (ongoing project, following approval of the revised project cost by the Cabinet in January 2013, work has resumed gradually from March 15.
- *Construction of Afghan Parliament building.*
- *Setting up of five toilet-cum-public sanitation complexes in Kabul.*
- *Upgradation of telephone exchanges in 11 provinces* (completed and handed over);
- *Expansion of national TV network by providing an uplink from Kabul and downlinks in all 34 provincial capitals* for greater integration of the country (completed and handed over).

The above list is not exhaustive.

b. *Humanitarian Assistance*, including the following:

- provision of free medical services and medicines through *Indian Medical Missions (IMMs)* located in Kabul and other cities of Afghanistan.
- *Provision of food assistance of 1 million MT of wheat* in the form of HEB distributed to approximately 2 million school children across Afghanistan, daily under a 'School Feeding Program' administered by the WFP.
- *Assistance of 2.5 lakh MT of wheat* to Afghanistan.
- *Reconstruction and renovation of Indira Gandhi Institute of Child Health (IGICH) Gifting of ten ambulances.*

c. *Capacity Building initiatives* like:

- Reconstruction and renovation of the Habibia School in Kabul;
- Award of 500 ICCR long-term university scholarships (for undergraduate and post graduate degrees) and 500 short-term *Indian Technical and Economic Cooperation (ITEC)* vocational training slots for Afghan nationals annually from 2006 to 07 onwards (since 2009, both ICCR and ITEC slots were increased to 675 annually and it has been decided to grant 1000 scholarships for Afghan Nationals (administered by ICCR) during the period 2012–13 to 2020–21.);
- Up to 258 Special *Discretionary ITEC* slots have been offered to Afghan Ministry officials for training programmes in India—over five such training programmes have been organised and the Ministry of Commerce and Industries, the Ministry of Agriculture and so on. have already had their personnel trained in various disciplines under this new scheme;
- Deputation of 30 Indian civil servants under UNDP's Capacity for Afghan Public Administration (CAP) programme; ongoing Indian contribution to UNDP's *National Institution Building Program (NIBP)* which finances attachment of Indian civil servants as Capacity Development Advisors (CDAs) in Afghan government institutions—there are ten Indian CDAs currently working in various important Ministries of the Afghan Government;
- Signing of 'twinning agreements' between related Indian and Afghan Ministries;
- Setting up of an India–Afghan Vocational training centre for training 3000 Afghans in carpentry, plumbing, welding, masonry and tailoring;
- Project by Indian NGO SEWA for setting up Women's Vocational Training Centre in Bagh-e-Zanana (Kabul) for training 1000 women in garment making, nursery plantation, food processing and marketing.
- 614 *Agriculture scholarships* (BSc, Msc and PhD) have been made available to Afghan students under an Indian Council for Agriculture Research (ICAR)-administered scheme. Sixty Afghan agriculture students are presently studying in various Indian agriculture universities and more than 100 have been accepted for the academic year 2013–14.

d. *Small Development Projects, community-based*, in vulnerable border areas, in the fields of agriculture, rural development, education, health, vocational training and so on. that can have direct and visible impact on community life, and with focus on local ownership and management. The Small Development Projects were implemented in two phases—the first in July 2006 comprising projects worth US$11,216,179 and the second in June 2008 comprising projects worth US$8,579,537. Sixty-five per cent of the projects are reported to be 100% complete. Some of them are awaiting final clearances of concerned authorities for completion certificate. Seventy-six projects have been completed, 34 projects are ongoing, 6 projects await tender finalisation with Afghan line Ministries, while ten projects await MEA approval. Till date, US$13.135 million has been released to our Mission under phases I and II of Small Development Projects. The implementation of the projects is done entirely by Afghan government agencies (with advisory inputs from Indian Embassy), which helps in building local capacity towards project management. A MoU for implementation of the third phase of the SDP scheme was signed during President Karzai's visit in November 2012 with an additional provision of US$100 million. Administrative and financial approvals for 60 projects, at an estimated cost of USD 14.223 million, under the third phase of the SDP scheme have been received from MEA in June 2013. The MoUs (in English and Dari) for each of these 60 projects have been finalised and waits signing. The third phase of SDPs is to be completed by 2015–16.

The future contours of the Indian assistance programme in Afghanistan were illuminated during the visit of the Indian Prime Minister, Dr. Manmohan Singh, in May 2011. The PM had announced a further increase in India's aid commitment to Afghanistan by USD 500 million, thus raising the cumulative Indian commitment to US$2 billion.

New Schemes

- Donation of 1000 buses for the Kabul and other municipalities with provision for maintenance support, training and infrastructure. Afghanistan has selected Delhi Integrated Multi-modal Transit System (DIMTS) as the Consultant to manage the process of procuring the buses and creating the structures for their maintenance and running. DIMTS has submitted a revised proposal.

- Donation of 500 tractors for Afghan farmers; provision of seeds and other assistance for the agricultural sector.
- *Medical package* consisting of the treatment of Afghan patients in select hospitals in India over the next three years to be implemented through the Afghan Ministry of Public Health;
- *Rehabilitation and professional upgradation* of the National Malaria and Leishmaniasis Centre of Afghanistan; and the
- *Upgradation* of the Indira Gandhi Institute of Child Health, including the neo-natal and maternal care unit.
- Setting up of a *National Agricultural University.*
- *US$50 million Buyers Credit Line* to promote exports and attract Indian business to Afghanistan.
- *Grant of US$10 million for preservation* and revival of Afghanistan's archaeological and cultural heritage and cultural exchanges.
- Grant of US$4 million to the Government of Afghanistan for the restoration of the historic Stor Palace in Kabul.
- Assistance in setting up an Afghan National Institute of Mines. To begin with, the Government of India has offered training at ISM, Dhanbad, for up to 180 resource persons in the Ministry of Mines, Government of Afghanistan from April to December 2013. Training is to be imparted in 12 disciplines related to Mining for batches of 15 each. Five training modules (for 15 × 2 = 30) resource persons have been completed.
- Assistance in setting up of a computer laboratory at Habibia School.
- Supporting the second phase of the Confederation of Indian Industry (CII) Skills Development Program for providing vocational training to Afghan nationals.
- Establishment of a Jawaharlal Nehru Chair of Indian Studies at Kabul University

In pursuance of the decision of Prime Minister of India and President of the Islamic Republic of Afghanistan to support the ARCS to treat Afghan children suffering from CHD, Government of India has decided to grant financial assistance of US$5 million to ARCS over a period of five years beginning 2015. Financial assistance provided by India will be utilised for the ongoing treatment by ARCS of Afghan Children at Artemis, Max and

Fortis Hospitals in New Delhi. These hospitals have offered special concessional rates for treatment of these children. The first tranche of US$1 million has already been disbursed to ARCS and additional disbursement would be made over the next four years.

Annex III: List of Persons with Whom the Afghanistan–India Partnership was Discussed

(Team consisting of Lt Gen PK Singh (Retd), Lt Gen PC Katoch (Retd), Maj Gen BK Sharma (Retd) and Mr Shakti Sinha at Herat, October 2/3, 2015; Kabul September 3/4 and November 21/22, 2015, and Mazar-e-Sharif, December 17/18, 2015)

1. Dr Rangin Dafdar Spanta, Chair AISS Advisory Board, former foreign minister, former NSA
2. Dr Sayeda Mojgan Mostavi, Deputy Minister of Publications, ministry of Information & Culture
3. Dr Davood Moradian, Director, Afghan Institute of Strategic Studies
4. Azizullah Royesh, educational consultant, Marefat Civil Capacity Building Organisation
5. Habibullah Fouzi, Member, International Relations Committee, High Peace Council
6. Shahmahmood Miakhel, Country Director, United States Institute of Peace
7. Abbas Noyan, general secretary, Rights and Justice Party
8. M. Ashraf Haidari, Research Fellow, AISS/Director of Policy & Strategy, Ministry of Foreign Affairs (MOFA)
9. Eng Sebghatullah Tamim, Excellent Planning & Construction Company
10. Ahmed Saeedi, political expert, civil society
11. Lt Gen Abdul Hadi Khalid, former Deputy Minister of the Interior
12. Dr Moheb Spinghar, Director General, Institute for Diplomacy, MOFA
13. Mr Mohammad Ismail Rahimi, Deputy minister, Ministry of Economy
14. Ehsanullah Zaki, Chief of Staff to First Vice President, former MP and Jumbish party activist

15. Wahidullah Shahrani, former minister of mines, former commerce minister and opposition politician
16. Eng Kohistani, acting Deputy minister/DG, Ministry of Energy & water
17. Eng Osmani, Minister of Energy & water
18. Mr Murad, Minister of Economy
19. Mustafa Aria, Director, Aid Coordination, Ministry of Finance
20. Amrullah Saleh, former Director NDS and opposition politician
21. Mohammad Naeem Aubzada, Director, TEFA, Kabul
22. Ahmad Sulaiman Aslam, Ministry of Finance
23. Feridudin Ilham, Deputy Head of Public Relations and Outreach
24. Humayun Khairi, Office of First Vice President
25. Maj Gen Masood Ahmad Azizi, Deputy Minister of the Interior
26. Mrs Homayra Etemadi, Deputy Chief of Staff under President Karzai
27. Abdul Jabbar Ariyaee, Senior Advisor, Ministry of Education
28. Mrs Nasrine Abou Baker, Office of CEO
29. Dr Mirwais Balkhi, Centre of Strategic Studies
30. Prof Rafiullah Niazi, Director, Academy of Science
31. Hashem Rasouli, The Voice of Afghanistan

Plus many members of the media, think tank researchers, senior officials in ministries of economy, energy and water, agriculture, finance, independent directorate of local governance, independent administrative reforms and civil service commission, Ambassador of India and his staff.

Notes

1. This section (India as donor) draws heavily on Rani D. Mullen, 'India's Development Assistance: Will it Change the Global Development Finance Paradigm?' Prepared for the Workshop on *Innovation in Governance of Development Finance: Causes, Consequences & the Role of Law Conference* April 8–9, 2013, Gießen & New York University School of Law. Can be accessed at http://www.iilj.org/newsandevents/documents/mullen.pdf And Lt Gen PK Singh, above cited.
2. Mullen, *op cit.*
3. Mullen estimates that a thousand dollars would easily allow for a person's three weeks' training in India.
4. This has allowed India to expand its development partnership portfolio considerably without a concomitant charge on its budget, with govern-

ment's own commitment limited to the interest subvention charges. Exim Bank raises its capital from international bond markets since it needs hard currency for its borrowers.

5. Information from compilation by IDRC, found in Mullen, *op. cit.*, based on Government of India Budget, Grants & Loans to Foreign Governments, Statement 11 of the Expenditure Budget, Ministry of External Affairs, Government of India.
6. Mullen, *op cit.*
7. Discussions with senior officials at the Ministry of Energy and Water, Government of Afghanistan, November 21, 2015.
8. Extensive discussions were held with the officials of the Ministry of Economy, Kabul and with concerned Embassy staff, September third and November 21, 2015.
9. Cell phone coverage in Afghanistan is over 60% of the population.
10. These discussions were before the December 2015 supply of the four promised helicopter gunships (Mi 25).
11. Mullen, *op cit.*

References

Al-Madani, Abdulla. 2005. Implications of Afghanistan's Inclusion in SAARC. *Middle East Transparent*. http://www.metransparent.com/old/texts/abdullah_elmadani/abdullah_elmadani_implications_of_afghanistan_inclusion_in_saarc.htm

Arora, Kashyap, and Rani Mullen. 2017. India's Development Cooperation with Bangladesh: Lines of Credit (LOCs). *Indian Development Cooperation Research Blog*. http://cprindia.org/sites/default/files/op-eds/India%E2%80%99s%20development%20cooperation%20with%20Bangladesh%20Lines%20of%20credit%20%28LOCs%29%20%281%29.pdf

Asian Development Bank. 2009. Energy is Life: Bringing Power to Afghanistan. https://www.adb.org/sites/default/files/publication/29647/energy-life.pdf

Ayres, Alyssa. 2015. Why the United States Should Work With India to Stabilize Afghanistan. *Council on Foreign Relations*. http://www.cfr.org/afghanistan/why-united-states-should-work-india-stabilize-afghanistan/p36414

Chanana, Dweep. 2009. India as an Emerging Donor. *Economic and Political Weekly* 44 (12): 11–14. http://www.epw.in/journal/2009/12/commentary/india-emerging-donor.html

Department for International Development (DFID). 2010. *Building Peaceful States and Societies: A DFID Practice Paper*. London: .DFID. https://www.gov.uk/government/uploads/system/uploads/attachment_data/file/67694/Building-peaceful-states-and-societies.pdf

Dornsife, Cinnamon. 2013. BRICS Countries Emerging as Major Aid Donors. *Asia Pathways*. http://www.asiapathways-adbi.org/2013/10/brics-countries-emerging-as-major-aid-donors/#sthash.sZgEOgAi.dpuf

Gupta, Swati. 2015. 4 Things to Know about India's Summit with African Leaders. *Time*. http://time.com/4093951/india-africa-summit-diplomacy-takeaways/

Haidari, Ashraf. 2015. India and Afghanistan: A Growing Partnership. *The Diplomat*. http://thediplomat.com/2015/09/india-and-afghanistan-a-growing-partnership/

Indian Technical and Economic Cooperation Program. 2013. About ITEC. https://www.itecgoi.in/about.php

International Commission for Red Cross (ICRC). 2014. From Aid to Partnerships: India's Humanitarian Assistance. https://www.icrc.org/en/document/aid-partnerships-indias-humanitarian-assistance

Karp, Candace. 2006. Leading by Example: Australia's Reconstruction Task Force and the NGO Civil-Military Relationship in Afghanistan. *Security Challenges* 2 (3): 1–8. http://www.regionalsecurity.org.au/Resources/Files/vol2no3Karp.pdf

Mathew, Joe E. 2015. Exim Bank extends 200th Line of Credit to Finance Exports to Developing Countries. *Business Today*. http://www.businesstoday.in/sectors/banks/exim-bank-extends-200th-line-of-credit-to-finance-exports-to-developing-countries/story/224186.html

McCloskey, Megan, Tobin Asher, Lena Groeger, and Sisi Wei. 2015. Behold: How the US Blew $17 Billion in Afghanistan. *Public Radio International (PRI)*. http://www.pri.org/stories/2015-12-18/behold-american-taxpayer-what-happened-nearly-half-billion-your-dollars

Ministry of External Affairs Report. 2012. India and Afghanistan: A Development Partnership. Accessed March 1, 2013. http://www.mea.gov.in/Uploads/PublicationDocs/176_india-and-afghanistan-adevelopment-partnership.pdf

Mullen, Rani D. 2013. India-Afghanistan Partnership. Indian Development Cooperation Program, Centre for Policy Research. http://cprindia.org/sites/default/files/policy-briefs/India-afganistan%20brief_0.pdf

Organization for Economic Co-operation and Development (OECD). 2012. Development: Aid to Developing Countries Falls Because of Global Recession. http://www.oecd.org/newsroom/developmentaidtodevelopingcountriesfallsbecauseofglobalrecession.htm

Pan-African e-Network. 2016. Pan-African e-Network Project. http://www.panafricanenetwork.com/

Price, Gareth. 2013. India's Policy towards Afghanistan. *Chatham House* 2013/04. https://www.chathamhouse.org/sites/files/chathamhouse/public/Research/Asia/0813pp_indiaafghanistan.pdf

Ramachandran, Vijaya. 2010. India Emerges as an Aid Donor. *Centre for Global Development*. http://www.cgdev.org/blog/india-emerges-aid-donor

Roopanaraine, Les. 2013. China: 'Rogue' Donor or Beacon of South-South Cooperation. *The Guardian*. http://www.theguardian.com/global-development-professionals-network/2013/apr/02/china-aid-africa-development

Sachdeva, Gulshan. 2012. The Delhi Investment Summit on Afghanistan. *Institute for Defence Studies and Analyses*. http://www.idsa.in/idsacomments/TheDelhiInvestmentSummitonAfghanistan_gsachdeva_260612

Smith, Bernard. 2012. Afghan Hospital in Coma for Poor Workmanship. *Aljazeera*. http://www.aljazeera.com/indepth/features/2012/10/20121021024352O232.html

Strand, Arne. 2014. Maintaining Development Momentum or Just Providing Aid. *ISPI Analysis* 261. https://www.cmi.no/publications/file/5194-http-www-ispionline-it-sites-default-files-pubbl.pdf

Shakti Sinha is Director, Nehru Memorial Museum and Library, New Delhi.

CHAPTER 8

Thinking Outside the Compound: Turkey's Approach to Peacebuilding in Somalia

Onur Sazak and Auveen Elizabeth Woods

Introduction

Turkey's engagement in Somalia is one of the most visible examples of a rising power's approach to a conflict-affected country. Since its high-profile intervention during the height of the famine in 2011, Turkey has elevated its level of engagement with Somalia and has committed to robust humanitarian assistance, development aid, and civilian capacity to resuscitate the fragile state. Over the years, a "Turkish model" of engagement has emerged. It is characterized by the quick delivery of assistance and programs with Turkish personnel on the ground. The Turkish model is also noted for its emphasis on soft power attributes such as business interests and cultural affinity such as Turkey's Muslim identity. This approach is in contrast to other "traditional donors" in Somalia who are often accused of being overly bureaucratic, slow, and isolated, either bunkered in the airport in Mogadishu or providing aid remotely from other neighboring countries (Wasuge 2016).

However, there are a myriad of actors with different interests and objectives engaged in the country. These range from the neighboring states of

O. Sazak (✉) • A.E. Woods
Sabancı University, Istanbul, Turkey

C.T. Call, C. de Coning (eds.), *Rising Powers and Peacebuilding*, Rethinking Peace and Conflict Studies,
DOI 10.1007/978-3-319-60621-7_8

Djibouti, Kenya, and Ethiopia, to traditional donors such as the United Nations and the UK, as well as more recent regional actors such as South Africa, the United Arab Emirates (UAE), and Turkey. Despite the longevity and level of financial investment, none of these actors have received the level of international attention that Turkey has since its high-profile intervention in the country in 2011. This chapter seeks to shed light on Turkey's activities in Somalia, particularly its approach to peacebuilding. It draws on interviews with Somalis to explore their perspectives on Turkey's engagement, while also placing these activities firmly in the context of other external actors in the country and Somalia's conflict dynamics.

Somalia Context

On February 8, 2017, Mohamed Abdullahi Mohamed (Farmajo) was elected as the ninth president of the Federal Republic of Somalia. He has inherited a weak and fractured state, with the previous government failing to achieve many of the benchmarks it set for itself when it came to power in 2012 (Arman 2017). Much of the lack of progress stems from the fragile nature of the state—as one recovering from a long civil war. This is a point put succinctly by the Finnish Minister for International Development, Pekka Haavisto: "When fragile states lack legitimacy and the trust of their own people, rapid state-building efforts can actually work against rather than for peace building, inspiring resistance from those who fear how state authorities will wield their new power" (Menkhaus 2014). On top of that, Al-Shabaab continues to launch attacks on the government and the African Union Mission in Somalia (AMISOM), upon which the government is dependent upon for its existence. Adding to the government's challenges is the high number of internally displaced people (IDPs) in the country. There are an estimated 1.1 million IDPs in Somalia, with 369,000 people thought to be displaced in and around Mogadishu alone (UNHCR 2016). Most are headed by women. About 4.9 million people are in need of humanitarian assistance (UNHCR 2016). Additionally, there are third-generation Somalis in refugee camps in Yemen, Ethiopia, Djibouti, and Kenya who are slowly returning to the country and pose a unique security risk as a vulnerable group. There is also continued animosity among the different clans and regional administrations such as Puntland and Jubaland, who simply do not trust the fledging federal state.

The root cause of Somalia's current predicament was the collapse of the Somali state infrastructure in 1991. While there had been increasing interclan warfare and atrocities since the late 1970s, the overthrow of the Siad Barre government (1969–1991) and the destruction of state institutions instigated over two decades of conflict and fragility that the country has yet to recover from. In the absence of an effective government, warlords and armed groups loosely affiliated to clans have vied with each other for power and dominance throughout the country. The current structure of the Federal Government is still based on the exclusionary 4.5 formula. This equally distributes seats among the four major Somali clans (the Darod, Dir, Hawiye, and the Digil and Mirifle). The minority clans, who are sometimes referred to as the Fifth Clan, are together allotted just half the number of seats of one whole clan receiving 0.5 percent representation. This is a deeply unequal system that sidelines all minority class, regardless of their population size.

The two main sources of conflict in Somalia are the clan structure of Somali society and competition over resources and their distribution (Somali Peace Line 2016). This has been particularly prevalent regarding the role of the state and its resources. Clans are a source of patronage, security, and justice for most Somalis—a status that has only been heightened in the stateless paralysis of the country. On the one hand, there is a strong culture of blood revenge or alternatively blood compensation (*Diya*) that can further heighten conflict. On the other hand, the clan system is also the source of traditional Somali conflict-resolution methods such as the *Shir Beeleed* (clan assembly), led by the clan Elders or Guurti. The *Shir Beeleed* is a slow and time-consuming negotiation and dialogue technique that can last for weeks or even months (Balthasar 2013).

This delicate balance between peace and conflict in the clan system has been further exacerbated by international interventions and meddling by neighboring countries, ostensibly due to security concerns. Since the Cold War, development and humanitarian aid has been diverted into the Somali war economy, first under President Siad Barre and later by clans. In the early 1990s, a series of UN-led peace operations attempted to support a statebuilding process and provide security for aid workers in the spiraling insecurity and famine ravaging the country. These missions, however, quickly became mired in the politicization of aid and became targets of the worsening interclan and warlord infighting (Harper 2012). The situation continued to escalate, culminating in the infamous Black Hawk Down incident in 1993 and the withdrawal of USA and other troop-contributing countries.

The result of these debacles has been enduring. A decade would pass before the next generation of peacekeepers arrived in Somalia with the launch of AMISOM in 2007. Meanwhile, the neutrality and security of humanitarian aid workers were compromised by these events, forcing donors to relocate their headquarters and international staff away from Somali communities and adopt a hands-off approach. This often meant operating outside the country, for example, in Nairobi, and employing intermediaries inside Somalia to deliver aid. The result of this approach meant that Somali recipients were burdened by a slow, bureaucratic aid system with little to no consultation with communities and the frequent diversion of aid into local war economies. This long-distance approach is the modus operandi that developed for many traditional donors working on Somalia. Traditional donors are often identified as state agencies or international NGOs from Development Assistance Committee (DAC) countries of the Organization for Economic Co-operation and Development (OECD), such as Norway, the USA, Italy, and Canada.

Since the mid-1990s, Somalia has been the site of proxy wars among Ethiopia, Kenya, Eritrea, and Djibouti, all of whom have, at times, allied with various Somali clans, regional administrations, or political groupings in order to destabilize a rival or gain access to a resource. Ethiopia invaded Somalia in 2006 to oust the Union of Islamic Courts (UIC) in south-central Somalia. While this was achieved quickly, Ethiopia was forced to stay until 2009 to prop-up the unpopular but internationally recognized Transitional Government of Somalia. It was in response to the harsh counter-insurgency operations employed by Ethiopia that Al-Shabaab emerged (International Crisis Group 2012). Ethiopia and Kenya continue to align with regional administrations in Somalia to support a federal system with a weak central Somali state. The decision to add Ethiopian and Kenyan soldiers to AMISOM alongside Ugandan and Burundian troops has been considered a controversial move given the hostility and suspicion most Somalis feel toward both countries (Geeska Africa Online 2015).

Turkish Foreign Policy Priorities: Explaining Turkey's Involvement in Somalia

Much has been made of Turkey's high-profile intervention into the devastating 2011 famine that stalked south central Somalia. The perceptions regarding this singular event often belie the historical relations between the two countries and the growing interest of Turkish authorities in

Somalia in the years preceding it. Turkish and Somali officials have emphasized the historical relations between both countries, which stretch back to the Ottoman Empire in the sixteenth century. At the height of World War I, the Ottomans armed Somalis in their rebellion against the British. Despite a cessation in Somali–Turkish relations for much of the Cold War, Somalia was nonetheless one of the few locations in Africa where a Turkish embassy was opened, in 1979. The embassy remained active until its closure in 1991 at the beginning of the country's civil war. It was reopened on November 1, 2011. With the exception of General Çevik Bir as force commander for UN Mission to Somalia (UNOSOM II) in 1993, the Turkish state had no relationship with Somali authorities until the visit of President Sheikh Sharif of the Transitional Federal Government in 2009, which began to pique the interest of Turkish authorities.[1]

There are a number of factors that underpin Turkey's engagement in Somalia. Humanitarianism was the underlying motive behind Turkey's initial engagement in 2011. At the height of the famine, which coincided with the holy month of Ramadan in August 2011, a period of fasting and charity, a huge public awareness campaign was run by Turkish NGOs and celebrities showing images of emancipated women and children. The impact of this campaign was decisive in mobilizing the Turkish public and state attention on the plight in Somalia. An estimated $57 million was raised from private donations alone (TIKA 2013) while around 500 Turkish nationals arrived in Mogadishu to help deliver aid (Lough 2012).

Humanitarian aspirations remain a motivation for Turkish engagement in Somalia. In March 2011, Turkey gave $122 million work of humanitarian aid to Somalia (Daily Sabah 2017). Turkey's broader activities, however, should also be seen within the broader foreign policy priorities context, in particular Turkey's image as rising power. Over the past few years, Turkey has pursued a range of activities such as gaining a seat at the UN Security Council (2009–2010), high-profile events like the World Humanitarian Summit in 2016 and increased commitment to aid and security support in general. Between 2012 and 2014 alone, Turkey's Official Development Assistance (ODA) increased by nearly 30 percent from $1.2 billion in 2012 to $3.6 billion in 2014 (TIKA 2014). Turkey's desire to promote its image as a rising power is succinctly highlighted by a 2012 Turkish International Cooperation and Coordination Agency (TIKA) report that states, "In 2012, there has been a decrease in the amount of development assistance provided by traditional donors; whereas Turkey's development assistance increased by 98.7% in one year. In this framework, Turkey is now defined as an "emerging donor" and strengthens its "donor" role each passing year" (TIKA 2013, 21).

In many ways, Somalia has become an opportunity for Turkey to illustrate not only its commitment to addressing shared international issues, but also to project its image as a rising power. Turkey's discourse reflects these aspirations. At the UN's High-Level Partnership Forum on Somalia in Istanbul in February 2016, President Erdoğan said, "Somalia, which was on the verge of destruction and totally hopeless back in 2011, is rising to its feet with the efforts we and our international partners make… With Somalia, the Turkish model of aid has gained recognition in literature" (Presidency of the Turkish Republic 2016). Such discourse is aimed not only at the international community but also at Turkey's own citizens. Turkey's engagement in Somalia, for example, has boosted the image of the ruling Justice and Development Party (AKP) and its leader Tayyip Erdoğan, appealing in particular to the Party's constituency of conservative and religious voters (Sucuoglu and Stearns 2016).

In addition to being an example of Turkey's rising power status, Somalia should also be seen in the context of Ankara's efforts to expand its economic and political relations. Over the past decade, Turkey has expanded its engagement in areas beyond its traditional sphere of the Balkans, the Middle East, and Central Asia. In 2014, Turkish ODA reached 29 African countries (TIKA 2016). Like other rising powers, economic interests are intricately linked to Turkey's foreign policy and its aid. In what has become a template replicated in other countries, the Turkish state's presence in Somalia was accompanied by the opening of a new embassy, TIKA offices, new Turkish Airlines routes, and an influx of development programs and commercial activities. Turkish exports to Somalia have increased from an estimated \$3.5 million in 2009 to \$115 million in 2016 (Turkish Statistics Agency 1996–2017). Turkish Airlines has a lucrative route to Mogadishu, and Turkish companies have secured numerous contracts in Somalia.

In February 2016, President Erdoğan and then-President Hassan Sheikh Mohamud co-hosted a Private Sector Investment Conference in Istanbul to promote Turkish investments in Somalia across a range of areas such as energy, information and communications technologies, and agriculture. There has also been interest in Turkish companies expanding beyond Mogadishu to Puntland in the north and Juba in the south (Sucuoglu and Stearns 2016). Additionally, Turkish state aid, which focuses on technical assistance and infrastructure development, combines both economic and development opportunities for Turkey and the recipient country.

Rebuilding of infrastructure such as roads and construction of hospitals and mosques has created jobs for both local Somalis and Turkish companies (Achilles et al. 2015). Somalia offers not only an untapped market for Turkish businesses but also a gateway into other African countries. Interviewees from Uganda, Burundi, and South Sudan have all expressed interest in Turkey's activities, highlighting its work in Somalia (Rising Powers Conference 2016).

The top three donors of gross ODA for Somalia between 2014 and 2015 were the USA with $205.4 million, followed by the UK at $195 million and Turkey, which provided $194 million (OECD 2015). EU institutions were the fourth largest donor to Somalia with $180 million and Sweden the fifth with $72 million (OECD 2015). Turkey is among one of the top donors to Somalia and is the only non-DAC member of this group. Yet its engagement in Somalia differs remarkably.

Soft power has underpinned Turkey's engagement in Somalia. Its image as a relatively prosperous democratic Muslim-majority country with historical ties to the country distinguished Turkey from traditional donors and made it an attractive partner. The visible engagement by Turkish officials and Turkish projects on the ground, and the high visibility of their projects such as from refurbishing buildings, has supported its positive image. Finally, the high-profile visits of President Erdoğan, the opening of Turkey's huge embassy in downtown Mogadishu, and the establishment of direct flights between Mogadishu and Turkey have all bolstered the ties between the two countries. In addition to this use of soft power and cultural affinity, Turkey's engagement in Somalia is characterized by the high visibility of its projects and their quick and direct delivery of aid on the ground. Turkey has a holistic approach, engaging in diplomacy, humanitarian relief, and development programs simultaneously in Somalia.[2] The Turkish model is also noted for its emphasis on business interests. Interviews with Turkish aid officials, NGO representatives, and beneficiaries on the ground have revealed three central principles that seem to drive Turkey's success. These are unconditionality, bilateralism, and non-securitization of aid and personnel.

Securitization has become more visible in the twenty-first century. Commonly referred to as the "securitization of personnel" or "compounding of aid" (Duffield 2010), representatives of international humanitarian agencies and relief organizations are confined to heavily fortified living and working quarters in conflict zones. These render agents of traditional actors immobile and alien to the needs of beneficiaries on the ground. This bunkered mentality has been particularly prevalent in traditional donors' approaches to Somalia since the 1990s. For many years, international diplomats and other personnel that worked on Somalia have been based in Nairobi and fly into the Mogadishu airport for a few hours, staying in the compound, and turn around and depart the same day.

By contrast, Turkey's engagement in Somalia has, in part, been defined by the presence of officials and personnel on the ground. While security is taken seriously with guards at Turkish offices, Turkish personnel still live in Somalia. Turkey has built one of its largest embassies in downtown Mogadishu, where Ambassador Olgan Bekar and other officials live. Turkey's consulate in Hargeisa, Somaliland, is occupied by a Turkish representative. Turkish aid groups, teachers, and others who work on Somalia continue to be based in the county, despite the fragile security situation (Wasuge 2016; Sucuoglu and Stearns 2016). This approach has a number of advantages over the bunkered practices of traditional donors. One is that it reduces the cost of programs by reducing the expense of brokers that are so frequently used by traditional donor agencies and country missions. Their presence on the ground also means that Turkish officials and personnel can react more quickly to changing dynamics. They can better monitor programs and consult with recipients on the quality and relevance of programs. Contrary to traditional donors, Turkey does not have rigid procedures or systems of delivery that must be adhered to. The daily flights provided by Turkish Airlines facilitate greater transportation of products and personnel when necessary.

Turkey works with a number of multilateral initiatives on Somalia. These include signing up with platforms like the New Deal for Somalia, hosting international meetings and supporting AMISOM. Despite this, however, bilateralism in general is still the defining attribute of Turkey's engagement to recipient countries. Roughly 90 percent of all Turkish aid efforts globally are coordinated directly between Turkey and the donor recipient country. For example, in 2014, just 2.4 percent of Turkey's ODA ($88 million out of $3.6 billion) was provided through multilateral contributions (TIKA 2016, 11). The main reason why Turkey prefers bilateral arrangements is the effectiveness of this model in expediting the process and delivering tangible results, according to the Turkish officials who have frequently commented on this issue.

There has often been criticism of Turkey for failing to coordinate with donors in Somalia and acting unilaterally. But there are a number of reasons for Turkey to work outside multilateral institutions. Speed and efficiency are highly valued by Turkish officials who are output orientated

(Sazak et al. 2015, 9). In contrast, Western donors and multilateral institutions focus on processes and systems. Such an approach, while intended to ensure that things are done correctly, is criticized by both Turkish officials and Somalis interviewed, for being too slow and bureaucratic. For example, Turkish diplomats apparently felt frustrated when they attempted to collaborate with AMISOM on training Somali soldiers in 2013. Their plan was met with resistance from some AMISOM partners such as the USA (Wasuge 2016). Frustrated with the lack of progress, Turkey decided to start working with the Somalia National Army bilaterally. Similarly, with the exception of a brief hiatus in 2013, Turkey has provided direct budgetary support to the Federal Government of Somalia. The payments have ranged from \$4.5 million to \$6 million in recent years (Olgan Bekar's speech, Rising Powers Conference 2016). This is an aspect of the New Deal that other donors have failed to do, citing concerns with transparency (Hearn 2016).

Some respondents noted that traditional donors' overly bureaucratic approach, with multiple offices, systems, and officials to work with, often overwhelmed and stifled the functioning of the recipient country's fragile state institutions.[3] Bilateral engagement seems to be more manageable for recipient states. However, the bilateral model also brings out a number of serious coordination problems, especially in the areas of personnel deployment (level of expertise and personnel insurance packages), absence of a reliable monitoring and evaluation model and language constraints. Turkey, nonetheless, remains acutely aware of the international analysis of global dynamics but prefers bilateral development assistance arrangements.

Turkey's Approach to Peacebuilding in Somalia

Since 2011, the majority of the Turkish state's activities have been engaged primarily in Mogadishu. This remains the case as officials interviewed for this study point out that it is the area with greatest need. Over these years, Turkey has, however, expanded its political engagement to include Somaliland, Kismayo, Puntland, Galkayo, Baidoa, and Beledweyne, among others (Olgan Bekar's speech, Rising Powers Conference 2016). There is no general framework or policy document publicly available that guides such activities or outlines the annual goals of Turkey's work in Somalia. Rather than having their own specific priorities, officials state that they try to develop projects in consultation with Somalis while conscious of their own available capacity and strengths.[4]

While each project may not be conceptualized in terms of a grander peacebuilding goal or "reconstruction" as Turkish officials term it,[5] Turkey's approach to Somalia, particularly south central, falls into two categories: statebuilding and social peacemaking. According to the Turkish Ambassador to Mogadishu, Olgan Bekar, providing humanitarian assistance, development aid, and statebuilding support simultaneously is key to lasting peace and stability in Somalia:

> "Peacebuilding and state building in Somalia require a comprehensive approach. This comprehensive approach also requires a humanitarian approach, humanitarian aid, political engagement, security and development assistance… A purely humanitarian approach to protracted conflict areas and conflict-affected countries offers only a short-term solution. Assisting affected countries simultaneously and in tandem with long term development tools increases the resilience and capacity of the beneficiaries. This in the long term reduces the vulnerability and increases the capacity of the recipient local actors to respond to humanitarian crisis themselves." (Rising Powers Conference 2016)

Dr. Kani Torun, Ambassador Bekar's predecessor in Mogadishu, also underlines the indispensability of statebuilding for peace in Somalia:

> State building is very important, because I have seen the kind of destruction that can happen to a society without a functional state as a result of a civil war … [Therefore] state building was our priority; we worked with the state particularly to improve the way in which the state operated … one area we worked with the government closely was the security area. Turkey worked with the police and army to build strong security forces to provide security. Security investment and other things will come. Even aid is related to security. (Rising Powers Conference 2016)

Turkey's holistic approach encompasses a wide range of projects. This includes rehabilitation of infrastructure such as buildings, institutional capacity building, social service support in communities, and direct engagement on social relations through education initiatives and cultural events. Ambassador Bekar illustrates the virtue of this approach with the Digfer hospital (renamed Erdoğan General Hospital in 2015) in Mogadishu:

> We demolished the old Digfer hospital and built a new Mogadishu research and training hospital. This was a big improvement with 220 beds. Then we

> equipped it and sent doctors and nurses and other personnel to run the hospital. But we did not run it on our own; we developed a good partnership with the Somali side and established a joint management with the Somali management staff. Today we provide internships and trainings for young Somali doctors. (Rising Powers Conference 2016)

At the international level, Turkey has been engaged in a number of multilateral initiatives on peacebuilding issues in Somalia. It has participated and hosted peace processes and donor conferences, including the Istanbul I and II conferences with the UN in 2010 and 2012, respectively. The 2012 conference focused on Somalia's post-transition future and brought together over 300 Somali civil society groups (International Crisis Group 2012). Turkish state representatives, including President Erdoğan, have also frequently pushed Somalia up on the international agenda through speeches and statements at UN meetings. Turkey is also a participating state in the Somali New Deal, has hosted its High-Level Partnership Forum in 2016, and is a co-chair with the USA on the working group on security. Signed in March 2013, the New Deal was meant as a guide for external actors engaging in Somalia and outlined a three-year statebuilding and peacebuilding roadmap (2014–2016). Of the seven states that have signed up to New Deal agreements, Somalia is the only country where the framework has been most successful, being used to define national priorities and align budgets. Prior to this, there were no existing frameworks or strategy agreements with donors, and the Federal Government of Somalia took early ownership of the New Deal to try to assert its burgeoning authority (Hearn 2016, 8).

At an interstate level, there are a range of Turkish ministries, and state and semi-state agencies working in Somalia. These range from TIKA, the Directorate for Religious Affairs (Diyanet), and the Turkish Red Crescent (Kızılay), to a myriad of State Ministries in the areas of health, education, and defense. Each of these ministries and state agencies are capable of enacting their own bilateral projects. In addition to these actors, the Turkish Ministry of Foreign Affairs and the Office of the Prime Minister have been involved in mediation attempts. There is a disagreement between burgeoning regional administrations such as Puntland, Garowe, and the central government in Mogadishu. The Turkish government has played a role in facilitating talks.

The most high-profile mediations facilitated by Turkey are ongoing discussions between the Somaliland government and the Federal Government in Mogadishu (Garowe Online 2016). Some of these mediation attempts have been overseen by former ambassador Dr. Kani Torun, who has initiated talks between the Federal Government and Somaliland. Describing his approach, Dr. Torun says, "When I talked to them, I did not talk the way career diplomats talk … by the book, if you will. I instead talked as if I were one of them. When they saw my sincerity as well as my open and frank engagement in discussion, they had trust and initiated the talks with the federal government" (Rising Powers Conference 2016). Progress has been slow, but Turkey has succeeded in getting representatives of the Federal Government and Somaliland to talk to each other more often.

Alongside this consistent intra-state engagement, Turkey's programs and approach to Somalia have evolved. Most of the Turkish state aid until 2013 can be classified as humanitarian assistance.[6] Turkish humanitarian aid dropped from $77 million in 2011 to $27 million two years later in 2013 (Global Humanitarian Assistance 2014). This aid was largely in the form of emergency food, medical services, and supplies to IDP camps in and around Mogadishu area. Since 2013, the Turkish state engagement in Somalia has focused on capacity-building and technical assistance programs. For example, in 2013, both the Turkish Ministry of Foreign Affairs and the Turkish Central Bank began to provide technical assistance and training to their Somali counterparts (Sazak et al. 2015). The Turkish Ministry of Foreign Affair had been helping its counterpart to establish its own internal server.[7] Since 2014, Somali diplomats have also participated in bilateral and international training programs with Turkey's Diplomat Academy in Ankara. These exchanges have been accompanied by greater cooperation and training between the Turkish and Somali Armed Forces through two agreements signed in 2010 and 2014 (Today Zaman 2012). Such activities are closely associated with statebuilding and peacebuilding for Turkish officials who argue that fundamental services and institutional capacity need to be strengthened to provide legitimacy to the Federal Government and, therefore, counter the allure of extremists.[8] Many of these state capacity programs are intended to improve local security and social services.

At a local level, Turkey's education programs such as scholarships, sponsorship of orphanages, and religious–cultural initiatives are specifically aimed at changing dynamics and conditions in local Somali society.[9] In particular, Turkish officials view education programs as important peacebuilding initiatives that can challenge the allure of extremist narratives. Since 2011, Turkish officials estimate that nearly 3000 scholarships have been provided to Somali students from both state and NGOs.[10] The presence of these initiatives, through the Turkish offices in the country or personnel directly delivering support to communities, also challenges one of the central conflict drivers in the country—brokers. According to one Turkish Red Crescent official, "Our representatives have always delivered their supplies to the recipients' camps on their own without involving any brokers. If the security situation is not conducive for us to go to a certain site, we don't go there, but we also do not entrust our supplies to some third entity who we know would not deliver it to the address it was supposed to go and would make profit out of it by selling it."[11] Ongoing security challenges that have targeted them have caused Turkish personnel to be more cautious. And yet, Turkish officials and personnel remain the most visible foreigners in Somalia, particularly in Mogadishu, through their offices and projects (Wasuge 2016).

Since 2013, Turkish peacebuilding in Somalia has also adopted a visible military presence. Turkey's pledge of financial and military training assistance to AMISOM indicated that its activities in Somalia would no longer be limited to humanitarian and development assistance. At the time, Turkey had committed $1 million financial support to AMISOM and had undertaken the training of a modest number of Somali troops and policemen in Turkey (Achilles et al. 2015). Furthermore, the Turkish military is opening a training facility for the Somali Armed Forces in Mogadishu in 2017. This is Turkey's first military base abroad. Reportedly, to be run by the Turkish Armed Forces personnel, the academy will have up to 200 Turkish officers and is expected to train over 10,000 Somali National Army troops as well as soldiers from other African nations (Hurriyet Daily News 2016). The academy is envisaged as a center for excellence for training missions encompassing the entire continent.

There was another marked shift in Turkey's approach to Somalia in 2015. Turkish public–private enterprises that characterized the frenzied environment until 2013 had evolved. Improvement in domestic security had been accompanied by an increase in private Turkish companies that won contracts in a number of key sectors. Mogadishu's Aden Abdulle International Airport is managed by Favori LLC (Favori LLC Website), as is Mogadishu Port by Albayrak (The Somali Investor 2015). There are also strong signals from bilateral investment conferences and meetings between officials from Turkey and Somalia that Turkish businesses intend to explore new opportunities in provinces such as Puntland (Sucuoglu and Stearns 2016, 25).

Since 2015, the capacity-building programs of the Turkish state have entered their second stage with a greater emphasis on sustainability and local ownership. This involves the transfer of responsibility and administration of Turkish programs to their Somali counterparts. An example of this is the garbage collection program in Mogadishu. The Turkish government has delivered equipment so that it will be run solely by Somalis.[12] Similarly, Sifa Hospital in Mogadishu, which is run by the Turkish Health Ministry, is being co-administered with the Somali Ministry of Health. Today, civil training programs are administered either on the ground in Somalia or more often in Turkey partly due to the continued insecurity in the country.[13]

Somalia is still the largest recipient of Turkish aid in Africa, but this is changing. The focus on collaboration and capacity-building programs has resulted in a decline in the spending and projects allocated to Somalia. Turkish officials, however, argue that this does not signal a declining commitment by Turkey.[14] In 2014, nearly 70 percent of TIKA's $8.3 million budget in Somalia went on health sector-related projects while administrative and civil infrastructure was at 20.5 percent (TIKA 2016, 136). This is equivalent to $5.7 million and $1.6 million, respectively. These numbers do not include spending from Turkish NGOs. Turkish officials highlight President Tayyip Erdoğan's visit to Mogadishu in January 2015 and on June 3, 2016. To them, these visits illustrate the importance of Turkey–Somali relations to Erdoğan's administration and signal the country's strong commitment to Somalia.

Response and Perceptions of Somalis

The Somali response to these myriad of Turkish activities and actors has been generally positive. Turkey's approach is seen as practical; their projects are tangible and of good quality, say most Somalis. "They brought orphanages, education. The best hospital was built by them. They train and build capacity, service delivery and business."[15] Through such projects, people feel that Turkey has contributed to the rejuvenation of the war-torn Mogadishu: "Look at the airport, for a country that has been out of touch for 25 years to have that kind of airport … They are planning to build- have built roads, the Turkish. They brought this town back."[16] This sentiment is shared by many interviewees. The Somali Ambassador to Turkey has stated that the "(Turks) ha(ve) returned a sense of normalcy to people, which is necessary."[17] Turkey's activities are credited with helping to change the narrative around Somalia as a failed state and the image of Mogadishu as a no-go-area. In particular, Turkey's approach has challenged the Nairobi-based model of long-distance aid that many traditional donors and international organizations have used for Somalia.

From a Somali perspective, Turkey is distinguished from other actors, even African states, by its impact on the ground, "The Turkish move around freely with no protection, no guns, nobody else can do that."[18] The visibility of both Turkish projects and personnel on the ground is perceived as a successful aspect of their approach, "They (the Turkish) are not politically visible, they are in the community and that is the most important aspect—a community-centered approach."[19] The community-centered projects of Turkey are felt to positively contribute to peacebuilding. According to a Somali civil society actor, Turkey "provides for basic needs. Terrorists recruit younger people with no hope for the future but through providing the basics, the Turkish help to mitigate the allure of what the terrorists promise."[20] This sentiment is reiterated by the Somali Ambassador to Turkey, who believes that Turkey's maximum value is in scholarships and programs which have provided opportunities for Somali youth.[21]

Despite the expansion of some projects to other parts of the country, Turkey's engagement in Somalia remains overwhelmingly focused on Mogadishu. With few exceptions, the benefits of these programs have been felt primarily by residents in Mogadishu. If the goal of these projects is to support the legitimacy and stability of the Federal Government, then it is geographically limited. Given the historical perception of Mogadishu as the center of patronage and oppression is still potent, Turkey risks being perceived as biased toward the capital. The potential negative implications of this have already been felt with Somaliland parties implying Turkey favoritism of the Federal Government's goal of a united Somalia.

In Somalia, Turkish nationals were seen through the prism of fellow coreligionist and not as another foreign power pursuing its own interest. This has started to change. A criticism levied by Somalis is that Turkish state agencies and business could do more to hire local people, "They are all Turkish companies not Somali private sector, we have nothing to do with it."[22] While there are no numbers to verify these claims, the perception that Turkish entities are excluding Somalis is significant. If Turkish state agencies and companies were importing Turkish workers to work on Turkish projects, it would create an insular dynamic that does not benefit local communities or youth. While such an approach may avoid some local conflict actors such as gatekeepers, it would also deprive communities of economic opportunities that could support peacebuilding and undermine the capacity-building efforts of Turkish state actors.

Somalis also highlight interstate conflict at the international level between Turkey and other states. In particular, the specter of the Somali state as a source of personal patronage reemerges in the minds of Somalis regarding the controversy over the awarding of Mogadishu Port tender to a Turkish company: "There was no transparency in the procurement of the tender for the port, which resulted in suspicions of foul play by the West. The Turkish were criticized as not being honest."[23] While donor officials stress that there is and must be international cooperation on Somalia, this does not allay the perception among Somalis that "(t) here is no coordination between the West and the Turkish which creates conflict."[24] International rivalry over business and contracts is a legitimate concern for Somalis given the history of the country and its susceptibility to regional and global shifts.

Other Actors in Somalia

There are a range of actors and countries engaged in Somalia. These include neighbors, donors, as well as new actors. When asked, however, which states they believe were conducting peacebuilding activities in Somalia, interviewees identified only Turkey. Other notable countries such as the UAE and, to a lesser extent, China were identified by interviewees as relatively new actors working in Somalia but not on peacebuilding. China is a relatively new actor, opening a small Embassy in the Jazeera Palace Hotel in Mogadishu in 2014. While China's activities in Somalia are minor compared to its ventures in other African countries, it has allegedly signed a number of trade deals, mostly recently with Puntland, to conduct oil explorations (Garowe Online 2016).

The Gulf States, in particular the UAE, were identified as another set of actors that are increasingly influential.[25] The UAE is reported to be focusing on the provision of basic commodities and services, similar to Turkey. However, there exists a perception that the UAE is attempting to compete with Turkey in order to gain influence and visibility (Somali Peace Line 2016). This has allegedly meant that although actors from the UAE are welcome, many are wary of their motives. The UAE's activities in Somalia have not been without controversy. It is alleged that it has been providing heavy ammunition to Puntland, Jubaland, and South West State.[26] The UAE plans to establish a military base in Somaliland and has signed a 30-year contract to manage its largest port, Berbera (Maina and Ibrahim 2017). This has been criticized as contradicting the sovereignty and integrity of Somalia (Radion Dalsan 2017), in which Somaliland is seen as a region of the country.

Local Somali actors that were interviewed clearly distinguished between the activities of states and non-state actors. In describing the activities of organizations such as the World Bank and the European Union, it was stated that they are service providers and focus primarily on systems.[27] Examples of these systems were cited as human rights, accountability, transparency, and good governance. This was contrasted to the approach of states that are perceived to be more practical in their engagement.[28]

Somali civil society members interviewed stated that the support from African states is not as welcome as that from Turkey, the Gulf States, and some Asian countries. In fact, it was stated in one interview that often other Africans are grouped with state actors from the Global North.[29] The main reason for this appears to be the historical tensions between Somalia and her neighbors, especially Ethiopia and Kenya. It was stated that local dynamics come into play and while on paper it appears that Al-Shabaab is being undermined, recruitment levels remain high. According to interviewees, Somalis feel betrayed by the African continent, particularly the African Union, which has permitted perceived interference from these regional actors who are believed to be pursuing anti-Somali agendas. Somali interviewees allege that the presence of peacekeepers from these regional powers has created a conflict of interest.[30]

AMISOM is considered a controversial force by many Somali respondents. Established in 2007, its mission, among others, is to reduce the threat of Al-Shabaab and provide security to enable stabilization, reconciliation, and peacebuilding processes in Somalia. The inclusion of Ethiopian and Kenyan troops has proved controversial and is a source for the distrust around AMISOM. However, in some instances, AMISOM itself has become a source of conflict. AMISOM troops have faced accusations of discrimination, rape, assault, sexual exploitation, and the killing of Somali civilians (Human Rights Watch 2015). For example, in July 2015, AMISOM troops were accused of killing six family members, as they were celebrating a wedding in the coastal city of Merka (Human Rights Watch 2015). These actions have made AMISOM unpopular in Somalia (Somali Peace Line 2016). Some AMISOM tactics have also alienated the mission from the very people they are supposed to protect. Somali interviewees mentioned that AMISOM troops frequently target Somali youth, particularly young men in Mogadishu, rounding them up and interrogating them on whether they are part of Al-Shabaab. Somali respondents noted that these actions have in fact turned some youth toward the group (Somali Peace Line 2016).

Perceptions are important, and they matter even more in fragile environments such as Somalia. As in most conflict-affected states, a large number of external actors are engaged activities in the country. Much work has been done to improve the livelihoods of Somalis. The effect of these many activities, initiated by different actors with divergent motivations and goals, can be very damaging given the conflict dynamics in Somalia. The motives behind the delivery of this support are not always transparent, and consequently benign intentions can be negatively perceived, as some of observations from Mogadishu confirm.

Conclusion

It is clear that the situation in Somalia is extremely complex and fragile. There are many latent issues that are not easily perceived from the outside. Statebuilding efforts in Somalia, which are an inherent conflict-riddled process, are a source of tension with disagreement over the structure of the Somali state. Another latent issue is the fragility of state institutions themselves that are unable to contain and address conflict through processes and systems. This leads political or business disagreements to spread to the public sphere. The inability of the Somali state to protect and support its citizens is also another issue which pushes civilians to seek alternative sources of power and survival.

In this complex and fragile context, the number and diversity of actors working in Somalia, from states to international institutions, and NGOs, with different values, approaches, and priorities, can cause harm. Based on the information gathered from the interviews, the approach of some actors in Somalia, such as the UAE, Ethiopia, Kenya, and AMISOM, is distrusted by Somalis.[31] A noteworthy point is the fact that rather than being the most welcome in Somalia, some actors from other African states are often the least welcome. This is important in highlighting that the sentiments and perceptions of the local population in environments emerging from conflict play a big role in the success of peacebuilding initiatives.

Not all activities conducted in the name of building peace appear to be contributing toward this objective. In the crowded donor environment and the fragile security situation in Somalia, the level of coordination and cooperation required for donors to be conflict sensitive is almost impossible without stifling the efficiency, aptness, and therefore effectiveness of programs. This is one of the main differences in the approach of traditional donors and that of other recent actors in Somalia. As previously mentioned, while traditional actors are said to focus more on systems, checks and balances, new actors such as the UAE and Turkey appear more concerned with the quick delivery of products or services. One interviewee stated that Somalis value tangible projects, and the problem for traditional donors is that systems cannot appear overnight and as a result of their focus on this, less is expected from them.[32]

Turkey's peacebuilding initiatives in Somalia highlight important alternative approaches, while offering vital lessons for all stakeholders to improve upon. The Somalia case study reveals several best practices, implemented by the Turkish state and its agencies that may be applied to other post-conflict reconstruction settings. Deployment of personnel in conflict-affect areas, consulting and responding quickly to stakeholder's and recipient's needs, refraining from securitizing and attaching conditions to aid, avoiding middle-men or brokers in order to avert security risks, engaging local partners, and not overcrowding the fragile institutions of the host country's vital bureaucracy are some of the approaches that Turkey brings to the spectrum. Some of these modes of engagement are similar to those espoused by traditional donors. However, while traditional donors appear to become stalled in the processes of ensuring principles are followed Turkey shows more flexibility and openness to changing procedures to meet the goal.

The Somali case study has also affirmed that there is still room for improvement for Turkey's peacebuilding activities in Somalia. The bilateral engagement on the ministerial level with Somali entities, without informing other Turkish state organizations, leads to overcrowding of the theater and waste of resources. Although Turkey has taken concrete steps to address some of these issues by coordinating some of its efforts with the international community and organizations, on a domestic level interagency cooperation still lags. Worse, institutional and legislative remedies to unravel this knot linger. Therefore, Turkey should use the Somalia case to single out some of its coordination issues and devise a solution that can be generalized to uproot similar problems that recur in Turkey's other overseas missions.

Turkey's diplomatic and humanitarian presence in Somalia demonstrates more than anything the resolve of rising powers to supporting fragile states in reconstruction. Somalia, contemplated by many as risky for humanitarian work, indicates the resolve of new actors in hedging the risks and intervening not just where there is peace to keep. This is quite in line with recommendations from the UN Advisory Panel for the review of the Peacebuilding Architecture, which posits that peacebuilding should cut across the conflict spectrum and not only come when normalcy has been established.

Notes

1. Interview with Turkish diplomat, 2014.
2. Interview with Somali civil society actor, 2015.
3. Interview with Afghan and Somali officials, Istanbul, 2016.
4. Interview with Turkish diplomats, 2015.
5. Ibid.
6. Interview with Turkish officials, 2015.
7. Interview with Dr. Kani Torun, Istanbul, 2014.
8. Interview with Turkish officials, 2015.
9. Ibid.
10. Ibid.
11. Interview with a senior executive from the Turkish Red Crescent on August 26, 2015.
12. Ibid.
13. Ibid.
14. Ibid.
15. Interview with Somali civil society actor, 2015.
16. Interview with official at the Office for Diaspora Affairs, Mogadishu, 2015.
17. Part of speech by Ambassador Abdullahi Mohamed Ali, Somali Ambassador to Turkey, Istanbul, 2015.
18. Interview with official at the Office for Diaspora Affairs, Mogadishu, 2015.
19. Interview with Somali civil society actor, 2015.
20. Ibid.
21. Part of speech by Ambassador Abdullahi Mohamed Ali, Somali Ambassador to Turkey, Istanbul, 2015.
22. Interview with official at the Office for Diaspora Affairs, Mogadishu, 2015.
23. Interview with Somali civil society actor, 2015.
24. Ibid.

25. Ibid.
26. Ibid.
27. Interview with official at the Office for Diaspora Affairs, 2015.
28. Interview with Somali civil society actor, 2015.
29. Ibid.
30. Ibid.
31. Ibid.
32. Ibid.

References

Achilles, Kathryn, Onur Sazak, Thomas Wheeler, and Auveen Woods. 2015. *Turkish Aid Agencies in Somalia: Risks and Opportunities for Building Peace*. Istanbul: Istanbul Policy Center.

Arman, Abukar. 2017. Blue Skies over Somalia. *Al Jazeera*. Accessed February 12, 2017. http://www.aljazeera.com/indepth/opinion/2017/02/blue-skies-somalia-170212083445301.html

Bekar, Olgan. 2016. Remarks at the Conference Entitled "Rising Powers and Peacebuilding: Innovative Approaches to Preventing Conflict and Sustaining Peace." Istanbul Policy Center, Istanbul, May 23.

Balthasar, Dominik. 2013. Somaliland's Best Kept Secret: Shrewd Politics and War Projects as Means of State-Making. *Journal of Eastern African Studies* 7(2): 218–238.

Daily Sabah. 2017. Turkey gives $122 Million in Humanitarian Aid to Somalia. *Daily Sabah*, March 9. Accessed March 9, 2017. https://www.dailysabah.com/africa/2017/03/09/turkey-gives-122-million-in-humanitarian-aid-to-somalia

Duffield, Mark. 2010. Risk-Management and the Fortified Aid Compound: Everyday Life in Post-Interventionary Society. *The Journal of Intervention and Statebuilding* 4(4): 453–474.

Favori LLC. n.d.. http://www.favorillc.com/

Garowe Online. 2016. Somalia: President Ali Signs Deals with a Chinese Company. *Garowe Online*, November 28. Accessed March 1, 2017. http://www.garoweonline.com/en/news/puntland/somalia-president-ali-signs-deals-with-chinese-companies

Geeska Africa Online. 2015. Uganda: AMISOM Peacekeeper's Position to Prolong AU Mission to Earn Money. http://www.geeskaafrika.com/uganda-amisom-peacekeepers-position-to-prolong-au-mission-to-earn-money/10086/#sthash.CMys14dp.dpuf

Global Humanitarian Assistance. 2014. Somalia Donors. Accessed February 28, 2017. http://www.globalhumanitarianassistance.org/countryprofile/somalia#tab-donors

Harper, Mary. 2012. *Getting Somalia Wrong: Faith, War and Hope in a Shattered State*. London: Zed Books.

Hearn, Sarah. 2016. *Independent Review of the New Deal for Engagement in Fragile States Cooperation*. New York: NYU Center on International Cooperation.

Human Rights Watch. 2015. Somalia: AU Forces Linked to Wedding Killings. Accessed February 25, 2017. https://www.hrw.org/news/2015/08/13/somalia-au-forces-linked-wedding-killings

Hurriyet Daily News. 2016. Turkey Finalizes Military Training Base in Somalia. October 1. Accessed October 14, 2016. http://www.hurriyetdailynews.com/turkey-finalizes-military-training-base-in-somalia.aspx?PageID=238&NID=104468&NewsCatID=510

International Crisis Group. 2012. Assessing Turkey's Role in Somalia. *ICG Africa Briefing No. 92*. http://www.crisisgroup.org/en/regions/africa/horn-of-africa/somalia/b092-assessing-turkeys-role-in-somalia.aspx

Lough, Richard. 2012. INSIGHT-Turkey Tries Out Soft Power in Somalia. *Reuters* June 3. Accessed January 11, 2016. http://www.reuters.com/article/somalia-turkey-idUSL5E8GP2LP20120603

Maina, Judy and Jamal Ibrahim. 2017. UAE Seeks to Open Military Base in Somaliland. *All East Africa*, January 11. Accessed March 2, 2017. https://www.alleastafrica.com/2017/01/11/uae-seeks-to-open-military-base-in-somaliland/

Menkhaus, Ken. 2014. If Mayors Ruled Somalia: Beyond the State-Building Impasse. *Nordic Africa Policy Institute*, Policy Note 2. http://www.nai.uu.se/news/articles/2014/04/29/154351/index.xml

OECD. 2015. Aid Statistics, Recipients at a Glance. http://www.oecd.org/countries/somalia/recipientcharts.htm

Presidency of the Turkish Republic. 2016. Somalia has Become a Symbol of the Relations We Wish to Establish With Our Brothers in Africa. Accessed March 5, 2016. http://www.tccb.gov.tr/en/news/542/39918/somalia-has-become-a-symbol-of-the-relations-we-wish-to-establish-with-our-brothers-in-africa.html

Radion Dalsan. 2017. Somalia Accuses UAE of Destabilising Country Terms Military Deal With Somaliland Illegal. Accessed February 16, 2017. http://radiodalsan.com/en/somalia-accuses-uae-of-destabilising-country-terms-miliatry-deal-with-somaliland-illegal/

Sazak, Onur, Thomas Wheeler, and Auveen Woods. 2015. Turkey and Somalia: Making Aid Work for Peace. *Safer World Briefing*.

Somali Peace Line. 2016. Transforming Conflict and Violence in Somalia through Effective Community Engagement. Workshop at the Istanbul Policy Center. Istanbul.

Sucuoglu, Gizem, and Jason Stearns. 2016. Turkey in Somalia: Shifting Paradigm of Aid. Report No. 24. Pretoria: South African Institute of International Affairs.

The Somali Investor. 2015. New Management at Albayrak Port in Mogadishu Creates Hope. Accessed February 16, 2016. http://somaliainvestor.so/index.php/travel/item/109-new-management-at-albayrak-port-in-mogadishu-creates-hope

Today Zaman. 2012. Turkey-Somalia Military Agreement Approved. November 9. http://www.todayszaman.com/news-297699-turkey-somalia-military-agreement-approved.html

Turkish Development and Coordination Agency. 2013. *2012 Annual Report*. Ankara.

———. Turkish Development Assistance 2014 Report. http://www.tika.gov.tr/en/publication/list/turkish_ development _assistance_reports-24

———. 2016. *2014 Annual Report*. Ankara.

Turkish Statistics Agency. 1996–2017. Exports by Country. Accessed February 28, 2017. http://www.tuik.gov.tr/PreIstatistikTablo.do?istab_id=624

UNHCR. 2016. Somalia: Overview Situation Report. Accessed January 20, 2017. http://data.unhcr.org/horn-of-africa/country.php?id=197

Wasuge, Mahad. 2016. Turkey's Assistance Model in Somalia: Achieving Much with Little. Mogadishu: Heritage Institute for Policy Studies. http://www.heritageinstitute.org/wp-content/uploads/2016/02/Turkeys-Assistance-Model-in-Somalia-Achieving-Much-With-Little1-1.pdf

Onur Sazak is an advocacy and coordination manager at Support to Life and a Ph.D. candidate in political science at Sabancı University, Istanbul.

Auveen Elizabeth Woods is a researcher, Istanbul Policy Center, Sabancı University, Istanbul.

CHAPTER 9

New Actors and Innovative Approaches to Peacebuilding: The Case of Myanmar

Lina A. Alexandra and Marc Lanteigne

We would like to show our appreciation due to the extensive support given by different institutions both in Myanmar and Indonesia which contribute to the conclusion of this report. In Myanmar, we would like to thank the Embassies of Indonesia, especially Dr. Ito Sumardi (Indonesian Ambassador to Myanmar 2013–2016), India, Japan, Norway, Switzerland to Myanmar; officials in the Strategic Studies and Training Department of the Ministry of Foreign Affairs (MOFA) Myanmar, Myanmar Human Rights Commission, and representatives of the Myanmar Armed Forces (Tatmadaw) and the commissioners from the Myanmar National Election Commission on the subject of pre- and post-election security in the country.; academics and researchers in the Yangon University, the Myanmar Development Research Institute (MDRI) /Center for Strategic and International Studies (CSIS), Myanmar Institute of Strategic and International Studies; the Mingalar Myanmar and the Shalom (Nyein) Foundation. We would like to thank also senior-level officials from the Indonesian Ministry of Foreign Affairs, especially Dr. Hassan Wirajuda (2001–2009); the Institute for Peace and Democracy (IPD); the former Indonesian Ambassador to Myanmar, Dr. Sebastianus Sumarsono (2008–2013); the Indonesian National Election Commission; Indonesian parliament member (Commission I); and The Habibie Center.

L.A. Alexandra (✉)
Centre for Strategic and International Studies (CSIS), Jakarta, Indonesia

M. Lanteigne
Centre for Defence and Security Studies, Massey University, Auckland, New Zealand

C.T. Call, C. de Coning (eds.), *Rising Powers and Peacebuilding*, Rethinking Peace and Conflict Studies,
DOI 10.1007/978-3-319-60621-7_9

Introduction

The positive movement towards political and economic reformation in Myanmar, (also known as Burma), began in the wake of reform processes since 2010 to the current administration under President Thein Sein, and has attracted the attention of various international actors interested in assisting the Myanmar government, economically and politically. Central to this attention has been the ongoing peacebuilding process in Myanmar, specifically the potential war-to-peace transition in the country as cease-fires and other political agreements between the Myanmar government and armed opposition forces are crafted. Both traditional partners as well as new actors in Myanmar diplomacy have developed policies and have approached the country's government to gather more information about how they could contribute positively to building sustainable peace in the country. This question became more pressing during the period leading up to the state elections on 8 November 2015. This vote, while not perfect, was the most inclusive in the country in decades, and was seen as a barometer on the overall reform process as well as ongoing attempts to develop a peace plan for the periphery of the country. The landslide win by the National League for Democracy (NLD), headed by former dissident Aung San Suu Kyi, promised to jump start many needed reforms in the country. Although the military-backed constitution prevented Ms. Suu Kyi from assuming the position of president, she currently serves as 'State Councillor', a position akin to that of a prime minister, and also holds the positions of Foreign Minister and Minister of the Office of the President. Her colleague within the NLD. Mr Htin Kyaw, assumed office in March 2016. After her first year in office, she acknowledged that much more work needed to be down in the areas of governmental reform, economic development and peacebuilding, and in March 2017 suggested that she would be in a position to step down if the public was dissatisfied with her performance.

When speaking of the 'reform' processes in Myanmar at present, one can identify four separate streams which can be differentiated but are nonetheless very closely tied together as this report will examine:

1. A transition from military rule to an intermediate 'mixed' system of civilian-military governance, with the promise of a return to full civilian administration and democratic institutions in the near term.
2. The end of civil conflicts in the periphery of Myanmar as governmental and opposition forces agree to a cease-fire and a peaceful

resolution to political disputes which have plagued the country for over five decades.

3. The conversion of the Myanmar economy from a command system to a liberalising one, developing stronger trade ties and private business development. This is key to alleviating the ongoing problem of widespread poverty, which is viewed not only as a socio-economic crisis but also a security threat.
4. The expansion and diversification of Myanmar's diplomatic contacts not only with other Asian governments, (including ASEAN), but also with major international actors including Western Europe and the United States.

This study of new actors in peacebuilding focuses on the role of external players in the second of these four processes, but mindful of how that process relates to the other three vital areas of reform that Myanmar has been undertaking. The study focuses especially on two countries which have played differing but prominent roles in peacebuilding, namely China and Indonesia. These countries represent three distinct types of actors in terms of their engagement in the country. Indonesia represents an emerging actor in Myanmar's diplomacy, both as a single player as well as a prominent member of ASEAN. Indonesia is still often categorised as a developing country but for the last decade or so has been viewed as an emerging market and as a stabilising force in Southeast Asian security. Jakarta has been seeking to develop its peacebuilding policies in recent years, with Myanmar being as a key case study. Bilateral relations were established during the early period of Indonesia's independence in January 1948, and solidified after Myanmar joined ASEAN in 1997, a move supported by most governments in the region, including Indonesia.

On the other hand, China represents another new actor in peacebuilding arena with different characteristics. In some ways, calling China a 'new' actor in Myanmar peacebuilding is a mis-categorisation, given that the two neighbouring countries have had longstanding diplomatic and economic contacts since the independence of Burma, and Beijing was one of the few regional governments to maintain ties with Myanmar during that country's period of diplomatic isolation between the late 1980s and 2010. However, in recent years China has been seeking to improve its identity in Myanmar through various diplomatic initiatives, due to public concerns about both its dominant role in the Myanmar economy as well as its previous good relations with the pre-reform military governments (SLORC and its successor, the SPDC).

Since 2014, there have been disputes across the Sino-Myanmar border, as well as signs of a cooling in political relations between the two states. Beijing nonetheless continues to see Myanmar as a vital partner both in energy trade as well as the ambitious plans of President Xi Jinping to develop port facilities in the Indian Ocean as part of China's 'Belt and Road' regional development initiatives first introduced by the Xi Jinping government in 2013. Beijing is wary of the possibility of enhanced Western engagement in Myanmar, seeing warming relations with the United States as especially difficult given the current strategic 'rebalancing' policy in Asia announced by the Obama administration in 2011 which many policymakers in China have perceived as tacit containment of Chinese power.

As a response, Beijing has been seeking to develop greater soft power in Myanmar in the face of developing diplomatic and trade competition from the West, especially the United States, Western Europe, and Australia, but also from Japan, India and other governments in Asia. Although it is likely that the next government in Myanmar will continue to diversify the country's foreign policy and possibly return to a more non-aligned strategic identity which was the norm before the end of the 1980s, Beijing by necessity will continue to be a major part of Myanmar's regional relations given China's status as a rising power and due to geographic realities.

This project seeks to compare the approaches to peacebuilding undertaken by these three external actors to gauge their policies as well as measure their successes on different levels in the transition period leading up to the November 2015 elections and beyond. After the analyses of these case studies, it will useful to briefly analyse comparative cases of other distinct peacebuilding actors in Myanmar, namely Norway as well as India, Japan and Switzerland, to provide further information regarding similarities and differences in approaches to peacebuilding concepts and practices. These four external actors for reasons of economy, focus and parsimony, but there are of course many other examples of foreign actors which have also begun to engage Myanmar, both economically and politically.

The two main cases of China and Indonesia are perceived as new (or emerging) actors, although arguably neither term is wholly accurate, whereas Norway and Switzerland are more 'traditional' Western donors. Japan can be seen as a 'returning' actor given that Tokyo's diplomatic and economic presence in what was then Burma was very strong until the 1980s, and India is certainly not a stranger to Myanmar politics, but has been at best a minor actor in peacebuilding but is seeking to take advantage of the developing reforms to better improve its position, both on a unilateral basis as well as due to concerns about Beijing's growing strategic presence in the Indian Ocean.

Indonesia's Engagement in Myanmar

Rationales and Strategic Objectives

While Indonesia's engagement in Myanmar's transition, particularly in the area of peacebuilding, can be viewed as relatively recent, the foundation of the relationship between the two countries goes back more than half a century. Burma was listed as one of the first countries to recognise Indonesia's struggle for independence, and the two governments appreciated each other's independence struggles with European colonial powers. In 1947, only two years after Indonesia's founding fathers President Soekarno and Vice-President Mohammad Hatta declared the country's independence from colonial powers, the Burmese government gave permission to open an Indonesian Office in Rangoon (now Yangon). The Burmese leaders at that time even addressed the Indonesian diplomats as representatives of the Republic of Indonesia in front of the Dutch authorities who at that time refused to acknowledge Indonesia's independence.

During those difficult times, in 1949 the Burmese government accepted the request of the Indonesian government to allow for Indonesian *Dakota RI-001* aircraft to land in Mingladon Airport, Rangoon and later helped to set up the first commercial Indonesian Airways in Burma. Furthermore, the Prime Minister of Burma, U Nu, together with Indian Prime Minister Jawaharlal Nehru, continued to rally support for Indonesia's struggle against its former colonial power by organising the Conference on Indonesia in New Delhi to condemn military activities conducted by the Dutch (Indonesia Embassy 2001).

Bilateral relations were very much watered down during Myanmar's isolationist period. Myanmar under the socialist system, which led to later economic traumas, created even less incentive for ASEAN countries, including Indonesia, to revoke its relations with the country. Hopes that Myanmar would be in a position to join ASEAN were dashed in the wake of the uprising which broke out in August 1988, followed by the consolidation of military rule in the country and the annulment of the results of the 1990s elections. ASEAN as the only regional organisation in the area, was heavily pressured to respond to the situation. Even after Myanmar joined ASEAN, relations between the country and other members were brittle, especially in the wake of the 2007 'Saffron Revolution' and the government's mishandling of aid after Cyclone Nargis in May 2008.

Compared with China, Indonesia has fewer geopolitical and geo-economic interests in Myanmar. Indonesia shares no border with Myanmar, and strengthening bilateral economic ties has been a struggle especially due to the low interest from the Indonesia's business sectors in venturing into Myanmar's still-emerging market. One of the results from the Second Joint Commission for Bilateral Cooperation (JCBC) between Indonesia and Myanmar in late December 2011, the two leaders committed to increase the trade volume to US$500 million by 2015 (Zaw 2012). Then around one year later, during the third meeting of the JCBC, as a follow-up to President Yudhoyono's state visit to Naypyitaw in April 2013, the two countries raised the expectation to achieve US$1 billion trade value by 2016 (Winarti 2013). Nevertheless, there are several means to explain Indonesia's motivations to engage with Myanmar. The first is at the domestic level. Based on the elaborations above, a long-term relationship which was established since the early period of Indonesia's independence between the two countries has created a solid basis for the Indonesian government throughout the history to develop ties with Myanmar. Due to generous pre-independence support given by Myanmar in the past, Indonesian policymakers have an implicit 'indebted' feeling, which has obliged the country to return the favour to Myanmar.

The second domestic factor is a combination of Indonesia's internal need and ambition to spread its newly adopted value—democracy—in the region in order to create an improved environment for its own democracy to grow at home. In the wake of the 1998 protests and the first direct presidential elections in 2004 which brought to power Susilo Bambang Yudhoyono, Indonesia managed to overcome its internal political and economic challenges to install a civilian government after thirty-two years of semi-authoritarian government during the New Order era (1965–1998), and embrace democracy as its new identity. Besides implementing various policies at the domestic level to deepen its democratic project—direct elections, autonomy, security sector reform, and so on, interestingly Indonesia has been also aiming high to project its democracy abroad, in order to create a supporting environment for its own democracy to grow to the fullest. As elucidated by former Foreign Minister Hassan Wirajuda, '[S]ince a democracy works best in a democratic environment, we should also like to see the further growth of democratic values in our own neighbourhood.' (Wirajuda 2005).

Myanmar has become a focus for Indonesia to project its democracy for various reasons. Other than historical debts, more importantly because the two countries see some similarities between them. Indonesia was once under the rule of General Soeharto during the 32 years of New Order era, which is very much the situation Myanmar is currently in. During the era of President Yudhoyono, who was a retired general, Indonesia enjoyed special relationships compared to other countries which allowed its engagement with Myanmar to flourish, even allowing for some dialogue on sensitive issues such as the ongoing Rohingya question. One of the reasons, as mentioned by an Indonesian foreign ministry official is simply because the Myanmar government is comfortable working with a government which has a history of 'military thinking', and still has military issues to resolve in politics (Macan-Markar 2013). This is particularly true as both countries are facing challenges of ethnic conflicts as well as separatism in their territories. Both governments are also facing gaps in the relations between the majority and minority groups, notably along the religious lines—Indonesia is majority Muslim while Myanmar has a Buddhist majority. Therefore, at least from these aspects, there are some modalities to tap on for Indonesia to projecting its democracy.

Regional factors have also shaped Indonesia's recent policies. Myanmar's location in the Southeast Asian region, and also its proximity to China and India, means that whatever happens in Myanmar immediately comes to the attention of countries in the region and of ASEAN itself. Indonesia's interest in engagement is further fuelled by its more consistently defining itself as a natural leader in the region and in ASEAN, which Myanmar officially joined in 1996. Indonesia has more or less shared the same interests with other ASEAN member countries' founding members on the need to embrace the Indochina countries and bring them into ASEAN, particularly in the case of Myanmar, which the organisation granted observer status to in 1991. The biggest interest of ASEAN at that time was to restrain increasing Chinese influence in the region which was seen as breaking Myanmar's traditional neutralism and transforming the country into China's 'satellite' in the region as well as creating an entry point for Beijing to better influence Southeast Asia, given China's long border with Myanmar and the latter country's placement on the Indian Ocean (Weatherbee 2009), which has emerged as an essential maritime trade route for Beijing as it enhances its trade with Africa and the Middle East.

Moreover, ASEAN's founding members, including Indonesia,[1] viewed engagement with Myanmar as crucial to close the loophole for major powers, especially Western countries, to intervene unilaterally in the region. Due to severe criticism from those outside powers, particularly the United States, over Myanmar's human rights violations, there has been a very strong interest from ASEAN countries for Southeast Asia to become an autonomous regional order where the members become masters of their own region, as indicated in Indonesia's initiatives back in 1971, and even now in the post-2015 agenda, to establish the 'Zone of Peace, Freedom and Neutrality' (ZOPFAN) in ASEAN (Anwar 2005). Relations between Myanmar and other ASEAN members, especially Thailand, remain problematic in some areas, but since the reform process in Myanmar began five years ago more doors have been opened for a deepening of the Myanmar-ASEAN relationship.

Types of Engagement

Generally, Indonesia's engagements with Myanmar have been established in most sectors, especially in political, economic, development, and military ones. Compared to other actors in the region, such as Singapore, Thailand and China, Indonesia can be considered as relatively newcomer in term of its economic engagement with the country. It can be said that Indonesia has within the past few years begun to reap some economic benefits from the country's carefully tended engagement with the military regime in Myanmar.

In 2014, total exports from Indonesia to Myanmar reached US$566 million in value which dominated by non-oil commodities, such as palm oil, cigarettes, clothing (*sarong*), and traditional medicines. Alternatively, Indonesia's imports from Myanmar rose significantly from US$73 million in 2013 to US$122 million in 2014, and dominated by non-oil commodities such as beans, especially mung beans and soybeans and also seafood products (Kompas 2009). In 2015, the Indonesian government was exploring the establishment of direct banking connections and to allow more flight connections between the two countries (Garuda Indonesia 2015). Then, to boost investments in Myanmar, current Indonesian President Joko Widodo, during the ASEAN Summit in Naypyidaw in 2014, announced plans to augment Indonesia's investments in Myanmar in three sectors: mining, telecommunications and infrastructure (Dunia 2014).

Non-Political Engagements

There are several sectors in the Myanmar economy which Indonesian companies have just recently become involved in within the past five years, including construction, telecommunication, and banking. Some leading construction companies such as Ciputra Group, Lippo Group, and Wijaya Karya (WIKA) have shown interest in taking advantage of almost 15% increase within the period of 2009–2013 in Myanmar's construction needs. WIKA has undertaken a US$270 million multifunctional development project in Yangon, involving commercial and residential units to be accomplished in 2017. Lippo Group, on the other hand, has been planning to invest US$1 billion to building 20 hospitals over the next three to five years and also aimed to seek opportunities in retail sector (Firdaus 2015; Antara News 2015). In 2013, the Indonesian state-owned telecommunication company Telkom won the tender to participate in modernising the information and communication technology in the country (Telkom 2013). Later on, in banking sector, the Indonesian state-owned bank, Bank Negara Indonesia (BNI) just built its first representative office in Yangon in November 2014 (Sipahutar 2014).

In the development area, Myanmar has been regarded as one of key partners to be engaged under Indonesia's framework of South-South and Triangular Cooperation (SSTC) of Indonesia. As a result of the second Joint Commission on Bilateral Cooperation (JCBC) between Indonesia and Myanmar, as recorded in the Blue Book on Indonesia-Myanmar Capacity Building Partnership, Indonesia has committed itself to providing assistance in the form of training and seminars/workshops as well as experts in the area of small and medium enterprises (SMEs), microfinance, national reconciliation, agriculture, local governance and media during the period of 2013–2015 (Ministry of Foreign Affairs 2015). The Indonesian government, through its state-owned electricity company, also committed itself to providing technical consultation assistance to help Myanmar to address its national electricity losses which reached up to 26% (Xinhua 2013). Besides this regular assistance, Indonesia has also helped Myanmar during emergency situations including the aftermath of Cyclone Nargis in 2008.[2] Jakarta also donated US$1 million to the Tripartite Core Group, composed of three members from the Myanmar government, three members from ASEAN and three representatives from the United Nations, for the victims of Cyclone Nargis (Shin 2009).

In terms of military engagement, there are limited interactions, there have been limited interactions, including regular military training courses and particularly on medical courses provided by the Indonesian armed forces so far. For the past two years, the Indonesian military has engaged in sharing specific knowledge and experiences on the role of the military in a democratic state. As of now, there are three military officers in Indonesia attending courses in the National Defence Institute (*Lemhanas/Lembaga Ketahanan Nasional*) in Myanmar.[3] Recently, there has been interest from the Myanmar government to purchase various defence products produced by Indonesian companies to enhance the capabilities of Myanmar's military and police (Tempo 2014).

Political Engagement

In addition to these economic and development engagements, Jakarta has been focusing further in its political engagements with Myanmar. However, this initiative, rather then being placed in a bilateral framework, was instead framed in a regional setting, especially through Indonesia's aspiration to nurture its leadership role in ASEAN. The country has tried to regain its central role within ASEAN as soon as it was relatively able to cope with its internal struggles between 1998 and 2002. When Jakarta chaired ASEAN in 2003, it came up with a very aggressive proposal of creating ASEAN Security Community (ASC)—which later modified into ASEAN Political Security Community (APSC).

The most critical ideas brought forward by Indonesia within ASEAN at that time was to insert the new principles of democracy, good governance and rule of law, as well as the promotion and protection of human rights as ASEAN's shared norms and values—points which were unthinkable or even an anathema for ASEAN to mention in the past, since some member countries are still categorised as 'non-democratic' or 'semi-authoritarian' states. Within this context, Indonesia has played an active role in persuading the non-democratic member countries of ASEAN toward observing these new ASEAN's common values and norms—which then later even brought higher by creating the Bali Democracy Forum (BDF) movement in 2008, with a mission to convert ASEAN countries into more robust democracies.

Indonesia's political engagements—after Indonesia's reformation era—with Myanmar started in 2003 when the Indonesian foreign minister Ali Alatas, a very capable diplomat, visited the country, after he was appointed as the United Nations special envoy to Myanmar. From the outset, no major breakthrough seemed to take place since the military junta continued to run the Myanma political affairs as usual. Even four years later, in

2007, when President Yudhoyono sent a retired reformist general, Agus Widjojo, to Myanmar, officially to attend the funeral of former Prime Minister Soe Win, but with a mission to convince the military junta to start thinking about political reform following the brutal military crackdown of anti-government protests led by Buddhist monks, nothing can be claimed as a significant result. The Indonesian president could not even get a guarantee that his plan to visit the country would bring some significant outcome, which then made him eventually postpone his visit indefinitely simply not to lose face. The momentum then arrived for Indonesia to again reassert its role, this time in a deeper fashion, after Cyclone Nargis.

Immediately after the disaster laid waste to much of Myanmar, the military junta shut down access for humanitarian aid to enter the country and help the victims, despite the authorities' lack of capabilities to provide such emergency relief. Indonesia's then-foreign minister, Hassan Wirajuda, known for pushing ASEAN to embrace new principles of democracy and human rights, took the initiative to place ASEAN at the forefront, since entreaties from many Western governments to persuade the junta to allow emergency ingress into Myanmar came to no avail. Aside from Indonesia's humanitarian assistance to send capable experts involved in dealing with Indian Ocean tsunami disaster in Aceh back in 2004, more importantly Jakarta played an instrumental role to persuade the military junta, with some pressure, to reconsider its restrictions on foreign disaster assistance. The foreign minister, in one meeting, basically offered the Myanmar government two options. First, it can allow an ASEAN-led mechanism to help coordinating the whole humanitarian assistance that were coming in to the country. Second, the junta could simply do nothing but would have to explain what was the meaning of Myanmar joining ASEAN in the first place. As a result, ASEAN then was given the role of aid coordination as the Myanmar belatedly opened up access for humanitarian assistance to flow into the country.

It is important to note that rather than being a one-way effort, Indonesia's overall engagement with Myanmar was made possible due to Myanmar's developing interests towards Indonesia's political processes from the very beginning. Under the New Order era, led by President Soeharto, a Burmese delegation at that time led by the then-Chief of Intelligence Unit Lieutenant General Khin Nyunt visited Indonesia in December 1993 to study the Indonesian military's 'dual function', defence and politics, system. Such interest has still been expressed today, since such a system has been perceived by many stakeholders in Myanmar as providing a gradual and stable transition from military into full civilian-led government in later years. Furthermore, many stakeholders in Myanmar also expressed interest in learning about *Pancasila*, the formal philosophical foundations of the State of Indonesia, particularly the idea of *Bhinneka Tunggal Ika* ('Unity in Diversity'), the official maxim of Indonesia, since the two countries have shared almost similar challenges with ethnic diversity and associated periodic political tensions.

While there has been some internal criticisms of the Indonesia government to be late when it comes to reaping the benefits of its early political investments in Myanmar, to some extent there is an interesting finding that such 'unfortunate' situation has somehow situated Indonesia in a better position compared to other actors, such as China, India and Japan, which have expanded their economic interests in the country (Chachavalpongpun 2010). Indonesia has been able to secure more trust to play a role of peace-builder, which will be elucidated in the next section, due to its relatively low-key presence in terms of business or economic activities in Myanmar so far.

Role in Peacebuilding/Peace-Related Areas

Indonesia's governmental role in peacebuilding in Myanmar is unique, in the sense that it has been directed more towards larger and more high-level contexts, including projecting democracy as the basic foundation to create sustainable peace. Here, Jakarta has been focusing itself to share its experiences in democratic transitions, including on how to manage with the 'messy' side effects of such processes. What makes it different is the emphasis on the usage of 'democratic' methods that are different from what the traditional actors, mainly Western countries, used to apply.

It is certainly not an easy task to grasp how the Indonesia policymakers define the term peacebuilding. When directly asked about their understanding on the term, most of them relate it with the UN definition, in which peacebuilding is a set of activities conducted after peace has been relatively achieved through the sigining of peace agreement between the conflicting parties. Within this context, then, some argued that peacebuilding itself is relatively a new experience for Indonesia and the country has just started to learn the process during the Aceh peace process which taken place after the Tsunami disaster severely hit the province in the end of 2004. As stated by one general, "Peacebuilding is also something new for Indonesia. We learn it in the case of Aceh. There is no template, we just follow the needs of the ground."[4] This argument has been confirmed by Indonesia's former Minister of Foreign Affairs, as he went on to describe how the Indonesian government at that time involved in the process to bring former combatants from Free Aceh Movement (*Gerakan Aceh Merdeka*) group members to enter into normal civilian life, including to regulate the distribution of lands and establishment of local government.[5]

Then, when asked whether Indonesia's roles in Myanmar can be categorised as peacebuilding efforts, most of them were not too sure. This is reflected from the comment given by the former Indonesian Ambassador to Myanmar (2008–2013), Sebastianus Sumarsono, when being interviewed regarding Indonesia's active role in the country:

> I am not sure whether those things are part of peacebuilding ... Not only in peacebuilding, but in many aspects of life we participate in helping Myanmar.

Such a view was also confirmed by Minister Wirajuda as he argued that it is hard to say that peacebuilding has taken place in Myanmar since peacemaking has not taken place in the country.[6]

Principles

There are several principles upheld by the Indonesian government to indicate democratic ideas in its engagement with Myanmar. The first, and the most important, is sharing. Fully aware of differences between the two countries, the idea behind this sharing is to provide Myanmar, once an isolationist state, with real evidence that transition into a democratic civilian-led government is not an impossible idea, as demonstrated in the Indonesian case. It is always debatable whether Indonesia's past experience, with its dual-function military and semi-authoritarian regime, is a good example to present. However, one argues that at least the Indonesian case presents an alternative to the Myanmar's leaders for the country to follow in walking the path of limited democratic reform and economic development (Renshaw 2013). Based on interviews with several Indonesian stakeholders, the 'sharing' activities conducted so far are aimed not only to share best practices, but also more importantly discuss Indonesia's mistakes of the past, which should not to be repeated in Myanmar. Moreover, by elucidating the concept of 'sharing', Indonesia positions itself not as being superior to its Myanmar counterpart, with the former dictating to the latter, but rather as a partner on equal footing.

The second principle, which is the consequence of the 'sharing' approach, is to work at the pace that is comfortable for all, especially the partner country, while giving some pressures when necessary. For the engagement to achieve success, Indonesia believes that it is important spend more energy and time to build confidence and trust, especially with the government, and wait until the initiative for change comes from the local stakeholders in order to grow the sense of ownership of the reform process. According to one director in MoFA, the approach should be based 'on their request, not ours because it involves changing of the culture and mindset of the society [regarding the democracy promotion]'.[7] Such an approach often been criticised not only by Western countries, but also by some segments of Indonesian society, as being too accommodative, powerless, or even ineffective. However, the Indonesian government particularly believes that it is very crucial not to give an impression of seeking to impose a worldview on others, as it may create counterproductive results. Former Minister Hassan Wirajuda when confronted with this criticism, made an interesting argument as he described Indonesia's approach to Myanmar when it persuaded the military junta to receive an ASEAN-led humanitarian assistance into the country in the aftermath of Cyclone Nargis disaster. According to him, Indonesia at that time actually made a straightforward movement by 'taking the bull by its horn' when the Indonesian government challenged the regime in Myanmar to consider the meaning of its participation in ASEAN should the ASEAN-led proposal also being rejected. While he strongly disagree with sanction mechanism to 'punish' Myanmar, as implemented by many Western countries, Wirajuda argued that there is no reason not to be able to apply what he called as 'constructive engagement' as shown from the case above. The spirit, according to him, should be like helping a family member in which 'rebuking' is justified to the extent that such action would bring better result than sanctioning.[8]

Projects

There are various projects related to peacebuilding efforts in Myanmar which have been implemented so far. The major theme for Indonesia's peacebuilding engagement in Myanmar is to sharing experiences in democratic transition on topics such as military reform, election processes, capacity building for parliament and political parties, and recently also managing ethnic relations, especially related to ethnic minority groups and questions of local autonomy/decentralisation. Those projects mainly took form in activities, such as visit, training, workshop, dialogue and so on which conducted by different agencies, starting from ministries, think tank institutions, local non-governmental organisations (NGOs) as well as international NGOs. The main implementing agency so far is the Indonesian Ministry of Foreign Affairs (MoFA), particularly the Directorate of Technical Cooperation which is responsible on all programmes within the framework of Indonesia's South-South and Triangular Cooperation (SSTC), including Indonesia's peacebuilding projects in Myanmar. Almost all of the projects,[9] organised by government agencies as well as non-governmental institutions, were funded through a triangular framework, meaning that they received funding from the third parties.

One implementing institution, which is closely linked to the Indonesian MoFA, is the Institute for Peace and Democracy (IPD). The IPD, which is independent from the government in terms of its management and funding, was formed by the Indonesian Foreign Ministry, with the support of the state-run Udayana University. Its original primary function was to implement the Bali Democracy Forum (BDF)—Indonesia's ambitious intergovernmental forum to promote democracy by gathering countries which regard themselves as democratic to share their experiences to non-democratic countries but have 'aspired to be more democratic'. The participants are from across the Asia-Pacific as well as the Middle East, and Myanmar is also a member.[10]

Recently, the organisation has been transformed into a fully independent institution which makes it no longer under the aegis of Udayana University. Specifically in Myanmar, IPD has organised different activities related to promotion of peace and democracy. Before designing certain programs/activities, the IPD first conducted the scoping mission in Myanmar to undertake needs assessment and scoping analyses, with the results being used to develop suitable programs and activities which would meet the expectations of different stakeholders in Myanmar.[11] Based on consultations with the local stakeholders, the IPD implemented several activities in Myanmar, as illustrated in Table 9.1 below. Within those activities, most of the programmes were focused to provide capacity building in democracy and peace building, the role of media, parliament, political party, election, regional autonomy, ASEAN leadership, (especially when Myanmar was preparing to assume the ASEAN chair in 2014), a national human rights body, as well as administrative reform, development (agriculture) and economic decentralisation.

Table 9.1 IPD's programs in Myanmar 2013–2014

Program	*Place*	*Date*	*Counterparts/beneficiaries*
1. Indonesia-Myanmar dialogue on democratic transition: building democracy and sustainable peace	Yangon, Myanmar	26–28 June 2013	Myanmar MoFA, MISIS, MDRI and other government officials
2. Indonesia-Myanmar dialogue on decentralization, democratization and peace building	Yangon, Myanmar	24–25 September 2013	Myanmar MoFA, MISIS, MDRI
3. Two-days dialogue on leadership and political party reform	Denpasar, Bali	9–10 November 2013	Fifty delegates from various institution in Myanmar, i.e. political parties, parliament members, MISIS, MDRI, Myanmar Peace Centre, Union Solidarity and Development Party (USDP), National League for Democracy (NLD), media and non-government organisations
4. Indonesia-Myanmar dialogue on parliamentary building 2014	Bali	7–9 April 2014	Attended by 25 participants from Myanmar
5. Election visit program to the indonesian presidential election 2014 and workshop for the Indonesian presidential election	Jakarta, Indonesia	8–10 July 2014	MDRI, Myanmar Center for Strategic and International Studies
6. Workshop on sharing experiences on development institutions: can decentralization bring peace, democracy and local development?	Yangon, Myanmar	17–18 March 2015	Myanmar MoFA, MISIS Academics, policy makers and government officials from Myanmar, Lao, and Vietnam

Sources: IPD's website, and information from the Directorate of Technical Cooperation, Ministry of Foreign Affairs

On the subject of elections, Indonesia has carried out different programmes, such as capacity-building in election monitoring and security maintenance, during the Myanmar electoral process. Here, it is interesting to note that while few projects were initiated and coordinated by the

Indonesian government, some others were actually initiated and carried out by non-governmental organisations (NGOs), including international NGOs, while Indonesian cases have been selected as references for Myanmar to take the lessons from. Here, we can see some useful collaborations existing between traditional Western donors with Indonesian partners who have the knowledge and experiences to better engage with Myanmar under reform.

For example, during the Myanmar election in 2010, the Indonesian embassy in Yangon sent a team to five different regions in Myanmar as observers.[12] Toward the upcoming national election in November 2015, Indonesia through the cooperation with different agencies has also been engaging to provide its support. As reported by local media, Indonesia has managed to provide some consultations to the Myanmar police in their preparation for election security requirements (Htoo 2015). Regarding the technicalities of election preparation, recently the Asia Foundation sponsored a tour for a delegation from Myanmar's Union Election Commission (UEC) to visit Indonesia which included a meeting with the chair and commissioners of the Indonesian National Election Commission, the local election commission in Yogyakarta, as well as non-governmental organisations, such as Perludem, (the Indonesian Association for Elections and Democracy), Google's Jakarta office on how it engaged Indonesia's voters and provided access to 2014 elections information using online services, the Institute for Inclusion and Advocacy of Persons with Disabilities (SIGAB), and *Solidaritas Perempuan* which particularly focuses its advocacy work for women's rights in Indonesia (Lee and Myint 2015).

Moreover, in the area of law enforcement, the Indonesian government in cooperation with the Myanmar government and the British government organised an International Training on the Strengthening of Law Enforcement in Jakarta on 4–13 June 2015. The training was implemented by Police Educational Institution, (*Lembaga Pendidikan Polisi Republik Indonesia/Lemdikpol*), and attended by twenty-five members of Myanmar Police force. According to the press release, such training was particularly designed to enhance the capacities of the local police in maintaining safe environment in the upcoming election in November 2015. The Indonesian National Police has been specifically selected due to its previous experiences to provide similar capacity-building for Timor-Leste in 2013 and Afghanistan in 2014 (Ministry of Foreign Affairs 2015).

Another noteworthy project was recently organised by the Habibie Centre (THC), which is a think-tank institution in Indonesia, in early August 2015 in collaboration with the Henry Dunant Centre

(HD Centre) Singapore. The project facilitated a study tour of the members of the Union Election Commission (UEC) from Rakhine State in order to learn about Indonesia's experiences to conduct peaceful elections in the post-conflict areas, particularly in Aceh and Ambon where segregation among the former conflicting parties still relatively exists. The delegation learned about the roles of the National Election Commission (*Komisi Pemilihan Umum*/KPU) and the National Election Monitoring Commission (*Badan Pengawas Pemilihan Umum*/*Bawaslu*), as well as the roles of the local NGOs and international NGOs to monitor the election process.

In terms of security sector reform, besides the usual military-to-military engagement mentioned earlier, there were some projects carried out by think tank institutions. For example, the Centre for Strategic and International Studies (CSIS) in Jakarta conducted two workshops on security sector reform in 2013 and 2014. The first workshop was held in Jakarta in September 2013, and attended by fifteen participants from Myanmar, comprised of ten high-ranking military officers and five representatives from think tanks and NGOs. The second workshop was organised in January 2014 in Yangon, through the collaboration with local NGOs, and attended by around thirty local participants comprised of high ranking military officers, police officers, parliament members, advisers to the President, and high ranking officers from the Indonesian Ministry of Home Affairs, as well as academics and NGOs representatives. In those two workshops, the Indonesian counterparts, especially the Indonesian retired generals who involved in the reform process shared about Indonesia's military transition process from the dual military system to becoming a professional military, democratic civilian control, human rights, as well as law enforcement to sustain peace process in conflict-prone areas. The Myanmar representatives specifically expressed their enthusiasm to learn from Indonesia's experiences in promoting conflict resolution in Aceh, specifically in regards to the Aceh insurgency from 1976 to 2005, as well as on addressing the root causes of other communal conflicts in Indonesia.

Another issue, which probably the most salient one in Indonesia's peacebuilding activities in Myanmar, is the commitment to assist the Myanmar government in dealing with problems related to ethnic groups, especially in relation to the controversial Rohingya issue. Members of the Muslim Rohingya community in Rakhine State in western Myanmar claim that they are a legal minority within Myanmar, but members of the Myanmar government do not recognise that status, and often eschew the very term 'Rohingya', instead referring to the persons in question as 'Bengali' and implying that they are migrants from neighbouring Bangladesh without claims to Myanmar citizenship. As a country with the world's largest Muslim community, Indonesia needs to address the concerns and pressures from its constituents at home to stop the massive violence and discrimination against the Rohingya ethnic group. Such pressures turned out to be a serious regional security threat as a group of Muslim extremists launched bomb threats against Buddhist religious facilities, as well as the Myanmar embassy in Jakarta, in 2013 (Institute for Policy Analysis of Conflict n.d.). At the same time, Indonesia also faces real challenges due to the influx in mid-2015 of Rohingya boat people from Myanmar entering into its territory by boats. Indonesia and Malaysia have so far agreed to provide temporary shelters for seven thousand Rohingya Muslims refugees and migrants from Myanmar and Bangladesh (Guardian 2015). However, violence in Rakhine state between Myanmar armed forces and Rohingya militants continues to plague the current Myanmar government.

Indonesia has provided development assistance to the Rakhine state in the form of financial and technical aid. While such action is not necessarily distinct, what is important to highlight is the way the Indonesian government took on a more balanced approach in order to quench the perception of Rohingya problem as a religious conflict of Muslims vs. Buddhists. Indonesia decided not to give support on the OIC's (Organization of Islamic Countries) approach to only aid the Muslim community in Rohingya, despite of its status as a member in the organisation, a move which would undoubtedly be rejected by the Myanmar government (IRIN News 2012). Indonesian Vice President Jusuf Kalla, who was the Chairman of the Indonesian Red Cross (PMI), back in 2012, stated that the PMI would be, by necessity, non-partisan in its assistance in Rakhine state, as he reflected on the ways which the Indonesian government addressed similar ethnic conflicts in Indonesia itself in the past (Taufiqurrahman 2012). One year later, Indonesia also built four schools in Rakhine state, using a donation from the Indonesian government with a total of US$1 million (Antara News 2014). Two schools have been dedicated to the Muslim community while two others were built for the local Buddhist community.

Aside to government's efforts, NGO also plays certain peacebuilding role in dealing with ethnic problems in Rakhine state. Muhammadiyah, for example, as one of the largest religious based NGO in Indonesia has collaborated with other NGOs in the region, including one local NGO in Myanmar, to explore possible areas of peacebuilding where it can participate in dealing with the Rohingya issue.[13]

Achievements/Measuring Results

Despite Indonesia's active engagement in peacebuilding in Myanmar, so far the government has not developed any standard monitoring and evaluation mechanisms in order to measure achievements as well as to evaluate past mistakes/failures from the projects. It is indeed a challenging task to measure of what has been achieved so far from Indonesia's engagement in peacebuilding in Myanmar for two reasons. First, there is simply no standard mechanism created by the government to monitor and evaluate projects of this nature. What normally exists is internal project evaluation applied by the donor/funding institutions or agencies, which cannot be shared for public consumption. For projects implemented by government agencies/ministries, each implementing body or ministry usually does not have any obligation to conduct any monitoring and evaluation processes. Even if such monitoring does take place, the data collected is usually not shared with the public.

Second, and more importantly, Indonesia has been focusing its engagement more on the political aspects of the Myanmar reform process and long-term projects more than working on short-term and specific or clearly defined areas. The 'sharing' approach basically emphasizes the sharing of ideas, knowledge and experiences and it is almost impossible to measure it quickly to what extent such ideas or experiences have been taken and influenced the policies of the Myanmar stakeholders.

The best indicator to measure results or achievements, as suggested by Myanmar and Indonesian stakeholders, would be to see the level of trust and confidence shown by the elites in Myanmar towards Indonesia's active engagement in the country. For example, the interest expressed from high-ranking military officers, high-level public officials, and also recently from the representatives of ethnic groups from Myanmar to participate in various events that involved Indonesian institutions as resources have shown a considerable success. Based on the interviews with different Indonesian stakeholders, they have been urged to continue the projects or even to come up with new projects.[14] But have we seen any changed behaviour? Interestingly, the request for more exchanges in the educational sector to better introduce Indonesia to more sectors of Myanmar society, especially among Myanmar's youth, can be seen from both sides.[15] From a positive perspective, it can be another indicator that Myanmar society welcomes Indonesia's deeper engagement in the country, but from a more negative perspective we can also see that Indonesia's activities so far have only been concentrated on elites, and have not reached the greater Myanmar society, yet.

Such trust could also be seen in the most sensitive issue of ethnic relations in Rakhine state. While initiatives from many countries and international organisations to help were turned down by the Myanmar government, President Thein Sein formally asked Indonesia during the 21st ASEAN Summit in Phnom Penh in November 2012, despite the fact that the country is majority Muslim, to help his government in resolving ethnic tensions in Rakhine state (Santosa 2012).

Another interesting piece of evidence appeared when President Joko Widodo was received as the first guest, among other ASEAN countries, by President Thein Sein on the sidelines of the ASEAN Summit in November 2014 in Naypyidaw, although not many issues were directly discussed by the two leaders. Indonesia has been welcome to expand its economic engagements in Myanmar, as President Thein Sein has encouraged his Indonesian counterpart to increase its investments, particularly to take advantage of the new policy that allows foreign banks to operate in the country (Otto 2014).

One unanticipated positive result from these engagements, as argued by some Indonesian stakeholders, is that instead of Myanmar simply learning from Indonesia's experiences, a two-way learning process has evolved, in which Indonesia is also learning from its Myanmar counterparts. For example, according to Lt-Gen. (ret.) Agus Widjojo, who was actively involved in the Indonesian military reform process, Myanmar actually has a better sense of the supremacy of law as compared with Indonesia's political system. According to him, before the Myanmar military deployed in conflict-prone areas, such as in the northern regions, the government first issued a state of emergency status, while in the Indonesian case military action, in most cases, took place before issuing any regulations, placing the legality of the military actions into question right from the outset.[16]

Another example, as shared by a leading think-tank based in Jakarta, is the degree of openness shown by the stakeholders from Myanmar, including from some of the country's politicians. During one discussion held recently by the Habibie Center in Jakarta which addressed the topic on election in post-conflict areas, the participants were involved in a very frank dialogue, an outcome which was not really expected due to the sensitivity of the issue related to the minority group in Rakhine state.[17]

On the other hand, one of the concerns is about whether the high level of interest by Myanmar's military towards Indonesia's 'dual function' military policies in the past would suggest a delay in the process toward democratisation in Myanmar. At present, the constitutional amendment which requires twenty-five percent of seats in the upper and lower houses of the Myanmar parliament to be assumed by members of the Myanmar military will not be eliminated in the near future. Indonesia, by comparisons, is also struggling to ensure that its own democratisation process would not go backward. Former Indonesian Minister of Foreign Affairs Hassan Wirajuda described this description succinctly by noting:

> During a workshop on security sector reform that I attended in Yangon earlier this year, senior Myanmarese military officers told me they had no intention of playing an active role in politics, unlike the Indonesian military of the past. [...] They continued to ask the Indonesians why in the wake of reform, our military was able to quickly withdraw from its political role in 2004, because they said they didn't think they would be capable of doing it as fast as we did in Indonesia.
>
> From the Indonesian side, we understood that their situation is different, but we reminded them that when Myanmar becomes a more democratic society in line with universal democratic values, the military will have to ultimately withdraw from the political stage. They are seriously considering this, but in terms of timing, it will not be as fast as what we achieved in Indonesia. This is nonetheless part of the process of Myanmar becoming an open and democratic society. (Wirajuda 2014)

Based on discussions with various Indonesian stakeholders, many challenges tend to come from within, rather than posed by the conditions in Myanmar. The first challenge is the view from some segments of Indonesian society that Indonesia is still far from having the capacity to project its own democracy and solutions to human rights problems, including some ethnic conflicts at home. Secondly, there is the problem of a lack of coordination among different agencies in Indonesia, especially among government institutions. Within the government, for example, while the Ministry of Foreign Affairs conducted its diplomacy activities to open up communications and gain trust from the Myanmar government, the other relevant ministries are not really following up to take advantage by bringing in more investments into the country in order to reap some tangible economic benefits.

China's Engageement in Myanmar

Strategic Objectives

China is considered a 'new' actor in the Myanmar peacebuilding process despite the longstanding history between the two states since it has been only recently that Beijing has sought to modify its 'hands-off' approach to domestic politics in Myanmar and instead seek to participate more directly both in the war-to-peace transition in Myanmar as well as that country's economic reform processes. What also makes the China case distinct is that the PRC is widely acknowledged to be rising great power and potential challenger to American policies in Asia, and has been traditionally very sensitive to the security of its borders.

There has been a largely unbroken political partnership between the two states ever since Burma became one of the earliest governments to recognize the People's Republic in June 1950. Burma was also the first non-communist country to recognise the Maoist government in Beijing. Shortly afterwards, a period of what was called '*Pauk Phaw*' (Sino-Burmese kinship) began, based on both states' support for the ideas of peaceful co-existence and decolonisation (Yue 2014). However, Sino-Burmese relations experienced difficulties, and Burma found it difficult to escape the political eddies which were buffeting its northern neighbour during the Maoist era. In the late 1980s, when Myanmar began a period of intensified diplomatic isolation, spearheaded by the United States and Europe. China was one of the few major countries to maintain political and economic relations with the military junta.

By the 1990s and after, there were growing impressions by Western observers and policymakers that Myanmar had become a *de facto* subaltern state to Beijing, an impression which has often been overstated given the more complex political relationship between the two governments during the cold war period. Military ties in the form of arms sales increased after that period, and Chinese legal and illegal migration to Myanmar also increased (Steinberg 2013).

Since the 1990s, energy cooperation has become a core interest in the Sino-Myanmar relationship. Oil and gas development projects proliferated, and in January 2015 the Maday Island oil pipeline which runs from the Myanmar coast to the Chinese city of Kunming in Yunnan province, formally began operations. Beijing has been seeking to develop alternative energy transit routes as an alternative to the Malacca Straits, through which about eighty percent of China's imported oil travels through from Africa and the Middle East (Meyer 2015). Despite the rapid drop in fossil fuel prices since the end of 2014 and the slowing Chinese economy in 2015, access to foreign energy supplies remains a priority for Beijing, given the inherent uncertainty of long-term access. Myanmar remains an important partner in the development of these alternative routes as China seeks greater access to the Indian Ocean and a diversification of trade routes both for trade and for energy imports from the Middle East and Africa.

Other areas of bilateral energy cooperation have been more problematic, such as the Myitsone hydroelectric dam project, located in Kachin State in northern Myanmar and worth about US$3.6 billion and expected to provide power for China's Yunnan province upon completion. Construction began in December 2009, but further work has been in abeyance since September 2011 out of concerns from the Myanmar government about the environmental and political impact of the project. In June 2014, Chinese Premier Li Keqiang called upon the Myanmar government to restart the project, and Beijing remains hopeful that the construction can resume (Harvey 2011). Economic interdependence between China and Myanmar also grew considerably after the late 1980s, with Beijing seeing its southern neighbour as an idea test case for China's developing 'going out' (*zouchuqu* 走出去) policies of expanding Chinese business interests on the regional and international levels. In addition to Myanmar's utility as a transportation corridor into the Indian Ocean, Myanmar's supply of raw materials and fossil fuels were also of great interest to Beijing as the Chinese economy began its 'take-off' phase (Yun Sun 2015). In 1988, as Myanmar was sinking further into diplomatic ostracism, Beijing signed an enhanced trade agreement with its southern neighbour, legalising direct cross-border trade and opening the door to military aid from Beijing (Legene and Ytzen 2014).

Despite some political differences, China is also remains a major supplier of aid to the government of Myanmar, and here has been bilateral consultation on a variety of areas including industrial development, education, corporate social responsibility, and environmental protection. Much Chinese aid and assistance has been in the form of infrastructure, including transportation (roads and railways) as well as ports and communication.[18] China has stressed the idea that peace and stability in Myanmar should be directly linked to combatting poverty and underdevelopment, especially in rural areas, and so much of China's economic assistance has focused on rural regions of Myanmar including in the north.

The border regions remain a security problem for both states, however, as illustrated for example by the 2009 Kokang Incident, when fighting between the Myanmar military and the rebel Myanmar National Democratic Alliance Army (MNDAA), a remnant of the CPB, resulted in an estimated ten thousand, and possibly as many as twenty thousand, refugees crossing the border into China's Yunnan Province. This was the largest refugee flow into China since the Vietnam conflict in the 1970s, and the numbers of refugees crossing into Yunnan caught Chinese officials completely off guard (Storey 2009; Thant Myint-U 2011). The 'Kokang Incident' also explained Beijing's ongoing interest in Myanmar peacebuilding. Any uptick in violence in northern Myanmar could result in further refugee flows into China at a time when Beijing was seeking to push forward austerity measures in the wake of its economic slowdown after 2014.

Border security continues to be a sensitive issue between Beijing and Naypyidaw. On the Myanmar side, there have been concerns expressed in Myanmar policy circles that Beijing was maintaining at least tacit support to armed rebel groups along the border, including the United Wa State Army (UWSA) in northern Myanmar (Lintner 2015).[19] Myanmar officials have been concerned Beijing views these northern armies as potential bargaining chips in maintaining a solid diplomatic and economic relationship with its southern neighbour.

Bilateral Economic Relations

Despite the perception that China's influence would be seriously diluted in the wake of the opening of Myanmar to new trading partners, including the West, as well as developing political differences, overall trade has continued to be strong, jumping from US$4.9 billion in FY 2012-3 to approximately US$7.2 billion in FY 2014-5 (Central Statistical Organization 2015). The addition of new potential trade and investment partners in Myanmar may actually be an advantage, rather than a liability for China since a diversification of economic partners would dampen the impression among some Myanmar policymakers that Beijing has too strong an influence on the Myanmar economy.

As well, the issue of illegal logging, supported by Chinese labourers, came into focus in July 2015 when 155 Chinese nationals were sentenced to life imprisonment for illegal logging activities in northern Myanmar, a case complicated by the fact that the Myanmar government was reportedly seeking to send out a warning to foreign actors not only about engaging in such activities but also about conducting private business deals with ethnic militias in the north. Although all the Chinese workers sentences were released as part of a widespread amnesty by the Thein Sein government later that month, the incident further chilled Sino-Myanmar economic relations (New York Times 2015). Chinese authorities also expressed disappointment at the slow pace of the Letpadaung copper mine project in the Sagaing Region of north-western Myanmar. Protests against the project have been common since 2012, and as one Chinese analyst argued, delays in the project could be traced to Myanmar's 'existing social contradictions' that specifically targeted Chinese business interests in the country (Song 2015; Parameswaran 2015). Overall, there does appear to be growing support within the government of Myanmar to better vary its trade partners.

China and Myanmar also have the opportunity to strengthen their economic relationship via new multilateral initiatives. Myanmar was a founding member of the Beijing-led Asian Infrastructure Investment Bank (AIIB) in March 2015, and Myanmar became an early potential recipient of development funding via the financial institution as the bank began operations in 2016. A US$20 million power plant at Myingyan in the Mandalay region is currently under consideration for AIIB funding.[20] China's 'Belt and One Road' (*yidai yilu* 一带一路), and its accompanying 'Silk Road Fund', with an initial value of US$ 40 billion, organized by Beijing since 2013 may also be of future benefit to Myanmar. In an April 2015 interview with the Chinese news agency *Xinhua*, the Chair of Myanmar's ruling USDP and presidential candidate, U Shwe Mann, expressed appreciation for the Silk Road projects, which are very likely to involve Myanmar given the country's key geographic location (Wang 2015).

Chinese Diplomacy before and after the Elections

Although China wishes to maintain robust relations with the current Myanmar government, Aung San Suu Kyi, the head of the opposition National League of Democracy (NLD), was invited to Beijing in June

2015 and had a direct dialogue with President Xi Jinping, a sign that China was still placing a great deal of importance on its Myanmar relations after the elections and is preparing for a time when the number of Myanmar's foreign policy links will grow and become more diverse.

Cognisant of the current challenges to its reputation in Myanmar, the government of China has sought to take more of a soft power approach towards its southern neighbour. First, Beijing has attempted to play a mediating role in the ongoing peace talks in Myanmar and has offered overall support for the successful completion of the negotiations. China, along with Thailand, has also hosted recent peace talks (Aung Naing Oo 2015). Second, the Chinese Embassy in Yangon has attempted to play a more active role in regional aid and assistance, as illustrated by the response of the Embassy to massive flooding which took place in western Myanmar in August 2015. Beijing released US$300,000 in aid to the region shortly after the flooding began and the newly arrived PRC ambassador to Myanmar, Mr Hong Liang, personally oversaw the delivery of relief supplies to the storm-affected Sagiang region of the country, while individual provinces in China, including Yunnan, also sent aid and supplies (CCTV 2015). China has also been active in developing university exchanges, including with the University of Yangon, and seeks to promote further linkages among research institutions in Myanmar.[21] It remains to be seen, however, to what degree Beijing's attempts at building soft power in Myanmar will counteract growing concerns about Chinese influence in the post-2015 government and politics in the country.

Chinese Views on Peacebuilding: Towards a Greater Pragmatism

Since China joined the United Nations in 1971, there has been a significant evolution of Beijing's overall views on internal intervention in war-to-peace transitions, including in the areas of peacekeeping and peacebuilding. These views have greatly changed from negative to positive, as demonstrated for example in Chinese views on participation in United Nations operations. Once China began to participate in UN missions, there was a preference for sending observers only, during the 1990s, with one exception being the UN Transitional Authority in Cambodia (UNTAC) in 1992–1993 where two separate Chinese engineering battalions were deployed, becoming China's first true 'blue helmets.' At the turn of the century, China agreed to send civilian police units as liaisons to the UN mission in East Timor (Permanent Mission of PRC to UN 2009).

These events suggested that Beijing was growing increasingly comfortable with peace operations under the UN banner, at least in East and Southeast Asia.

Under the administration of Hu Jintao (2002–2012), the Chinese government slowly began to accept both the concept of soft power in international relations and the debates behind it. However, there were occasional indications that Beijing viewed soft power, like hard power, as a source of competition and even possible danger. While the idea of soft power began to circulate in the United States and elsewhere in the West during the 1990s, the concept only began to make tentative appearances in Beijing official statements in the following decade. President Hu, in one of the first official mentions of soft power, stated during a 2006 speech that 'how to identify the orientation of China's cultural development to create a glorious new national culture, and enhance the international competitiveness of our culture, to enhance the soft power of the State, is a major practical issue before us.' (People's Daily 2006).

However, once the concept of 'peaceful rise' began to be discussed at greater length by Chinese policymakers, soft power matters grew beyond questions of culture, becoming increasingly folded into spirited debate by both government and academia over what role soft power might play in gauging the country's overall power levels, especially vis-à-vis the United States. For example, in a landmark 2006 article on the subject of China's developing 'comprehensive national power' (*zonghe guoli* 综合国力), Yan noted that if soft power were to be added to the overall measurement of power levels, Chinese comprehensive power would still be 'inferior' to that of the United States (Yan 2006a, 2006b). Under the Hu government, international law, including the observance of UN protocols, was an increasingly visible part of China's views on foreign policy and international institutions as a way of improving this perceived shortcoming in comprehensive national power. Southeast Asia has become a crucial test case from Chinese attempts to improve its prestige and soft power, through various revised policies including developing a more nuanced approach to peacebuilding.

Soft power also began to be debated in China since the turn of the century within the framework of foreign policy development as the government considered the merits of continuing to adhere to the Deng Xiaoping–era doctrine of keeping a low global profile (Li 2008). Included was the question of whether China's rise meant that its foreign policy should focus on responsibility to match growing Chinese power. As China began to expand its foreign policy interests under President Jiang Zemin in the 1990s, the ideas stressed by Deng during the previous decade about maintaining a low profile and not taking the lead in international affairs, and 'hiding one's light' (*taoguang yanghui* 韬光养晦) began to be viewed as less viable (Guo 2013). China, at this stage, was in the process of making its transition from 'large developing country' to 'rising power'. In Beijing's 2011 White Paper on 'peaceful development' (*heping fazhan* 和平发展), support for building a peaceful global environment was stressed along with the idea that China's armed forces would develop as a defensive force and support military exchanges and develop partnerships both on the regional and the international levels (PRC State Council 2011).

However, China's economic successes and its overall rise, it has been argued, have not removed international (and regional) concern about a possible 'China threat'. This has especially been an issue in the United States, where it was noted that a weaker and divided China tended to be viewed more favorably by the United States while, conversely, a strong and externally oriented China is looked upon more negatively. Thus, Beijing needed to seek ways of developing its strength while continuing to avoid the appearance of challenging the international order. This has proven difficult for a variety of reasons. First, China's rise has been both strategic and economic, with both 'rises' taking place very rapidly and affecting more and more of the international system. The current disputes between China and members of ASEAN, especially the Philippines and Vietnam, over maritime sovereignty in the South China Sea has accentuated concerns that China is playing more assertive and revisionist role in Southeast Asian security. As noted above, Myanmar is seeking to avoid being caught in regional disputes between Beijing and Southeast Asian governments and may be seeking to return to a more non-aligned stance in its foreign policy, placing greater distance between itself and China.

Second, China's military spending, while still nowhere near American levels, has nonetheless increased considerably under Hu Jintao and Xi Jinping, and has resulted in greater power projection capabilities, particularly at sea. This has led to questions about whether Beijing would seek to address long-standing maritime disputes as noted in the introduction to this paper, and even whether China would seek its own *de facto* version of a Monroe Doctrine, an implied sphere of influence in the western half of the Pacific (Yoshihara and Holmes 2011). Third, it was suggested that despite the country's soft power development there remained a high degree of foreign policy 'inconsistency' on Beijing's part, which has made it difficult for the Chinese government to make optimal use of its soft power (Gill and Huang 2009). This has been caused at times by nationalism, concerns over potential 'containment' policies by the West, and internal differences over the future direction of China's international relations. As such, one of the most visible ways by which Beijing is attempting to satisfy the dueling demands of building both military and soft power internationally, while under considerable global scrutiny, is through its commitments to UN peacekeeping.

China's increased engagement with international peacekeeping missions has been acknowledged as a necessary building block for the development of Chinese soft power, as well as promoting the idea of China as an 'internationally socialized country' (Guo 2007; Wuthnow 2008) and a 'responsible power'. The latter concept, facilitates the development of Chinese peacekeeping policy by allowing Beijing to define its own peacekeeping role, to further integrate into the international system without necessarily adhering to Western foreign policy models, to critique the international system, and to underscore that China is developing into an atypical great power which respects international sovereignty (Richardson 2011). Moreover, China's peacekeeping commitments since the 1990s have allowed that country's military to operate far away from Chinese soil without triggering anxieties from its neighbors or the United States in the wake of Beijing's expanded military budgets and capabilities.

By the beginning of this century, China was openly supportive of the peacekeeping idea both as a way of prompting peaceful multilateral settlement of disputes and as a means to include its armed forces in 'Military Operations other than War,' or MOOTW, including humanitarian missions, disaster relief and increasingly peacekeeping missions. The concept was borrowed from American post–Cold War military terminology to refer to noncombat military operations (Gill and Huang 2009; Fravel 2011). Southeast Asia had been a major beneficiary of Beijing's changed views on peacekeeping, as Beijing was supportive of the development of the UN Transitional Authority in Cambodia (UNTAC) in 1992–1993 despite China's difficult history with that conflict. China was also willing to send civilian policy to assist with the United Nations Transitional Administration in East Timor (UNTAET), despite the fact that the major element of that deployment was to prepare for the independence of Timor-Leste (Lanteigne 2014). China has been traditionally wary of international intervention in separatist crises out of concern for precedent, but has begun to better differentiate between 'good' and 'bad' forms of intervention in the name of peacebuilding. War-to-peace traditions via the UN are considered ideal models for China and far better options than unilateral or great power-led peacebuilding initiatives. For example, Beijing was highly critical of NATO operations in Serbia-Kosovo in 1999, and more recently the American and European operations which toppled the Gaddafi government in Libya in 2011, actions which Beijing blames for starting the ongoing civil war there.

A major element of China's success in developing its peacekeeping practices as a factor in its soft power development is that the country has consistently approached overall peacebuilding practices via policies more consistent with 'middle-power' status rather than that of the great power it was quickly developing into. Beijing's lack of history as a colonial power, and its policies dating well back to the Maoist era of solidarity and support for developing countries and regions including in South and Southeast Asia, (the so-called 'Bandung Spirit' of the mid-1950s) (Cao 2005), have helped underscore the perceptions which Beijing is seeking to put forward that China as a state that eschews the great power chauvinism and at times hegemonic conduct of previous great powers, especially the West.

In its diplomacy in developing countries, China retains many vestiges of previous 'large developing country' thinking which, in the case of its peacekeeping and peacebuilding policies, have served Chinese interests very well. However, in light of China's increasing power and growing ever closer to traditional great-power status, an argument can be made that the country's middle-power approach to peacekeeping may be less viable in the future. This would have an adverse effect on China's ability to promote peacekeeping as a key component in its soft power development. Nonetheless, China continues to maintain ties between soft power development and engagement with various forms of peacebuilding/war-to-peace transition policies. In September 2015, this commitment was further underscored during President Xi's speech to the United Nations General Assembly. Xi offered to commit eight thousand Chinese personnel for a standby UN peacekeeping force, as well as offering greater support for Un requests for engineering and medical staff, on the condition that 'exit strategies needed to be timely formulated and executed.' (Martina and Brunnstrom 2015).

China and Myanmar Peacebuilding

As a core member of the group of actors seeking to shepherd a successful cease fire agreement in Myanmar in the next year, Beijing has attempted to soften its reputation in the country in the wake of mistrust both from elements of the Myanmar government and the public, while at the same time discourage a 'Western drift' in Myanmar's foreign relations given the important role the country plays in China's future regional development plans. As well, the events since the beginning of 2015 have also underscored the close connection between China's southern border security and the successful completion of the peace process. Due to its sensitivity to being perceived as a spoiler or a revisionist power in all four streams of the Myanmar peace process, China has chosen to emphasize the role of education, anti-poverty measures, and infrastructure in Myanmar as its main contributions to the peacebuilding process.

These approaches have been in keeping with its traditional policies of aid and assistance which favour keeping a strong separation between governance and economics, while also drawing a distinct connection between poverty and underdevelopment on one side and insecurity on the other. As noted above, Beijing is also stressing that it is willing to work with any successor government after the November 2015 vote, as illustrated by the willingness of the Xi government to open communications with the NLD and Ms Suu Kyi. At the same time, China is also developing a peacebuilding policy in Myanmar that incorporates sub-governmental activities including educational and training programmes in rural regions, especially in the northern provinces, to stress the need for more balanced development in the country.[22]

China, as a participant in the ceasefire process in Myanmar, has also been notably active in calling for an end to hostilities between the MNDAA and the Myanmar government as part of Beijing's desire to pacify the border between the two states. In June 2015 it was announced that a ceasefire would go into effect after four months of coercive diplomacy by China (McLaughlin and Zaw 2015). Beijing continues to support a wider pacification of the Myanmar border region s through the development and signing of a National Ceasefire Agreement (NCA). According to Chinese officials based in Yangon and Jakarta, China has approached the Myanmar peacebuilding process based on its traditional views of the sanctity of state borders and a high regard for sovereignty and the rights of the people of Myanmar to take the lead in their political interests. As well, China remains Myanmar's top trade partner and has been in the best position to promote economic development in the country. China's interest in developing a strong ceasefire, according to Beijing representatives, was the concerns that the border region become stable and open to legal cross-border trade. China has also been a supporter of the BCIM (Bangladesh, China, India, Myanmar) trade corridor as part of Beijing's views that anti-poverty policies and peace are closely linked.

However, according to many persons interviewed in Yangon, China still has much work to do in promoting itself as a force for peace and stability given its long history with the military governments in Myanmar. A senior member of the ceasefire negotiation team, representing the Myanmar Peace Centre, issued a statement in September 2015 that Beijing was interfering with the process and encouraging two groups, the United Wa State Army (UWSA) and the Kachin Independence Organization (KIO) to eschew an agreement out of a desire to keep a high degree of control over the China-Myanmar border region. These charges were vehemently denied by Beijing, with the government stressing its support for a complete and comprehensive cessation of hostilities throughout Myanmar (Wee 2015; Meng 2015).

Comparative Cases of Peacebuilding Actors

Norway

Norway has developed a longstanding, if at times controversial, relationship with the governments of Myanmar over the past decade. The country developed a reputation for being an 'honest broker' due to its willingness to communicate and negotiate with the pre-reform military governments in Myanmar. With the 1991 Nobel Peace Prize being awarded to Aung San Suu Kyi (2010), Norway had been viewed as helping the question of the peace process of Myanmar to gain further international stature. Some Myanmar opposition figures have been unhappy with the decision by Oslo to meet directly with the military government of Myanmar, but Norway has established itself as a key mediator in the peace process. Norwegian businesses, most notably the telecommunications firm Telenor, also have a high profile in Myanmar (Telenor 2017). However, with the reform process continuing and with other countries in Europe, such as Germany, increasing their contacts with Myanmar in recent years, there is the question of whether Norway's special role in the country can be maintained.

Norway played a primary coordinating role among donors in Myanmar around peace issues. On the governmental level, there has been much in the way of institution-building between Norway and Myanmar in the area of peacebuilding. For example, Norway established the twin institutions of the Myanmar Peace Support Initiative (MPSI) and the Peace Donor Support Group (PDSG) in 2012 at the request of Myanmar authorities (Government of Norway 2013). The MPSI was established to engage the Myanmar government, the country's military, as well as non-state armed and political groups, civil society actors and communities, in addition to international actors, to provide concrete support to the ceasefire process and emerging peace process. Various projects have been initiated via the MPSI in ceasefire areas and in conjunction with relevant stakeholders.

Yet, the reputation of Norway in Myanmar as a peacebuilding actor has been mixed in recent years largely due to the approach which Oslo has taken regarding direct contacts and mediation efforts with the disputants in Myanmar. It has been argued that Norway's 'normative' approach to the peacebuilding process in Myanmar was conducted along similar lines as Norwegian mediation activities in Sri Lanka during that country's long civil conflict (Sánchez-Cacicedo 2014). While Oslo distinguished itself among other Western actors, including the United States, Australia, Canada and other Western European countries, which largely sought to isolate the military regime in Myanmar since the 1990s, Norway's status as a 'white knight' did fall under some criticism from some actors in Myanmar and elsewhere in Asia both for Oslo's willingness to engage with political and military institutions in the country which have been accused of gross misconduct, but also that Norway's approach has lacked depth and greater understanding of political and socio-economic conditions 'on the ground', especially in the embattled northern regions on the country.[23]

Nonetheless, Norway has maintained a distinct status in the country both as a result of its peacebuilding efforts and the legacy of the Peace Prize, an act which brought the political and security situation in Myanmar to global attention and prompted greater international pressure for Ms. Suu Kyi's release and for reforms both in governance and foreign policy as well as a halt to the ethnic conflicts in the country (Johnsen 2015). Ms. Suu Kyi was finally able to accept the Prize in person in Oslo in 2012. In her speech, she stated,

> The Burmese concept of peace can be explained as the happiness arising from the cessation of factors that militate against the harmonious and the wholesome. The word *nyein-chan* translates literally as the beneficial coolness that comes when a fire is extinguished. Fires of suffering and strife are raging around the world. In my own country, hostilities have not ceased in the far north; to the west, communal violence resulting in arson and murder were taking place just several days before I started out on the journey that has brought me here today. (Suu Kyi 1991)

Norway has been seeking to develop its soft power in the months leading up the elections, through various forms of aid and assistance to urban and rural areas as well as relief efforts in the wake of the August 2015 cyclone and subsequent flooding in the western regions of Myanmar. The government of Norway pledged NoK10 million (US$1.2 million) in aid to the region after the flooding began, and has worked towards better early warning facilities in order to reduce the number of casualties after future such disasters. However, other donations which Oslo made to Rakhine State were met with some criticism in Myanmar due to concerns this aid was favouring the Rohingya peoples, which are not considered a legal minority by authorities in Myanmar, and in a broader sense that Norwegian businesses were profiting on the coattails of Oslo's role in the peace process (News and Views from Norway 2014; McGregor 2015) Two Norwegian firms which have greatly increased their visibility in Myanmar since the peace process began has been the telecommunications corporation Telenor and the state energy firm Statoil. In 2015, an agreement was pending to allow Statoil access to a maritime block in order to survey for potential oil and gas.

There have been calls, especially from local educational actors, for Oslo to better diversify its aid and assistance portfolio in Myanmar by offering greater research links, student and faculty exchanges, and joint programmes in the country.[24] There are plans for the Norwegian Embassy in Yangon to move within the city to a more central location, and to be based within a 'Nordic House' which would share facilities with the embassies of Denmark, Finland and Sweden, presenting more of a Nordic model of diplomacy to Myanmar.[25] Norway has been caught up in the final states of the National Ceasefire Agreement, as some of the ethnic minority actors involved have requested that Oslo, along with the United States, Great Britain, Japan and the European Union be included. Earlier in 2015, the government of Myanmar agreed to expand the list of witnesses from solely the United Nations, ASEAN and China to include Thailand and India (Lun Min Mang 2015). Norway, however, was accepted by the Myanmar government as an election observer for the November 2015 vote, along with the European Union, Canada and Switzerland (Bangkok Post 2015). Although Norway may find itself having to compete with a larger array of foreign partners in Myanmar, including other Western European actors such as the UK and Germany, should the reform processes succeed and the peacebuilding process take root, Oslo is still in a strong position to maintain a distinct peacebuilding identity in Myanmar.

India

India has developed particular interests toward Myanmar, especially after the implementation of its 'Look East' policy in the early 1990s. Although India is the largest democracy in the world, its engagement with Myanmar has focused on economics and development, with no deliberate promotion of democratic values even during the opening process in Myanmar five years ago. While New Delhi has been open to the idea of 'sharing' its democratic experiences, the Indian government has insisted that the initiative should purely come from Myanmar, and that nothing should be done before India sees a more positive signal from Myanmar. As one regional specialist noted, India's initiative to promote democracy abroad is based on 'realist' political concerns, which emphasises the country's strategic aims, especially countering the expansion of Chinese influence in the Southeast Asian region and gaining support in the fight against separatist forces in the Indian northeast, and economic interests rather than an idealistic motivation (Cartwright 2009).

Second, in spite of the great improvement in relations between India and Myanmar, especially due to the investment activities in infrastructure including road and air links, banking services, and information technology, the Myanmar government has been very careful to balance its relations with India by continuing to engage with China. Yet, at the same time, Myanmar is trying as much as possible to maintain this delicate balance in order not to step between these two rising Asian giants. Therefore, as argued by Kanwal (2010), Myanmar's deliberate engagement with China, framed in economic and military cooperation, has been particularly aimed to 'keep India off balance and prevent its rise as a competing regional power.' Although it has been suggested that New Delhi will benefit by default from the current expansion of Myanmar's foreign policy interests and desire to move away from an overdependence on Beijing, there has been little sign that India is any position to directly compete with China on the economic or diplomatic front, and there are perceptions in Myanmar that India is more interested in balancing Chinese influence than deepening long-term investment in Myanmar (Jaishankar 2015).

Indian interests in peacebuilding in Myanmar have been framed by a strong perceived link between promoting economic development and regional stability and a consolidation of the war-to-peace transition in Myanmar. Before the military era, Indian entrepreneurs had an high profile in Burma, especially in Yangon, but cross-border relations foundered by the 1980s and did not recover until the beginning of the reform era and a thawing of relations in the wake of then-Myanmar President Thein Sein's visit to Delhi in 2011 when the beginnings of potential joint projects were discussed. The focus in India regarding Myanmar is about 'connectivity', meaning the building of roads, other transportation links and communications between the two states to promote trade and cooperation.[26] Related to these areas has been the prospect of developing links based on IT, financial institutions and tourism. In regards to the disarmament process, India is not a part of the cease-fire negotiations, unlike China, and New Delhi has expressed concern about the security situation in western Myanmar and especially Rakhine, (although specific mention of the Rohingya issue was avoided). Although Indian officials are reluctant to speak about diplomatic and strategic competition with China, there is an economic dimension to India's engagement of the region, including participating in the port project at Sittwe on the Bay of Bengal. Among Myanmar officials spoken to, there was some lingering scepticism about whether India's burst of diplomatic and economic activity in Myanmar is a direct product of the desire to 'check' Beijing in the Indian Ocean.

As well, India and Myanmar are still addressing border security differences, as well as lingering Burmese traditional resistance toward the Indians inherited from the unfortunate position of the Indians during the colonial era. It has been estimated that there are as many as one million Myanmarese of Indian origin. India's infrastructure projects are still relatively low-key and peripheral, (i.e. only situated at the border areas), compared to China, for example. Furthermore, Indian development assistance in order to improve the education and health conditions in Myanmar, hampered by low transnational connections between Indian NGOs and Myanmar NGOs, have not been sufficient to overcome its deep-rooted image deficit there (Egreteau 2011). Thus, such conditions have limited India's role, especially in peacebuilding in Myanmar.

Japan

Japan and Myanmar have a long post-WWII history of engagement. Japan was an occupying power during the Second World War between 1942 and 1945, but between 1955 and 1988, Japanese aid to the country was estimated at US$2.2 billion, and until 1988 Tokyo was by far the largest aid and trade partner under the military-socialist era in Burma between 1962 and 1988. During that period, the Burmese government embarked on a *de facto* 'Look East' policy with a strong emphasis on deepening ties with Tokyo.

However, as a result of the military coup and the beginning of the SLORC government in 1988, Tokyo soon lost much diplomatic and economic ground for many reasons. First, under Japanese law, Burma had to be re-recognized under the new military government, which caused legal and political red tape for almost a year after the coup. Second, the SLORC government was less inclined to view Japan as a key economic partner than its predecessor. Finally, the United States placed heavy pressure on Japan to join in the West's sanctions regime against the SLORC government, badly weakening Tokyo's economic presence in the country. Even today, there remains a bilateral diplomatic dispute as a result of the shooting of a Japanese journalist during the 2007 'Saffron Revolution' protests in Yangon, an incident which the Myanmar government has yet to make a formal apology for. Tokyo is therefore in a strong position to play a greater peacebuilding role in the future given Japan's growing economic interests in the Myanmar reform process.

Although Japanese trade with Myanmar remains smaller than China's, and has been rising at a much slower rate, estimated at only US$500 million in 2008, but rising after the reforms began to coalesce to US$1.5 billion in FY 2012-3 and then rising to US$1.7 billion in FY 2014-5 (JETRO 2014; CSO 2015), Tokyo has greatly increased its aid and development presence in the region since the 2011 reforms began. Summit diplomacy in Myanmar has also been a priority for Japan, as Prime Minister Shinzō Abe has made two visits to Myanmar during his second term in office. The first visit was in May 2013 when he agreed to write off about US$2 billion in remaining Myanmar loans to Japan while announcing new aid initiatives, and the second took place in November 2014 when new overseas development assistance loans for infrastructure improvements were announced.[27]

Other Japanese projects elsewhere in Myanmar included loans for improving communications in the capital of Naypyidaw, providing road construction equipment in Rakhine and weather monitoring systems for various parts of the country. Japan has also been active in developing infrastructure in Yangon, providing new grants via the Japan International Cooperation Agency (JICA) for waterworks, hospital upgrades and bridge construction, and providing technical assistance with Yangon port facilities upgrades and the Greater Yangon Urban Development plan since 2012.

In terms of more direct participation in peacebuilding initiatives in Myanmar, Tokyo is a member of the Peace Support Group (PSG) in the country along with the United States, Australia, Canada, the EU, Norway and Switzerland. During the signing of the cease-fire between the government of Myanmar and eight of the ethnic armed groups from the northern edges of the country, the Government of Japan was a participant in the signing, as well as the Nippon Foundation, a philanthropic organisation with longstanding interests in the peace process (Factiva 2015). However, according to the *Irrawaddy* news service, Japan's deeper participation in the peace process has been hampered by opposition from China, which has been against the inclusion of Japanese and Western actors into the ceasefire negotiations (Aung Zaw 2015).

Switzerland

In keeping with Switzerland's venerable foreign policy of neutrality, which had been in place for centuries and had been codified and internationally recognised after 1815 (Church and Head 2013), the country has sought to play a peacebuilding role in Myanmar through programs oriented towards arbitration and education. Switzerland has been active in the current preparations for the Myanmar elections by developing activities through the Swiss Agency for Development and Cooperation (SDC) and other parts of the Swiss government to assist with voter preparation and education. Switzerland has called for ongoing dialogue between all major actors in the electoral process, including political parties, election officials, the media, and civil society organisations. In conjunction with the government of Germany and the International Labour Organisation (ILO), Switzerland has also been teaching vocational skills in Myanmar, including in areas of industry and tourism.

Myanmar peacebuilding projects undertaken by the Swiss government have included drafting a Code of Conduct (CoC) in October 2014 for all participating political parties, (estimated to number about ninety by August 2015), in the November 2015 elections, educating voters and parties on the democratic process, and supporting civil society and media organisations. These projects were undertaken using a 'hands-off' approach which specifically avoids any impression of political bias according to one Swiss official.[28] Among the provisions of the CoC are pledges for all parties to respect the right to peaceful assembly and campaign activities, to settle disputes between parties in a cordial fashion, to avoid tactics synonymous with slander, to avoid discrimination during campaigning as well as the visible display of weaponry, and to avoid intimidation and dissemination of false information (FDFA 2014; Swissinfo 2015). The Embassy has also established mobile units for education on voter rights and responsibilities to more remote regions of the country. Plans are also underway for educational exchanges which would allow students to learn about politics and democratisation in Geneva and Bern. These courses would include case studies of federalism, which until recently had been a politically off-limits subject in Myanmar since for many years the military government in the country equated federalism with a unacceptable level of power devolution and a heightened risk of ethnic separatism.[29]

However, the spirit and letter of the CoC were threatened by laws which were implemented by the Myanmar government in the months leading up the elections, including a controversial ban on political parties from criticising the armed forces as well as disrespecting the country's 2008 constitution which guarantees the reservation of one-quarter of all seats in the upper and lower houses of the Myanmar parliament for the Myanmar Armed Forces/*Tatmadaw* (Slodkowski and Aung Hla Tun 2015). These restrictions, however, did very little to prevent the electoral landslide by the NLD after the November 2015 vote.

A large majority of political parties agreed to abide by the CoC and to participate fairly in the process. Switzerland has also been a supporter of human rights development in the country, and has advised on the Myanmar peace process via the Foreign Affairs Ministry's Human Security Division (HSD) (FDFA 2013). In the area of economic assistance, Switzerland has especially concentrated its Myanmar aid programmes in the country's south-eastern regions, including Kayin and Mon provinces. This region was chosen due to its compatibility with Swiss development initiatives for Myanmar, including promoting cohabitation between majority Burmese and ethnic minority groups, the possibility of a special economic zone being created in the Dawei region, and the promotion of legalised cross-border trade between Myanmar and its neighbours to the east, specifically Thailand.

Lessons Learned

The fieldwork completed for this chapter suggests a great deal of policy similarities between so-called 'old' and 'new' actors in Myanmar peacebuilding. Thus, collaboration between traditional actors and new actors is the most ideal framework to maintain, but the process should be undertaken on as much of an equal footing as possible. New(er) actors have the comparative advantage of having not too distant memories/experiences, or even still struggling with their own peacebuilding processes, as in the case of Indonesia:

1. Still relatively applicable for the host country.
2. New actors have more ability to have 'empathy' with the host countries as they might also encounter the same problems/challenges before.
3. Having the advantage to come in the position to 'dictating' or 'prescribing' but rather 'sharing' lessons learned, experiences, including past mistakes—equal footing.

China, as well, is addressing Myanmar peacebuilding with a great deal of local and regional concerns:

1. Safety of the Sino-Myanmar border, while ensuring cross-border trade can continue and grow.
2. Stress over the rights and responsibilities of being a great power in East Asia and moving away from its persons of being a large developing state.
3. Ensure it retains a place in the peacebuilding process despite the rapid introduction of new actors, including Japan, into the peacebuilding milieu.
4. Developing a more congenial identity in Myanmar after years of strong relations between Beijing and the Myanmar military regimes.

Traditional actors, on the other hand, also have their own comparative advantages, (including 'first mover' advantages which have been a boon some actors including Norway). These include:

1. Capacity to provide funding and related support

2. Ability to develop a more systematic approach with clear instruments to measure achievements and results.
3. Have more energy to focus on peacebuilding efforts abroad since the developed countries have settled their own peacebuilding process long-time ago.

Conclusion

On 8 November 2015, Myanmar held the second democratic election after the result of the first multi-party election in 1990 was cancelled by the military junta. Earlier anxieties that this election would end up in the same fate proved to be wrong as the ruling military government under the leadership of President Thein Sein congratulated the National League of Democracy as soon as the result indicated a landslight victory for Aung San Suu Kyi's party.

The Indonesian government, through the press statement released by the Foreign Ministry expressed appreciation for the peaceful election process taken place in the country. More importantly, Indonesia has reiterated its commitment to continue to suppport Myanmar in its efforts towards sustainable reform and democratization, through cooperation in bilateral and ASEAN framework (Kemlu 2015). However, such statement, according to certain element in Indonesia has been considered as not only too late as it was released almost in the end of the month, but even worse was failed to send a clear message to indicate Indonesia's 'constructive engagement' approach to ensure the democratization process to be still on track. Such message is crucial because Indonesia, as elucidated in the editorial of the *Jakarta Post* published on 12 November 2015, is "constitutionally and morally responsible for helping all parties in Myanmar, including its army generals, reach this goal, no matter how painful the sacrifices they have to endure during the transition to democracy." (Jakarta Post 2015) With this clear trajectory, then Indonesia can maintain its proactive role to continue sharing its experiences in sustaining democracy in the country.

Looking at the existing challenges faced by the country, it is most likely that its foreign policy will seek to invite more investments from different countries to pour into the country to boost its economic growth. But, at least there is one common position between the NLD and the Indonesian government regarding the foreign policy direction. Based on the 2015 Election Manifesto of the NLD, foreign policy will be directed to 'pursue an active and independent foreign policy, and to establish friendly and close political relations.' (NLD 2015) On this point, this is a good beginning for the two countries to enhance their cooperation into a higher level, especially to maintain ASEAN unity the midst of competition among the major powers to spread their influences in the Southeast Asia region. However, the new Myanmar's leadership interest towards ASEAN remains in question mark since the regional organisation has been perceived as being too accommodative to the military junta regime in the past due to non-interference principle upheld by ASEAN, which then limited its interactions with NLD as the opposition party at that time. (Myint Thin 2013)

Notes

1. The founding members of ASEAN when the organisation was created in August 1967 were Indonesia, Malaysia, the Philippines, Singapore, and Thailand.
2. Indonesia donated around 22.4 tonnes of food, clothes and medicines and deployed medical team comprised of 30 personnel. See "TNI Hercules Delivers Humanitarian Aid to Myanmar [Hercules TNI Angkut Bantuan Kemanusiaan ke Myanmar]," http://tni.mil.id/view-9696-hercules-tni-angkut-bantuan-kemanusiaan-ke-myanmar.html, accessed March 27, 2017
3. Interview with Chief Military Training, Myanmar Armed Forces, August 2015.
4. Interview with Lt. Gen. Agus Widjojo, August 12, 2015.
5. Interview with Hassan Wirajuda, August 11, 2015.
6. Interview with Hassan Wirajuda, August 11, 2015.
7. Interview with MoFA, Directorate of East Asian and Pacific Affairs, August 10, 2015.
8. Interview with Hassan Wirajuda, August 11, 2015.
9. In some capacity building projects, such as in agricultural sector, economic development, women's empowerment were funded by the Indonesian government. However, for trainings and workshops related to peacebuilding were funded externally from the third parties. The Institute for Peace and Democracy, for example, has been working closely with funding agencies from Australia, Denmark, Japan, the Netherlands, New Zealand, Norway, the United States and the European Union. Then, the latest specific training organised by the Indonesian government for the Myanmar police was supported by the government of the United Kingdom.
10. So far, 58 countries have been listed as participants, namely Indonesia, Afghanistan, Armenia, Australia, Azerbaijan, Bahrain, Bangladesh, Bhutan, Brunei Darussalam, Cambodia, China, Fiji Islands, Georgia, India, Iran, Iraq, Japan, Jordan, Kazakhstan, Kiribati, Republic of Korea, Kuwait,

Kirgyzstan, Lao PDR, Lebanon, Malaysia, Maldives, Marshall Islands, Micronesia, Mongolia, Myanmar, Nauru, Nepal, New Zealand, Oman, Pakistan, Palau, Palestine, Papua New Guinea, The Philippines, Qatar, Russia, Saudi Arabia, Singapore, Solomon Islands, Sri Lanka, Tajikistan, Thailand, Tonga, Timor Leste, Turkey, Turkmenistan, Tuvalu, United Arab Emirates, Uzbekistan, Vanuatu, Vietnam, Yemen. See https://bdf.kemlu.go.id/about/participants, accessed March 27, 2016.

11. From 26 August to 1 September 2012, IPD in collaboration with the Presidential Advisory Council of Indonesia and the Indonesian Embassy in Yangon visited the country to conduct the scoping mission. During the visit, the Indonesian delegation,et with the Advisors of the President of Myanmar, the Myanmar National Human Rights Commission, Myanmar Development Resources Institute, Group of Democracy (the group of political parties in Myanmar) and the Union of Election Commission. See http://www.ipd.or.id/democratic-transition-in-myanmar.htm, accessed March 27, 2016.
12. Interview with former Indonesian Ambassador Sebastianus Sumarsono. The ambassador managed to do the observation in the Northern part, while other officials went to the South, West, East and Cental regions.
13. Muhammadiyah activists have involved in intensive communications with colleagues from the Center for Peace and Conflict Studies (CPCS) and The Center for Diversity and National Harmony (CDNH) and given access to utilise the Need Assessment Report of the Rakhine Province regarding peacebuilding in the area which can be used in creating the action plan for Muhammadiyah's participation in dealing with Rohingya problem.
14. For example, CSIS has received urgent request to continue its activities in Myanmar by creating a project to share its experiences in managing ethnic relations in conflict-prone areas.
15. Interview with some lecturers in Department of International Relations from Yangon University, August 2015.
16. Interview with Lt. Gen. (ret) Agus Widjojo, August 2014.
17. Interview with Habibie Center, August 2015.
18. Interview with Chinese government officials, Yangon, August 2015.
19. Bertil Lintner, "Same Game, Different Tactics," *The Irrawaddy*, July 2015, 14–19.
20. Interviews with Chinese Embassy officials, Yangon, April 2015; "Myanmar: Myingyan Power Plant Project," *Asian Infrastructure Investment Bank* (AIIB), https://www.aiib.org/en/projects/approved/2016/myingyan-power-plant.html, accessed September 26, 2016
21. Interviews with administrators at the University of Yangon, Yangon, August 2015.

22. Interviews with Chinese Embassy officials, Yangon, April 2015.
23. Interviews with Myanmar policy officials and education specialists in Yangon, August 2015; Interviews with Myanmar foreign policy specialists, Beijing, July 2015.
24. Interviews with education officials and lecturers, University of Yangon, August 2015.
25. Interviews with Norwegian Embassy officials, Yangon, August 2015.
26. Interview with senior Indian Embassy official, Yangon, August 2015.
27. Interviews with Japanese Embassy officials, Yangon, August 2015.
28. Interview with senior Switzerland Embassy official, Yangon, August 2015.
29. Interviews with Embassy of Switzerland officials, Yangon, August 2015.

References

Anwar, Dewi Fortuna. 2005. *Indonesia at Large: Collected Writings on ASEAN, Foreign Policy, Security and Democratisation*. Jakarta: The Habibie Center.

Aung, Naing Oo. 2015a. Armed Conflict: The Beginning of the End. *Myanmar Times*, August 25. http://www.mmtimes.com/index.php/opinion/16137-armed-conflict-the-beginning-of-the-end.html

Aung, Zaw. 2015b. Of Pomp and Peace. *The Irrawaddy*, October 16.

Cao, Desheng. 2005. 'Bandung Spirit' Lives on after 50 Years. *China Daily*, April 19.

Cartwright, Jan. 2009. India's Regional and International Support for Democracy: Rhetoric or Reality? *Asian Survey* 49(3): 403–428.

Central Statistical Organisation. 2015. Ministry of National Planning and Economic Development. Myanmar. Accessed September 2, 2015. https://www.csostat.gov.mm/s1.4MA0201.htm

Chachavalpongpun, Pavin. 2010. Last Bus to Naypidaw. In *Myanmar/Burma: Inside Challenges, Outside Interests*, ed. Alexis Rieffel. Washington, DC: Brookings.

Church, Clive H., and Randolph C. Head. 2013. *A Concise History of Switzerland*. Cambridge and New York: Cambridge University Press.

Dunia. 2014. Jokowi: Indonesia to Invest in 3 Sectors in Myanmar [Jokowi: Indonesia Investasi 3 Sektor di Myanmar]. *Tempo*. November 12, 2014. Accessed November 15, 2014. http://dunia.tempo.co/read/news/2014/11/12/118621420/jokowi-indonesia-investasi-3-sektor-di-myanmar

Egreteau, Renaud. 2011. A Passage to Burma? India, Development, and Democratization in Myanmar. *Contemporary Politics* 17(4, December): 467–486.

Federal Department of Foreign Affairs (FDFA), Switzerland. 2013. Swiss Cooperation Strategy Myanmar, 2013–2017. Accessed July. https://www.eda.

admin.ch/content/dam/deza/en/documents/Laender/Swiss_Myanmar_strategy_2013_2017.pdf

———. 2014. Code of Conduct for Political Parties and Candidates. Accessed October. https://www.eda.admin.ch/content/dam/countries/countries-content/myanmar/en/Code%20of%20Conduct%20for%20Political%20Parties%20and%20Candidates_Eng.pdf

Firdaus, Farid. 2015. Lippo Group Inaugurates First Myanmar Hospital, Plans $1b Investment. *The Jakarta Globe*, June 7. http://thejakartaglobe.beritasatu.com/news/lippo-group-inaugurates-first-myanmar-hospital-plans-1b-investment/

Fravel. 2011. Economic Growth, Regime Insecurity, and Military Strategy: Explaining the Rise of Noncombat Operations in China. *Asian Security* 7(3): 177–200.

Garuda Indonesia. 2015. The Strategic Cooperation will Further Strengthen Both Airlines' Flight Network and Provide Seamless Yet Convenient Connections between Indonesia and Myanmar. Accessed March 27, 2017. https://www.garuda-indonesia.com/id/en/news-and-events/Garuda-indonesia-myanmar-airways-tandatanganikerjasama-codeshare.page

Gill, Bates and Chin-Hao Huang. 2009. China's Expanding Peacekeeping Role: Its Significance and Policy Implications. SIPRI Policy Brief, 1–7 (February).

Guo, Shuyong. 2007. Xin guoji zhuyi yu ruan shili waijiao [The New Internationalism and China's Soft Power Diplomacy]. *Guoji guancha [Global Perspective]* 2.

Guo, Sujian. 2013. *Chinese Politics and Government: Power, Ideology and Organisation*. London and New York: Routledge.

Harvey, Rachel. 2011. Burma Dam: Why Myitsone Plan is Being Halted. *BBC News*, September 30.

Htoo, Thant. 2015. Police Study Up on Election Rules. *Myanmar Times*, February 27. http://www.mmtimes.com/index.php/national-news/13252-police-get-training-ahead-of-election.html

Indonesian Embassy [Kedutaan Besar Republik Indonesia]. 2001. *Sang Merah Putih di Tanah Pagoda: Kenangan, Masa Kini, dan Harapan [The Red and White (Indonesian Flag) in the Pagoda Land: Memory, Now, and Future]*. Yangon: Indonesian Embassy.

Institute for Policy Analysis of Conflict. n.d. Indonesian Extremists and the Rohingya Issue. http://www.understandingconflict.org/conflict/read/9/INDONESIAN-EXTREMISTS-AND-THE-ROHINGYA-ISSUE

Jaishankar, Dhruva. 2015. Myanmar is Pivoting Away from China. *Foreign Policy*, June 15. http://foreignpolicy.com/2015/06/15/myanmar-burma-is-pivoting-away-from-china-aung-san-suu-kyi-xi-jinping-india/

Japan External Trade Organisation (JETRO). 2014. Japanese Trade and Investment Statistics. https://www.jetro.go.jp/en/reports/statistics/

Johnsen, Ingveld. 2015. Gifts Favour the Giver: Norway, Status and the Nobel Peace Prize. In *Small State Status Seeking: Norway's Quest for International Standing*, ed. Iver B. Neumann and Benjamin de Carvalho. London and New York: Routledge.

Kanwal, Gurmeet. 2010. A Strategic Perspective on India-Myanmar Relations. In *Myanmar/ Burma Inside Challenges, Outside Interests*, ed. Lex Rieffel. Washington, DC: Brookings Institution Press.

Kemlu. 2015. Indonesia Congratulates Myanmar for the Official Result of Myanmar Election. *Indonesian Ministry of Foreign Affairs.* November 24, 2015. Accessed March 27, 2017. http://www.kemlu.go.id/en/berita/Pages/Indonesia-Congratulates-Myanmar-for-the-Official-Result-of-Myanmar-Election.aspx

Kompas. 2009. Crucial, The Direct Trade Indonesia-Myanmar [Penting, Perdagangan Langsung Indonesia-Myanmar]. Kompas.com, July 6. Accessed March 27, 2017. http://bisniskeuangan.kompas.com/read/2009/03/17/05300219/Penting.Perdagangan.Langsung.Indonesia-Myanmar.

Lanteigne. 2014. Red and Blue: China's Evolving United Nations Peacekeeping Policies and Soft Power Development. In *Asia-Pacific Nations in International Peace Support and Stability Missions*, ed. Chiyuki Aoi and Yee-Kuang Heng, 113–140. New York: Palgrave Macmillan.

Lee, Susan and Mi Ki Kyaw Myint. 2015. Myanmar Election Commission Visits Indonesia. In *Asia*, May 20. http://asiafoundation.org/in-asia/2015/05/20/myanmar-election-commission-visits-indonesia/

Legêne, Josine, and Flemming Ytzen. 2014. International Actors. In *Burma/ Myanmar: Where Now?* ed. Mikael Gravers and Flemming Ytzen. Copenhagen: NIAS Press.

Li, Mingjiang. 2008. China Debates Soft Power. *Chinese Journal of International Politics* 2(June): 287–308.

Lintner, Bertil. 2015. Same Game, Different Tactics. *The Irrawaddy*, July 2015.

Lun, Min Mang. 2015. Govt. Agrees to More International Witnesses. *Myanmar Times*, August 7. http://www.mmtimes.com/index.php/national-news/15879-govt-agrees-to-more-international-witnesses.html

Macan-Markar, Marwaan. 2013. Indonesia's Special Relationship with Burma Faces Testing Times. The Irrawaddy, April 9. Available at https://www.irrawaddy.com/news/asia/indonesias-special-relationship-with-burmafaces-testing-times.html

Martina, Michael and David Brunnstrom. 2015. China's Xi Says to Commit 8,000 Troops for UN Peacekeeping Force. *Reuters*, September 28. http://www.reuters.com/article/2015/09/29/us-un-assembly-china-idUSKCN0RS1Z120150929#6ybGmIOcqkEcIvel.99

McGregor, Fiona. 2015. Norway Donates to Rakhine State, Denies Financial Interests. Accessed July 6. http://www.mmtimes.com/index.php/national-news/15357-norway-donates-to-rakhine-state-denies-financial-interests.html

McLaughlin, Timothy and Hnin Yadana Zaw. 2015. Under Pressure from China, Kokang Rebels Declare Myanmar Ceasefire. *Reuters*, June 11. http://www.reuters.com/article/2015/06/11/us-myanmar-rebels-ceasefire-idUSKBN0OR0T120150611

Meng, Jie. 2015. China Supports Myanmar's Peace Process from Start to Finish: Negotiator. *Xinhua*, October 15. http://news.xinhuanet.com/english/2015-10/15/c_134717144.htm

Meyer, Eric. 2015. With Oil and Gas Pipelines, China Takes a Shortcut Through Myanmar. *Forbes*, February 10. http://www.forbes.com/sites/ericrmeyer/2015/02/09/oil-and-gas-china-takes-a-shortcut/

Ministry of Foreign Affairs. 2015. Indonesia, in Cooperation with Myanmar and UK, Shares Experience on the Strengthening of Law Enforcement Personnel, Press Release. Jakarta, June 4, 2015. Accessed March 27, 2017. http://www.kemlu.go.id/id/berita/siaran-pers/Pages/Joint-Press-Release-Indonesia-in-cooperation-with-Myanmarand-UK-Shares-Experience-on-the-Strengthen.aspx

Myint, Thin. 2013. Why Suu Kyi Absent from ASEAN? *The Irrawaddy*, January 30. http://www.irrawaddy.org/commentary/across_irrawaddy/why-is-suu-kyi-absent-from-asean.html

Myint-U. 2011. *Where China Meets India: Burma and the New Crossroads of Asia*. London: Faber and Faber.

NLD. 2015. National League for Democracy: 2015 Election Manifesto [Authorised Translation]. December 2, 2015. Accessed March 27, 2017. https://drive.google.com/file/d/0B-Tuf9DZaVm9ZmFLdm9wUjh1TzA/view

Otto, Ben. 2014. Indonesia to Continue Push into Myanmar: Widodo. Accessed November 12. http://blogs.wsj.com/indonesiarealtime/2014/11/12/indonesia-to-continue-push-into-into-myanmar-widodo/

Parameswaran, Prashanth. 2015. China's Influence in Myanmar Facing Growing Scrutiny. *The Diplomat*, January 7. http://thediplomat.com/2015/01/chinas-influence-in-myanmar-facing-growing-scrutiny/

PRC State Council. 2011. China's Peaceful Development. Information Office of PRC State Council.

Renshaw, Catherine Shanahan. 2013. Democratic Transformation and Regional Institutions: The Case of Myanmar and ASEAN. *Journal of Current Southeast Asian Affairs* 1: 29–54.

Richardson, Courtney J. 2011. A Responsible Power? China and the UN Peacekeeping Regime. In *China's Evolving Approach to Peacekeeping*, ed. Marc Lanteigne and Miwa Hirono. New York and London: Routledge.

Sánchez-Cacicedo, Amaia. 2014. *Building States, Building Peace: Global and Regional Involvement in Sri Lanka and Myanmar*. Houndmills, UK and New York: Palgrave.

Santosa, Novan Iman. 2012. Myanmar Asks RI to Help Settle Rohingya Problem. *The Jakarta Post*, November 21. http://www.thejakartapost.com/news/2012/11/21/myanmar-asks-ri-help-settle-rohingya-problem.html

Shin, Aung. 2009. Indonesia Donates to Nargis Victims. *Myanmar Times*, September 7. http://www.mmtimes.com/index.php/national-news/6111-indonesia-donates-to-nargis-victims.html

Sipahutar, Tassia. 2014. BNI to Open New Myanmar Office in November. *The Jakarta Post*, September 13. http://www.thejakartapost.com/news/2014/09/13/bni-open-new-myanmar-office-november.html

Slodkowski, Antoni and Aung Hla Tun. 2015. Myanmar Bans Parties from Criticising Army in State Media. *Reuters*, August 29.

Song, Junying. 2015. China-ASEAN Relations: Managed Disputes and Sustained Cooperation. In *CIIS Blue Book on International Situation and China's Foreign Affairs*. Beijing: China Institute of International Studies, World Affairs Press.

Steinberg. 2013. *Burma/Myanmar: What Everyone Needs to Know*. 2nd ed. Oxford and New York: Oxford University Press.

Storey, Ian. 2009. Emerging Fault Lines in Sino-Burmese Relations: The Kokang Incident. *China Brief* 9 (18): 5–8. http://www.jamestown.org/single/?tx_ttnews%5Btt_news%5D=35468#.Vea5q-vZHds

Sun, Yun. 2015. China and Myanmar: Moving Beyond Mutual Dependence. In *Myanmar: The Dynamics of an Evolving Polity*, ed. David I. Steinberg. Boulder and London: Lynne Rienner.

Suu Kyi, Aung San. 1991. Aung San Suu Kyi—Nobel Lecture. As delivered on acceptance of the Nobel Peace Prize in Oslo. Accessed July 2017. https://www.nobelprize.org/nobel_prizes/peace/laureates/1991/kyi-lecture_en.html

Suu Kyi, Aung San. 2010. *Freedom from Fear*. London: Penguin Books.

Taufiqurrahman, M. 2012. Kalla Pledges Aid to Myanmar Rohingya. *The Jakarta Post*, September 10. http://reliefweb.int/report/indonesia/kalla-pledges-aid-myanmar-rohingya

Telenor. 2017. Telenor Myanmar. Accessed March 27, 2017. https://www.telenor.com.mm/pages/telenormyanmar/147

Telkom. 2013. Telkom Won Tender for Maynmar's International Network [Telkom Berhasil Memenangkan Tender Jaringan Internasional Myanmar]. July 28, 2013. Accessed March 27, 2017. http://www.telkom.co.id/en/telkom-berhasil-memenangkan-tender-jaringan-internasional-myanmar.html

Tempo. 2014. Myanmar Shows Interest in Buying Indonesia's Defense Products. *Tempo*. Accessed March 27, 2017. http://nasional.tempo.co/read/news/2014/09/13/055606685/myanmar-shows-interest-in-buyingindonesias-defense-products

The Guardian. 2015. Indonesia and Malaysia Agree to Offer 7,000 Migrants Temporary Shelter. May 20, 2015. Accessed March 27, 2017. http://www.theguardian.com/world/2015/may/20/hundreds-more-migrants-rescued-offindonesia-as-pope-calls-for-help

Wang, Yamei. 2015. Myanmar Ruling Party Leader Highly Appreciates China's Initiative on New Silk Road. *Xinhua*, April 25. http://news.xinhuanet.com/english/2015-04/25/c_134183984.htm

Weatherbee, Donald E. 2009. *International Relations in Southeast Asia: The Struggle for Autonomy*. 2nd ed. Lanham: Rowman & Littlefield.

Wee, Sui-Lee. 2015. Myanmar Official Accuses China of Interfering in Peace Talks. *Reuters*, October 8. http://www.reuters.com/article/2015/10/08/us-myanmar-china-idUSKCN0S22VT20151008#2v8VxIJLaJQIeWEd.97

Winarti, Agnes. 2013. Myanmar, RI Reaffirm to $1b in Trade. *The Jakarta Post*, June 13. http://www.thejakartapost.com/news/2013/06/13/myanmar-ri-reaffirm-1b-trade.html

Wirajuda, Hassan. 2005. Indonesian Foreign Policy: Strategy and Objectives. In *DUTA: Indonesia and the World*, 24, Cited from Rizal Sukma, Indonesia Finds A New Voice. *Journal of Democracy* 22 4(Oct. 2011): 117.

———. 2014. Myanmar Steps from the Shadows. *Strategic Review*, October–November. http://www.sr-indonesia.com/in_the_journal/view/myanmar-steps-from-the-shadows?pg=all

Wuthnow, Joel. 2008. The Concept of Soft Power in China's Strategic Discourse. *Issues and Studies* 44(2, June): 1–28.

Xinhua. 2013. Indonesia's Electricity Firm Plans to help Myanmar Cut Electricity Losses. *Xinhua*. March 27, 2013. Accessed March 27, 2017, http://www.globaltimes.cn/content/771091.shtml

Yan, Xuetong. 2006a. The Rise of China and Its Power Status. *Chinese Journal of International Politics* 1: 5–33.

———. 2006b. Zhongguo ruan shili youdai tígao yanxuetong [Chinese Soft Power Needs to be Improved]. Centre for China in the World Economy. www.ccwe.org.cn/ccweold/journal/2/1.pdf

Yoshihara, Toshi, and James R. Holmes. 2011. Can China Defend a "Core Interest" in the South China Sea? *Washington Quarterly* 34(2): 45–59.

Yue, Ricky Wai-Kay. 2014. Sino-Myanmar Relations: Is Pauk-Phaw Pragmatic or Rhetoric? *Journal of Comparative Asian Development* 13(2): 264–289.

Zaw, Win Than. 2012. Indonesia Trade to Hit $500 Million by 2015. *Myanmar Times*, January 9. Available at http://www.mmtimes.com/index.php/business/1291-indonesia-trade-to-hit-500-million-by-2015.html

Interviews

Interviews with Chinese government officials, Yangon, April 2015.
Interview with senior Indian Embassy official, Yangon, August 2015.
Interviews with Japanese Embassy officials, Yangon, August 2015.
Interview with senior Switzerland Embassy official, Yangon, August 2015.
Interview with Chief Military Training, Myanmar Armed Forces, August 2015.

Interview with Agus Widjojo, August 12, 2015.
Interview with Hassan Wirajuda, August 11, 2015.
Interview with MoFA, Directorate of East Asian and Pacific Affairs, August 10, 2015.
Interview with some lecturers in Department of International Relations from Yangon University, August 2015.
Interview with Habibie Center, August 2015.
Interviews with administators at the University of Yangon, Yangon, August 2015.
Interviews with education officials and lecturers, University of Yangon, August 2015.
Interviews with Norwegian Embassy officials, Yangon, August 2015.

Lina A. Alexandra is Senior Researcher, Centre for Strategic and International Studies (CSIS), Jakarta.

Marc Lanteigne is Senior Lecturer, Centre for Defence and Security Studies, Massey University, Auckland, New Zealand.

CHAPTER 10

Conclusion: Are Rising Powers Breaking the Peacebuilding Mold?

Charles T. Call and Cedric de Coning

Introduction

The growing international profile of countries like India, Indonesia, Brazil, Turkey, and South Africa has drawn considerable attention in scholarly and policy circles in the past decade (Carmody 2013; Fernández Jilberto and Hogenboom 2010; Mody 2011; Vieira and Alden 2011). Each of these countries has deliberately sought to strengthen its position in regional affairs and in global institutions (Flemes 2007; Hurrell 2006; Schirm 2012). They are all democratic regimes that have (along with China and Russia) opened up their markets in the past two decades and experienced dramatic economic growth. These countries have grown their middle classes and reduced the portion of those in extreme poverty.

These rising powers have also become notably more active in facilitating the economic development of other, less powerful, countries. India's

C.T. Call (✉)
School of International Service, American University, Washington, DC, USA

C. de Coning
Norwegian Institute of International Affairs, Oslo, Norway

Peacekeeping and Peacebuilding Unit, ACCORD, Durban, South Africa

C.T. Call, C. de Coning (eds.), *Rising Powers and Peacebuilding*, Rethinking Peace and Conflict Studies, DOI 10.1007/978-3-319-60621-7_10 development cooperation increased fourfold in the decade between 2003–2004 and 2013–2014 (Mullen 2013). India and Brazil created new agencies dedicated to development cooperation, and South Africa is in an advanced stage of creating a new agency, but it has been actively supporting other African countries since at least 2000 through the African Renaissance Fund (Besharati 2013). Brazilian development cooperation, for instance, rose from US$160 million in 2005 to over US$900 million by 2010 (Leite et al. 2014, 7). Over that period, its technical cooperation grew almost fourfold and its humanitarian cooperation exploded from less than $US1 million to US$161 million (Leite et al. 2014, 7). Admittedly, these totals remain small compared to traditional donors, and financial or political crises in Brazil, Turkey, and South Africa call into question the sustainability of even this level of cooperation. Nevertheless, these expanded development roles are politically meaningful for rising powers and their development partners.

Less attention has been devoted to the roles these rising powers play in facilitating peace processes and supporting efforts to prevent and end wars in other countries. Since 2002, each of these countries launched efforts at what we may call “peacebuilding.” Turkey, for instance, played a high-profile role in mediation and post-war recovery efforts in Somalia. South Africa has supported peace efforts in Burundi and the Democratic Republic of the Congo (DRC), just as Indonesia has supported peace processes in the Philippines and Myanmar. India is the fourth-largest donor in war-torn Afghanistan. Brazil has played leading roles in the United Nations (UN) Peacebuilding Commission and in UN peace missions in Haiti and the Guinea-Bissau.

All of these rising powers have emphasized the comparative advantages they bring to peacebuilding over traditional Western actors. Turkey and Indonesia, for example, see themselves as regional examples of transitions to secular democracy in Muslim majority countries. India and South Africa believe that their own anti-colonial struggles and liberation position them well to share experiences and capacities in an egalitarian and respectful manner.

Yet, little comparative and systematic research has been carried out on the peacebuilding roles of these new actors. New research on development roles has not extended as far into the roles in their new programs in post-conflict countries or to advance peace in fragile or war-torn societies (de Carvalho and de Coning 2014; Mathur 2014; Richmond and Tellidis 2013). This chapter offers some conclusions from the research carried out in 2015 and published in this book by our contributing partners from India, Indonesia, South Africa, and Turkey on their specific approaches to peacebuilding. We added a contribution on Brazil as well. The chapter begins with some of the conceptual findings of the book as regard to the very definition of peacebuilding. It then highlights some of the commonalities across these countries' policies and peacebuilding activities, followed by an analysis of some of the differences among the countries and implications for ideas and the practice of peacebuilding. We believe that these conclusions might serve as hypotheses about the new role of emerging powers in the relatively new field of peacebuilding.

Concepts: Different States, Different Understandings

Rising Powers, Development Partners

This book focuses on the role of what we call "rising powers" in and around peacebuilding. No term adequately captures the group of states examined here. We initially referred to "emerging powers," a term that derives from "emerging markets." However, countries like Brazil, Turkey, and India eschew this label since they either are or have in the past been powers in their own right. The term "middle powers" also is appropriate for some of these states, but derives from a realpolitik framework that emphasizes traditional military prowess and aspirations that do not reflect the way that these countries see themselves today. Countries such as Brazil and Indonesia reject a world order assigning position based on military power, and see their contribution as helping address global problems (de Carvalho and de Coning 2014).

"Rising powers" capture the role of Indonesia, South Africa, Brazil, India, and Turkey better than "emerging" since it reflects recent movement with a positive connotation. Turkish officials are more comfortable with a characterization that conforms to their self-image of increased regional influence. Nevertheless, diplomats of countries like Indonesia are uncomfortable with "rising power" since they do not wish to seem to elevate themselves above other countries in any way. Here, we use rising power to refer to the countries that have successfully sought to exercise a strategic influence in their regions and in multilateral fora. Although countries such as Russia, Nigeria, Mexico, and Egypt might warrant "rising power" status, we focus on countries that have played a particular role on peacebuilding issues—India, Indonesia, Turkey, Brazil, and South Africa.

Peacebuilding

One important finding of the book is a concept of "peacebuilding" among policy circles in rising powers that diverges in clear ways from how the concept is used by traditional donors and the UN system. In our initial conversations, project partners in India, Indonesia, South Africa, Turkey, United States, and Norway determined that we would not pre-determine a specific definition of "peacebuilding," but would let each nationally focused line of research articulate its own definition based on the policy context of that country. The main guidance agreed among the partners was that some "theory of change" needs to exist that reflect how a given activity is intended to influence peace and order, for it to be considered "peacebuilding." Thus, we did not beforehand seek to restrict the conceptual time frame to post-conflict, or limit its content in ways that excluded economic development activities or mediation support efforts or even humanitarian projects, so long as some theorized link to peace outcomes existed. What interested us was how policy communities in rising powers thought about peacebuilding and defined it themselves. We also did not pursue notions of peacebuilding defined as independent variables, that is, we were interested in peace-related outcomes rather than the impact of peacebuilding activities or their success.

Peacebuilding, it turns out, is not a clearly defined or well-developed concept in policy circles of virtually any rising power. In fact, it is rarely used in the domestic discourse of the rising powers studied. When it is used, it is most often in connection with discussions of UN peacebuilding. Domestically, the preference seems to be for a wide range of concepts that are descriptive of the activities undertaken, for example, technical exchanges, training, mediation, rather than of the overall intent. Rarely is an attempt made to group several such activities together under an overarching concept like peacebuilding. The term is more widely used, with a shared understanding, by some (e.g., Brazil) than others (e.g., India), often as a result of exposure to and active participation in multilateral fora such as the UN Peacebuilding Commission. Yet even Brazilians use the term in slightly different ways, depending on if it is used in the corridors of the UN, in the Ministry of Foreign Relations, or in mobilizing large infrastructure projects. In Turkey, the term connotes some link to ending human suffering in war-torn societies, and in South Africa officials are more likely to refer to post-conflict reconstruction.

Peacebuilding offers an example of concepts shaped by international organizations and their interaction with domestic bureaucracies. The traditional (viz., OECD) donors have shaped the Western understanding of peacebuilding as largely a category of programmatic activity that is funded for a specific purpose, different from "normal" development, and thus exempted from some of its requirements. Thus, the need, from a donor logic, to differentiate between funds spent on peacebuilding versus development played an important role in conceptualizing what is and what is not peacebuilding. This element seems missing among the rising powers. Their bureaucracies have no need to distinguish peacebuilding from development, mediation, or other categories, since they are not subject to the Organisation for Economic Co-operation and Development (OECD's) Development Assistance Committee regulations. In contrast, rising powers are incentivized to keep the concept vague and flexible, partly to avoid battles over turf and resources among ministries and departments. In the case of peacebuilding, it would appear as if international organizations have shaped the discourse in rising powers more than the reverse.

Perhaps it is best to begin with how the concept is deployed in the UN system and among traditional donors and the European Union (EU), albeit with differences. The UN's concept of peacebuilding has evolved, from a narrow one focused on political aspects of post-accord, post-conflict processes toward a concept that encompasses state institution-building, economic recovery, national ownership, and, most recently, sustaining peace (Call and Collin 2015). Nevertheless, the UN concept, at least until very recently, tended toward top-down and state-centric approaches that emphasize political and security institution-building over civil society and long-term economic development. Among Western donors, the concept also shares a focus on political and security institution-building, with some economic activities, and a general focus on post-conflict recovery. The EU has a broader approach that emphasizes prevention. It uses "conflict prevention" and "conflict mitigation" alongside "peacebuilding," which "tends to be associated with a wide range of long-term development activities designed to promote structural stability, or with short-term actions with direct conflict prevention objectives" (quoted in Stamnes 2016, 3).

A More Holistic Concept

Rising powers' concept of "peacebuilding" is closer to that of the EU but broader in time and content. The peacebuilding concept of the six rising powers studied in this book encompasses a broad swath of development and other activities in war-torn societies, as well as conflict prevention and mediation efforts in "pre-war" or peaceful societies seen as unstable. Thus, for them peacebuilding activities in war-torn societies extend to health projects, student exchanges, education support such as building schools, food security, infrastructure development of any sort, as well as political/security cooperation like security advisers, mediation support, dialogue facilitation, and elections support. In their chapter, Nyuykonge and Zondi say, for instance, "In terms of peacebuilding support, South Africa has provided states with substantial assistance in the areas of good governance, dialogue and reconciliation, human resource and infrastructure development, policy implementation, economic development and trade, information sharing and exchange visits among South African dignitaries, as well as humanitarian assistance." India's concept is the broadest of the countries examined here, going beyond the others in breadth. For India, virtually all development in a war-torn society, or societies where conflict may arise, is considered peacebuilding. Singh's chapter quotes one Indian official as saying that the attempt to distinguish between peacebuilding and other development assistance is "academic hair-splitting," a view "shared by others" in New Delhi.

At the UN, there is a process underway that is broadening the concept. In 2016, building on a review of the UN's peacebuilding architecture, undertaken by an Advisory Group of Experts and a review of UN peace operations undertaken by a High-level Independent Panel, the Security Council and General Assembly adopted resolutions on the UN peacebuilding architecture that embraced a new concept of "sustaining peace," that comports more closely with that of rising powers.

The "sustainable peace" concept has been influenced by the process leading to the adoption of the UN's Agenda 2030 including approval of a broad set of sustainable development goals (SDGs) in 2015. Among this new set of goals, 36 targets refer to the negative influence of violence and instability, and Goal 16 specifically aims to promote peaceful and inclusive societies for sustainable development, provide access to justice for all, and build effective, accountable, and inclusive institutions at all levels (UN 2015). Although not well defined, "sustainable peace" moves beyond post-conflict contexts to prevention, and suggests a greater emphasis on economic foundations for longer-term peace and addressing underlying causes of conflict. It also represents a shift in focus to local agency, as it operates from the assumption that to sustain the peace, local social institutions need to have the resilient capacity to absorb tensions and shocks that would otherwise risk a lapse into violent conflict.

As Youssef Mahmoud and Andrea Ó Súilleabháin have noted, this new expansive definition recognizes that sustaining peace is an inherently political process that spans prevention, mediation, conflict management, and resolution. They argue that with the sustaining peace concept, the UN approach to peacebuilding now puts UN member states and their populations in the lead; it further puts politics and political solutions front and center, gives prevention an uncontested home, and leverages the UN's three pillars—human rights, peace and security, and sustainable development—in a mutually reinforcing way (Mahmoud and Ó Súilleabháin 2016).

The new UN Secretary-General António Guterres, who took office on 1 January 2017, has embraced these developments and has made prevention and sustaining peace a central theme of his office. In his first statement to the UN Security Council on 10 January 2017, he noted the strong support for an integrated approach that connects development, human rights, and peace and security in both the 2030 Agenda for Sustainable Development and the General Assembly and Security Council resolutions on sustaining peace.[1] This broadening of the peacebuilding concept seems to fit well with the rising powers' approach that tends to be quite comprehensive and/or holistic, that is, inclusive of political, security, peace, justice, development, and economic elements. This broadening of the peacebuilding concept seems to fit well with the rising powers' approach that tends to be quite comprehensive and/or holistic, that is, inclusive of political, security, peace, justice, development, and economic elements.

Rising powers also see a closer link between humanitarian assistance and peacebuilding. This is the strongest in Turkey, where its efforts to support Somalia's response to famine in 2003 led to major peace-related initiatives in Somalia (Achilles et al. 2015; Tank 2013). But it is also present in other countries, such as Brazil, which saw its response in Haiti deepened after Hurricane Tomas hit that country in 2010, and South Africa that combined offers of humanitarian assistance to, for instance, Somalia, with a range of other initiatives aimed at conflict resolution and post-conflict reconstruction (Kok 2014; Nyuykonge and Zondi 2016; van Nieuwkerk

2014). Alexandra argues in her chapter that the frequency of natural and other humanitarian emergencies in Southeast Asia makes it a fertile opportunity to open up work related to peace: "While humanitarian action, including disaster relief, is normally separated from peacebuilding efforts, in the context of Indonesia, humanitarian assistance has been utilized to pave the way to conduct peacebuilding." Following Cyclone Nargis in 2012, the Indonesian government and its Red Cross drew explicitly on the post-tsunami Aceh experience to dialogue with the Myanmar government about the importance of opening up to the international community, democratization, and addressing the conflict in Rakhine state involving the Rohingya.

Institutional/Legal Incentives

Divergent histories and legal/political contexts also shape the global South's broader concept of peacebuilding. In the West, the need to justify ODA in the OECD Development Assistance Committee (DAC) and national legal and parliamentary oversight contexts has resulted in the need to delineate between peacebuilding funding versus development funding versus humanitarian aid. Because rising powers do not share this same history, they can be more flexible in their approach to peacebuilding and are not under pressure to define or delineate it from "routine" development.

Not Just Post-conflict

Activities such as mediation support, dialogue facilitation, and cross-ethnic programs in non-war settings—which might be considered "peacemaking" and "conflict prevention" in the UN system—also fall under the rubric of "peacebuilding" for many rising powers. Indonesia's efforts to facilitate a peaceful political transition in Myanmar, apart from the peace processes involving ethnic rebel movements in that country, are nevertheless considered a major peacebuilding activity undertaken by Indonesian officials. Mediation support efforts like Turkey's in Somalia and Indonesia's in the Philippines are also considered peacebuilding by many (Martin 2010). Similarly, many Indonesian, Indian, and South African officials make no distinction between peacekeeping and peacebuilding. They find it puzzling to exclude from "peacebuilding" the extensive operations historically undertaken by these countries in peacekeeping, dating back decades (India remains one of the largest troop contributors in the world). For instance, in 2004, the South African minister of defense combined these approaches when she introduced the new concept of "developmental peacekeeping" (Madlala-Routledge and Liebenberg 2004). Some Brazilian officials—mainly those who have been posted to New York—routinely distinguish between peacekeeping and peacebuilding, but many in Brasília do not (Charles Call interview with MRE officials, August 2015, Brasilia).

Context-Specific Usage

A tension also seems to exist between how rising powers use the concept at the UN in New York versus how they use it at home in their capitals. At the UN, rising powers tend to use the concept in a way that comports with the UN definition, and, at least before the latest "sustaining peace" evolution of the concept, eschews prevention which may be seen as an incursion on sovereignty. However, in their own foreign ministries and in exchanges with think tanks and civil society, these governments tend not to use the term much. When they do, it is a concept that is more pragmatic, flexible, and all-encompassing of activities such as mediation support, direct mediation, peace-related economic development projects, and indeed any development and infrastructure projects in a post-conflict setting.

Rising Powers' Peacebuilding Policies and Operations

Rising powers' recent experiences and their own characteristics have shaped their motives for embarking on new or expanded efforts to advance peace in other countries. Their experience shows a combination of distinct values and principles that mutually reinforced strategic interests. All these countries sought more influence in their own regions and in global affairs. Their greater role in providing development cooperation and in peacemaking and peacebuilding efforts reflect a sense that such middle powers can and should play lead roles in handling international responses to specific countries. Turkey tried to mediate the very challenging war in Somalia and, in partnership with Brazil, a nuclear deal with Iran. South Africa sought to help bring stability to its continent partly to secure more stable environment for investment and trade. In the only UN peacekeeping operation in the Western hemisphere, in Haiti, Brazil sought and received command of the military forces in that country, a role sustained without interruption since 2004 (Santos and Cravo 2014). India's expansive support for Afghanistan's transition took place in the shadow of its rivalry with Pakistan.

These rising powers have all eschewed unilateral military action, openly backing peacekeeping as a multilateral alternative, preferably with the consent of the host government. Their commitment to a less militarized world coheres with their comparative advantage of "soft power"—of which peacebuilding is one element—rather than traditional "hard" power of military troop deployments and operations. Civilian-led peacebuilding efforts offer a way to advance security objectives in a deliberately non-unilateral, non-militarized manner.

It is no coincidence that these efforts, and the expanded roles in development and peacebuilding, occurred on the heels of the crisis of legitimacy of the UN Security Council following the US invasion of Iraq without its consent in 2003. The elections of Recep Tayyip Erdoğan as prime minister of Turkey and of Luiz Inácio Lula da Silva as president of Brazil ushered in governments that sought more prominent and active roles in global politics. At times, these countries sought to alter the structure of global order, and at other times they sought to rise within that order (de Coning et al. 2015). South Africa, India, and Brazil campaigned for a revamped UN Security Council in which they would have permanent seats (McDonald and Patrick 2010; Pouliot and Therien 2015).

Material interests also drive investment and technical cooperation in risky war-torn environments. Abdenur and De Souza (2014) argue that development and peacebuilding interventions reflect direct economic gains as well as security or principled interests of rising powers. Brazilian diplomats acknowledge that opening markets in sub-Saharan Africa was a goal that converged with that country's concern to assist post-conflict Lusophone countries like Guinea-Bissau, Angola, and Mozambique (Charles Call interviews with various diplomats who requested anonymity, Brasilia, August 2015). China's access to raw materials and markets in Africa is an acknowledged benefit of its increased peacebuilding engagement.

Yet, interviews conducted for this book reveal that values and principles underlie choices to carry out peacebuilding in ways that reflect less hierarchy, less conditionality, less security-focus, and a greater commitment to longer-term accompaniment rather than urgent stabilization and exit. These motives and values are not the focus of this piece, but are relevant to the analysis that follows. Our aim here is rather to identify the main characteristics of these selected rising powers' approaches to peacebuilding, putting into relief their differences from traditional, Western approaches. It is important to note that these rising powers are democratic regimes whose policies may be even closer to Western approaches than non-traditional donors such as China, Russia, and the Gulf states.

Divergent Worldviews and Theories of Change?

The different approaches of rising powers may best captured in the context of broader understandings about development, and especially what was once known as "political development"—that is, how developmental states emerge over time and through what historical processes, and how stable polities and regional arrangements emerge and are sustained. In concrete terms, these are distinct "theories of change" in peace processes, peacebuilding, and institutional development. The peacebuilding approach of traditional donors—embodied by the OECD—is focused on preventing lapses or relapses into violent conflict. While it recognizes that there may be deeper root causes at work that need longer-term attention, it tends to focus on addressing more immediate tensions that, if left unaddressed, can become triggers for violent conflict.

Recent best practice in the "traditional donor" approach in any given setting is that peacebuilding interventions need to be informed by a conflict analysis that seeks to map the conflict by identifying the main actors, the conflict drivers, the political economy of the conflict, and the political history of the conflict.[2] This kind of technical analysis usually finds that conflicts are driven by political, social, and economic inequalities between groups. These groups are usually organized along ethnic, religious, or language identities, and the conflict is typically linked to one or more groups feeling marginalized, for instance, due to center–periphery inequalities. Economic actors and factors are not ignored, but are placed in the context of these group dynamics. They generally manifest an emphasis on the free flow of goods and services, especially capital. The traditional donor approach to peacebuilding in this context is typically aimed at trying to change the behavior of the political system that causes marginalization and inequality by introducing incentives that encourage greater political pluralism and political freedoms. It tends to focus on trying to address such inequalities in political processes and institutions, the civil service, the judicial and security sector, both by making these state institutions more representative of the population of a given country and by spreading state services to the periphery. The theory of change is that greater political access and participation will lead to greater social stability, which will be conducive to development and economic prosperity.

The rising powers seem to have a different theory of political, social, and economic change. Politics, development, and stability are seen as closely interlinked, with political complexity emerging in step with advances in development. Their experience suggests that the level of political competition that a society can manage peacefully is closely linked to the complexity of its social institutions, and thus its level of development. To ensure stability, political activity needs to be governed to stay within manageable levels, and the focus for social change should be on social and economic development. They argue that over time developmental progress enables a social system to become more political complex, and this enables a society to develop social institutions, which ultimately has to manifest in state institutions, to manage the political competition within society.[3] This is why the peacebuilding approach of rising powers tends to focus on the development of state institutions and why they tend to focus on socioeconomic development.

These differences in their respective theories of change may help to explain why the rising powers and traditional donors have different approaches when it comes to, for instance, differentiating between peacebuilding and development, measuring results, or working with civil society. For instance, on civil society, while rising powers are concerned about the peaceful development of the whole society, and while it may be involved in projects that involve the community, it prefers to do so through the institutions of the state, because sustainable development and sustainable peace require the development of responsible state institutions. Fragmented power across state and social institutions will not, in this view, help move the country toward stability or institutional and economic development. Rising powers are concerned that working through non-governmental actors to deliver social goods undermine the development of state institutions and thus ultimately delay and undermine self-sustainable peace and development. They thus prefer to work through state institutions and in this way try to stimulate and develop those institutions they view as most important to ensure self-sustainable peace and development.

When it comes to results, the lack of interest that rising powers seem to show for the kind of monitoring and evaluation systems favored by traditional donors could be partly explained by their theory of change that anticipate slow maturing long-term results. Rising powers realize that their approach to peacebuilding generates change over the medium- to long-term. While they may engage in community development (see India chapter) and other initiatives aimed at more short-term needs, their goal is to lay the foundation for peaceful development. They regard their peacebuilding support as successful as it results in steady progress toward self-sustainable peace. Rising powers thus tend to be less concerned about the politics and setbacks of the day. They prefer stability, so that the longer-term trajectory to development is not disrupted. They thus prefer to focus on infrastructure, agriculture, education, and public administration, because they argue that these are the basic socio-economic and governance capacities that any society and state need, regardless of the politics of the day. They also believe that infrastructure that links the periphery to the center, and education and agricultural development that uplifts all societies, will contribute to alleviate inequalities over the medium- to long-term. While this is not something they are concerned about monitoring in the short-term, they do, at times, articulate such goals (see Myanmar case study) that can be evaluated over time. At the same time, there does seem to be a growing interest among rising powers in the results frameworks employed by the traditional donors. The development agencies in Brazil, India, and South Africa have exchanges with their counterparts among the traditional donors. They seek to improve their tools and techniques, including their monitoring and results systems. This interest is driven by a functional or technical interest in improving practice, not by changes in their overarching theory of change.

The primacy of stable development in the approach of the rising powers to peacebuilding may also explain why they do not feel the same need as traditional donors to differentiate conceptually or in practice between peacebuilding and development. For the rising powers progress in the area of socio-economic development automatically means progress toward peacebuilding. Politics, development, and stability are understood as closely interlinked, with political complexity emerging in step with advances in development. The traditional donors have their own unique historic context within which development originated. As peacebuilding is a fairly recent addition, and as it differed in important aspects from development, traditional donor bureaucracies felt the need to explain how peacebuilding and development are different from each other. Growing impulses in Western capitals, especially legislatures, to monitor and measure the activities and outcomes of development assistance also drove distinctions to clarify distinctions between security-related and development-related efforts. This was driven in part by human rights concerns, and partly by bureaucratic tendencies to protect turf and budgets. The rising powers do not have these same bureaucratic pressures to differentiate between peacebuilding and development.

Another reason why the rising powers may have the "luxury" of a peacebuilding approach that is grounded in longer-term development and stability is because they do not feel responsible, to the same degree as traditional donors, for the day-to-day management of global peace and security. Rising powers regard the day-to-day maintenance and management of international peace and security as the responsibility of the UN and they contribute to that responsibility through peacekeeping and other contributions to the UN. They regard the UN Security Council, and the UN and related institutions, such as the Bretton Woods institutions, as dominated by Western powers, and thus view these powers as primarily responsible for the day-to-day management of international peace and security. In addition, they project a solidarity to humanity that leads them to engage in bilateral peacebuilding and development; however, this is not driven by, or understood as, a contribution to maintaining or managing the global order on a day-to-day basis. Rather it is seen as contributing to the medium- to long-term human development.

Below are some of the core characteristics our book has identified of rising powers' new approaches to peacebuilding.

1. Each rising power's approach to peacebuilding is shaped by its own identity and recent historical experiences.

Western powers' history and values shape the content of their development and peacebuilding approaches, so it is unsurprising that rising powers' experiences should influence theirs. However, rising powers tend to explicitly cite their own experiences in their policy statements and in their dialogues with partner countries. Thus, Turkey's peace efforts emphasize its recent experience in democratization and its unusual position as a secular Muslim democracy. India's peacebuilding is informed by its own postcolonial struggle for independence, with an emphasis on sovereignty and development, rather than security. As Singh says in his chapter, "India shares her experiences of democracy, pluralism and tolerance with the host countries, without interfering in their internal politics and social dynamics." South Africa's regional work advancing peace reflects the debt that the ANC-led government feels it owes to its African neighbors for their support during apartheid.

In her chapter, Alexandra points out that Indonesia's interactions with partners are shared "based on Indonesia's own experiences with democratic consolidation." Its Bali Democracy Forum invites Asia-Pacific leaders to share their experiences to foster international cooperation in peace and democracy. Alexandra finds that Indonesia's work on democracy is linked to its policy to advance the stability of Southeast Asia: its "experiences of democratic transition, which included installing the civilian government, returning the military to the barracks, and settling internal conflicts, have been considered valuable lessons which can be shared with other countries that are currently struggling with similar challenges." These lessons have shaped its relations with Myanmar more than discourse about stability or peace. The democratic character of these rising powers plays a special role in their peacebuilding policies. Indeed, recent democratization experiences are also seen as comparative advantages over traditional donors.

2. Longer time horizon for peacebuilding.

The UN and traditional donor approaches to peacebuilding have tended to focus on preventing relapse into violent conflict. This has resulted in a preoccupation with immediate risks and thus the short term. The UN approach until recently focused on "post-conflict" peacebuilding, rather than prevention, especially in forestalling relapse within six months to two years of war's end. Although the average length of UN peace operations grew from 5.62 years at the end of 1995 to 7.97 years by mid-2016,[4] these operations rarely privilege "root causes" and have more minimalist aims of demobilizing combatants, building basic state institutions and supporting elections before withdrawal of UN missions and return to a "normal" development process.

By contrast, the rising powers seem to have a longer-term approach to peacebuilding that reflects some degree of strategic patience and historic perspective. Their theories of change are typically long-term, believing that addressing underlying causes of conflict, which are often economic in nature, are the soundest way to prevent violent conflict. Of our cases, India is most emblematic of this long-range perspective. Singh argues in his chapter that for current Indian policy, development activities are peacebuilding: "India has not made the same distinction between development assistance and peacebuilding activities that the traditional actors seem to make." India is proud to count its scholarships for Afghans to study in India as part of its contribution to peace there. Somalia's ambassador to Turkey praises Turkish scholarships for Somalis. Its investment in infrastructure like the "ring road" in Afghanistan is also seen as a key contribution to peace. The road is useful for internal and international commerce, and useful for defense forces' mobility. It is an investment to support an embattled allied government, and investment in both internal peace and in regional stability. Turkey similarly invested in the Mogadishu port and in key roads there. Indonesia explicitly emphasizes its slow, deliberate support for dialogue in places like the Philippines and Myanmar.

At the same time, we see a contradictory aspect of rising powers' approach. These countries tend to eschew the lengthy bureaucratic processes of traditional donors, relishing quickly visible projects that governments have explicitly requested and that the population can see. Turkey's road and ports projects in Mogadishu are a case in point. Turkish officials stress that other donors' red tape led to many delays, and the Turkish government quickly approved a road project and the gift of four boats for the coast guard that Somalis saw as immediate, concrete contributions. Rising powers also envision a long-term relationship with the partner country that involves diverse sets of support to help economic development reach a level whereby stability is enhanced. They are less concerned with the immediate outbreak of hostilities and more concerned with a slow progression toward economic growth and stability that will have positive effects for the rising power's own commercial interests and for regional stability.

3. Heightened concerns about national sovereignty, and thus national ownership.

The rising powers uniformly emphasize national ownership in their peacebuilding approaches, often in the context of the UN Charter principles of sovereignty and self-determination. When the UN Security Council considered invoking its authority under Responsibility to Protect to send in assistance over the objections of the Myanmar government, Indonesia argued forcefully against any action defying the government's will. According to Alexandra, "consent from the host country is a must" in Indonesia's approach to engaging with other countries. She goes on to argue that:

> Indonesia's role is to support each country as it crafts its own peacebuilding process, rather than pushing it from the outside. This approach contributes to the establishment of a sense of national ownership that is critical to ensure the success of any peacebuilding effort.

Brazil, India, and Turkey have all underscored their emphasis on national ownership repeatedly. In 2012, for instance, India's acting Ambassador to the UN said that it is "important for the PBC [UN Peacebuilding Commission] to align its objectives with national priorities and ensure that all plans and programmes are implemented under national leadership and through national institutions so that gains are sustainable even if slow," (quoted in Singh's chapter). Over the past decade, a demand for greater national ownership from G7+ countries has converged with a similar stance among rising powers in the Global South to lead the UN, the EU and OECD countries to commit to national ownership in virtually all documents and discussions of peacebuilding.

The emphasis by emerging powers on sovereignty shapes their understanding of "national ownership." It means taking priorities first from the central government, and then also channeling resources through the state. For rising powers, this notion translates largely to accepting the government of the day as the embodiment of national ownership, with less emphasis on local or inclusive ownership. India's peacebuilding priorities in Afghanistan, for instance, are shaped very heavily by conversations between the Indian ambassador in Kabul and the Afghan president. Turkey reaches out more to local leaders, whose priorities determine how Turkish assistance will be used. Typically, rising powers do not invest in much broader consultations with lower level community leaders, civil society, or critics of the government in formulating priorities. They are concerned more about the capacity than the legitimacy of the partner state. Their vision is to invest in the long-term development of the state, regardless of the government of the day. In implementation, countries like India and Turkey may well then reach out to and meet with local beneficiary communities. Indian officials, for instance, seek warm relations of solidarity with partner countries and care about what local communities think of their programs and their effects. They may adapt their programs in response to dialogue with communities. However, in setting priorities, they principally and initially take their cues from the central government's preferences.

This approach contrasts with the growing understanding that Western donors have of "national" and "local" ownership that includes non-governmental actors, especially civil society organizations representative of salient social groups based on ethnicity, gender, youth, and religion. Rising powers' views on peacebuilding comport less with the trend among intergovernmental organizations, Western donors and the new SDGs emphasizing "inclusive politics."

4. A rejection of conditions on cooperation, reflecting a less securitized and more egalitarian vision of global order.

One of the consequences of values that seek to democratize the global order and of histories of colonial occupation is an emphasis on equality and mutual respect for partner countries. The implications of this posture go beyond a refusal to tell other countries what they should do to eschewing conditionality that has been and continues to be central to Western and traditional modes of aid and diplomacy. Rising powers openly reject conditioning their assistance on liberal political, democratic, electoral, or human rights benchmarks that have become the hallmark of North American and European assistance. As Singh points out in his chapter "Right from the outset, India's basic philosophy towards development assistance was that any aid/assistance would be demand driven, given without conditionalities, be administered in a decentralized manner and would not constrain the sovereignty of its partners in any way." Similarly Sazak and his co-authors argue that:

> As often reiterated by Turkish Foreign Ministry, and intermediary organizations, Turkey does not discriminate on race, religion, language and gender, nor does it place political or economic conditions on its resources to alleviate the suffering of victims of a catastrophe and restore human dignity.[5]

Yet, there is an apparent contradiction in the positions of rising powers. Their increased development and peacebuilding roles in the early 2000s reflected in part their desire to play a greater role on the world stage in order to democratize it. Thus, Brazil and South Africa are widely perceived to have expected some degree of support from new partner countries in their bids for permanent Security Council seats. Miguel Lengyel and Bernabé Malacalza (2011) point out the distinction between procedurally specific conditionalities on aid or technical cooperation, on the one hand, and implied or strategic conditionalities not tied specifically to aid but seen as part of a mutually supportive relationship on the other hand (Lengyel and Malacalza 2011, 15–16). Having denounced IMF conditionality on his own country and others, Brazilian President Lula embraced development and peacebuilding policies that did not include conditionality, for instance. Yet, this renunciation of strict conditionality in Lula's outreach to African countries can coexist with an expectation of partner countries' support on broader global questions.

5. Mutual respect, equality, and cultural understanding.

There is an emphasis on cooperation that is seen as mutually beneficial, as aid that is seen as one (superior knowledge and tools) part coming to the aid of a (inferior knowledge and tools) party. The rising powers we have studied claim that their technical advice reflects an exchange among equals rather than that of a benefactor giving resources to a beneficiary. Indonesia emphasizes that this relationship is not a one-way transfer but involves mutual learning: Alexandra argues that "rather than acting as an expert conveying its success stories, Indonesia tends to apply a two-way approach in which it shares its own experiences, but also learns from the host country." Alexandra further finds that "Indonesia emphasizes a mutual learning process when conducting peacebuilding activities." One of the two principles Alexandra highlights in Indonesia's approach to peacebuilding is the "comfort" level of the partner country: "The host government should reach the stage where it feels the need for and is comfortable enough to open up itself to receiving other countries' assistance in the peacebuilding process." Sazak and his co-authors quote one Somali non-governmental organization (NGO) official which they think reflect the Somali view of Turkey's assistance: "When we work with Turkish organizations, we feel like equal partners. The Turks respect the Somalis as equals" (Interview with a Somali NGO representative, quoted in Wasuge 2016, 23).

6. *More technical cooperation rather than aid.*

One reflection of rising powers' emphasis on mutual respect and equality is a greater reliance on technical cooperation than the transfer of aid. Traditional donors use technical advisers extensively, including in security ministries, courts, and finance ministries. However, the amount of bilateral and multilateral aid and loans that traditional donors provide dwarfs the monetary value of their technical advisors. In contrast, rising powers draw on technical advisers and cooperation as a greater percentage of their peacebuilding work, usually bilaterally. In many cases, these advisers are sent to places of cultural, historical, or linguistic affinity, improving the chances that the exchange will be sustained. More research is needed to analyze the impact of South-South technical cooperation before we can judge if their approach is having the intended effects.

Some partner governments and communities request or prefer Western aid, because it is perceived to result in more money or greater economic and social benefits for individuals or institutions involved, or because it addresses other political, economic or strategic interests (such as Myanmar seeking Western aid to counterbalance China's role). In addition, the reliance on technical advisers reflects a more constrained institutional and financial context than in many Western countries. It is less costly to pay the travel costs for one's own government employees to work abroad for six to 12 months than to provide aid for projects or pay the salaries and transaction costs of others. Brazilian law, for instance, provides for technical cooperation, but not for actual aid except through international organizations. Resource and legal constraints thus help explain the penchant for technical cooperation and for multilateralism.

7. Monitoring, evaluation, and impact.

Although more data are needed, rising powers also seem to differ from Western actors in the degree and character of their monitoring and evaluation of peacebuilding efforts. As seen earlier, rising powers' motives for peacebuilding reflect variously their humanitarian impulses, their ideologically-framed regional or global roles, their desire for neighborhood stability or their own interests in commerce or commercial and alliance or regional interests. It is worth reflecting on the strategic purposes of peacebuilding for rising powers. Western powers and traditional donors provide aid and peacebuilding support for strategic reasons of course. They seek stability in other regions and countries for their own security and to maximize commercial opportunities. They also seek to strengthen alliances and partnerships with other governments, and to propagate their values. For instance, a recent review commissioned by the Norwegian parliament, entitled "A Good Ally—Norway in Afghanistan 2001–2014," found that Norway's engagement with Afghanistan had achieved a strategic purpose of strengthening Norway's relationship with the United States, even as it largely failed to achieve virtually any of its project and programmatic goals on the ground in Afghanistan.[6]

Similarly, rising powers pursue peace-related programs for their own strategic reasons. These motives often reflect a desire to build relationships or strategic partnerships or trade relations. Such benefits rarely are captured by monitoring and evaluation frameworks. Yet to the extent that peacebuilding programs reflect strategic relationships or solidarity with countries in the global South, then those programs achieve their aims when relationships are strengthened. On a different level, the enhancement of legitimacy of a partner government is often viewed as strategic for an external donor as well as assisting legitimacy internally. In this view, the positive expression of senior Afghan officials about Indian projects is the most relevant criterion for success possible. Myanmar's governmental expressions of friendship and appreciation for Indonesia's role are more important to the foreign ministry than project-based evaluations.

Similarly, some rising powers acknowledge that their peace-related activities have a side effect of enhancing opportunities for commerce and investment by their own private sector. To the extent that these opportunities are seen as positive outcomes, they signify "successful" attainment of national interests quite apart from their impacts on peace. In addition, some rising powers' approaches center on long-term projects such as economic conditions and infrastructure.

Monitoring and evaluation of such projects will take years and not lend themselves to the sort of causal immediacy that conventional evaluation of short-term peacebuilding projects seek to ascertain. Instead, assessment will examine visible products like roads or schools completed, with less ability to identify connections to peace. The foreign ministries of rising powers have little culture of evaluation. Although their development agencies have growing monitoring and evaluation, they remain less institutionalized than their Western counterparts. Conventional project-based monitoring and evaluation are less commonly practiced by rising powers than traditional ones, but their governments are often more comfortable admitting how peace-related projects advance national interests.

Yet, assessment and learning are evident among rising powers. Several chapters note examples of an openness to incorporating effective elements of conventional practices, including adopting some practices that were earlier eschewed following a similar learning curve followed by traditional donors in past decades. After an avowed resistance to taking political considerations into its cooperation, for instance, China has in recent years recognized that it must heed issues of partisan and ethic exclusion or see its projects impeded. Turkey may yet confront some of the same problems encountered by Western powers of a military presence provoking perceived involvement favoring one side in Somalia. At the same time, Turkey has begun to recognize the need in Somalia for some degree of planning, coordination with other donors, and evaluation of its projects. And India is introducing ethical standards in its cooperation efforts. None of these rising powers is averse to multilateral approaches, but they are wary of seeing Western-led donor coordination processes become mechanisms to dictate the content of their assistance.

One arc of evolution and learning bears further research—how rising powers' peacebuilding activities redound on their internal policies regarding violence and insecurity. Abdenur and Call's chapter points out that Brazil's approaches to community violence and development in its peacekeeping mission in Haiti drew explicitly on the approaches of Viva Rio, a well-known NGO whose projects had helped improve household incomes and mitigate violence in Rio de Janeiro's most violent slums. Yet, there are few feedback mechanisms that draw on lessons from rising powers' peacebuilding activities abroad to shape policies at home. Few think tanks exist in these countries, and they have understandably focused on the relatively recent forays of some rising powers into peacebuilding abroad. They are not financially incentivized (by external or internal funders) to examine the implications of such activities for domestic policies, an endeavor that might also prove politically sensitive. Greater transparency public debate, and engagement with civil society and research communities might stimulate enhanced feedback loops between domestic and foreign experiences. Given high levels of poverty and insecurity in large swaths of rising powers' territories, their governments have also been hesitant to draw too much attention to sending their staff and money abroad.

Conclusions

This book seeks to identify and analyze the peacebuilding concepts, policies, and practices of a selected group of rising powers: Brazil, India, Indonesia, South Africa, and Turkey. Although the development practices of these new actors have been analyzed by scholars, their peacebuilding activities have not received much scrutiny. Our book finds a number of common elements, starting with different understandings of peacebuilding that bear further study and discussion. "Peacebuilding" for these countries is less narrowly understood than in Western settings or in the UN, and incorporates development, humanitarian, infrastructure, health, education, jobs creation, mediation, dialogue, and reconciliation activities, as well as more conventional post-war reconstruction and institutional support. Their notion of "peacebuilding" covers pre-war, at-war, and post-war countries, as well as those experiencing mass violence that falls short of armed conflict.

The peacebuilding policies and operations of these rising powers also reflect commonalities that distinguish them from traditional donors. They have a more holistic operational approach that draws on multiple ministries, including technical advisors from agriculture, health, and education sectors. They have a longer time horizon and strong emphasis on national ownership, often interpreted to mean governmental consent, than Western approaches. Their heightened sensitivity to sovereignty and a lack of immediate conditionalities on their peacebuilding cooperation, even when that cooperation advances strategic and economic interests, reflect their post-colonial trajectories and South-South solidarity. The limited scale of their funding and programs, as well as divergent political agendas among traditional donors and rising powers, combine to limit the extent to which peacebuilding policies and practice have evolved during their short lifetimes. However, important shifts in peacebuilding both converge with and have been influenced by the peacebuilding policies and activities of these countries as their roles have gained salience on the global stage.

A number of caveats are in order. First, it would be an exaggeration to say that the rising powers studied here represent *all* rising powers. This book systematically examined six important rising powers—Brazil, India, Indonesia, South Africa, and Turkey. These are all democratic countries whose recent (or not so recent in India's case) political transitions shape their regional and global roles and policies. Other countries that have become more active as development partners and peacebuilding actors—including Russia, China, Mexico, Colombia, Egypt, Nigeria, Saudi Arabia, and other Arab states, among others—are not analyzed here. These may have very different peacebuilding approaches that merit further study.

Second, although this book has identified some elements common to these countries, these countries exhibit variation among themselves in how they conceptualize and practice peacebuilding. Rising powers diverge, for instance, in the extent to which they equate peacebuilding with development. For most, peacebuilding is a distinct but related and overlapping concept with development. It is a particular peace-related set of activities that usually occur in the context of war-torn societies, and that aim to advance or sustain peace. India is an exception, as it equates virtually all of its development activity with peace support and peacebuilding. India, like China, also has a longer time horizon given its historical reference points; therefore, the longer-term emphasis means less concern with junctural political events and more concern with longer-term social and economic conditions for peace. Other variations exist in the extent to which countries contrast themselves explicitly with Western or traditional approaches, with Brazil being more prone to such statements, for example, than Indonesia.

Another area of variation among the rising powers is in the degree to which their cooperation is provided bilaterally versus multilaterally. One study shows that Turkey, Brazil, India, and Russia all shifted from bilateral assistance toward multilateral channels between 2005 and 2010 (White 2011, 7). Indonesia and China shifted in the opposite direction, and South Africa remained highly multilateral according to its official development aid figures (White 2011). Multilateral often does not mean working with and through the UN. These countries remain comfortable working in coordination with the UN, but this is not necessarily the preferred mode of cooperation. Rising powers have fostered work with and through regional organizations like the AU and ASEAN, partly because of greater influence in those fora. In addition, they work through multilateral groupings such as the BRICS and its New Development Bank, the India, Brazil, and South Africa (IBSA) fund, the AU's New Economic Partnership (NEPAD), the Organization of Islamic Cooperation (OIC) , the Brazilian Development Bank, and in the case of China, its Asian Infrastructure Investment Bank. Most of these mechanisms are relatively new, and hold additional potential to shape the peacebuilding priorities and financing.

Recent events raise doubts about whether rising powers will sustain their new roles in development and peace-related cooperation. Corruption indictments of senior officials have rocked the administrations of President Zuma in South Africa and sparked the impeachment of President Rousseff in Brazil. China has faced economic slowdown, and political crises plagued the government Recep Erdoğan in Turkey. Indonesia's development cooperation fell from \$27 million in 2012 to \$12 million by 2013. Brazil has cut the budget of its Ministry of Foreign Relations dramatically since 2013, slashing its program budgets (Charles Call interviews with Brazilian diplomats, August 2015, Brasilia). As a result, some scholars call into question the future impact of rising powers on global governance and international practices of development and peacebuilding (Chandhoke 2014; Quadir 2014; Stuenkel 2014).

What then can we say about the impact of these new peacebuilding roles in the institutions and policies and practice of peacebuilding globally? The dialogues and discussions thus far indicate that these rising powers have influenced the discourse and practices of development, but not transformed them. One area of apparent impact is the content of the SDGs, approved at the UN General Assembly in September 2015. Rising powers did not veto goals regarding peace and security, but they exercised important influence on the wording of those goals and targets, including Goal 16 on "just, peaceful, and inclusive societies." Rising powers helped shape Goal 16's "targets" to exclude the term "security" and to include capacity-building, commitment to a stronger role for developing countries in the institutions of global governance, violence prevention, and reduced illicit arms flows. Work on peacebuilding in the next 15 years will reflect these targets. Beyond the SDGs, rising powers have helped achieve more holistic notions of peacebuilding in policy statements that reinforce the work of development agencies and funds in this area. Their longer time horizons also support the role of the development and humanitarian actors in peacebuilding, in contrast to a narrower concept that privileges the UN's peace and security institutions.

The participation of rising powers in the peacebuilding architecture at the UN also contrasts with their reluctance to engage the OECD and its New Deal processes. Brazil has chaired the PBC, and Indonesia, India, and South Africa have all played prominent roles in PBC debates and decisions. That role has strengthened a commitment to national ownership in the rhetoric and work of the UN's peacebuilding work, including a tone of mutual respect in UN dealings with recipient governments. These countries' holistic notions have also helped ensure that economic recovery and jobs programs remain a part of the agenda of the UN peacebuilding and peacekeeping programming and discourse, including the UN Peacebuilding Fund. Their emphasis on national ownership has ensured a central place for that concept in all UN and other multilateral fora, visible also in the 2015 reviews of peace operations and peacebuilding. Their role has not, however, led to an end to conditionality. The tug-of-war between an expansive understanding of "national ownership" (as backed by Western donors) versus a narrow government-centered understanding of that term (reflecting usage by rising powers) persists in the UN.

Which direction, one might speculate, will the peacebuilding policies and engagement of the rising powers take in the coming years? At a workshop in The Hague in 2016, researchers debated whether the future would witness a convergence or persistent different tracks between traditional approaches and rising powers' approaches to peacebuilding. Much of that, of course, depends on the role and relative power of specific rising powers in global affairs in coming decades, discussed above. However, the role of partner countries themselves, and the understandings within multilateral institutions, will play an important role in determining whether and how alternative ideas will prevail in this mix. It is possible that some convergence will occur as traditional donors choose or are forced by the "development cooperation market" to accommodate longer timelines, less conditionality, more deference to governments. It is also possible that rising powers will "learn" to adopt more results-based and shorter-term approaches in response to their own domestic constituencies. They may also broaden their understandings of national ownership to include more NGOs. In the near term, distinct but overlapping parallel approaches are likely to persist. These need not be competitors, but may prove to be complementary and cooperative.

Ultimately, the impact of rising powers on peacebuilding institutions, policies, and practices is likely to derive more from their discourse, concepts, and moral authority as their resources. Their "talk" may influence more than their "walk," although the influence of their programs may vary depending on the resources devoted. From a partner government's perspective, a small alternative source of funding goes a long way to undercut conditionality even of a much larger donor. The research presented in this book documents how rising powers have set forth a common set of principles and rationales as the basis for a new approach to peacebuilding. That set of principles around the peacebuilding concept and its practice are likely to continue to serve as reference points for debates in the halls of Western donors, the UN and regional organizations, bolstered by non-governmental organizations. The pace and character of those interactions will shape peacebuilding on the ground in varied and important ways in coming years.

Notes

1. Remarks of the Secretary-General to the Security Council Open Debate on "Maintenance of International Peace and Security: Conflict Prevention and Sustaining Peace," 10 January 2017, accessed on January 31, 2017, https://www.un.org/sg/en/content/sg/speeches/2017-01-10/secretary-generals-remarks-maintenance-international-peace-and
2. See, for instance, the G7+ Fragility Assessment frameworks, the UK Stabilization Unit's Joint Analysis of Conflict and Stability, the State Department's Interagency Conflict Analysis Framework 2.0 (2013),

USAID Conflict Assessment Framework 2.0 (2011), the UNDP Conflict-related Development Analysis (2007), inter alia.

3. The approach is similar to Samuel Huntington's *Political Order in Changing Societies* (Yale University Press, 1968), but less concerned with order in the core, and more concerned with order as pre-requisite for domestic prosperity, capacity, and eventually legitimacy.
4. Calculations of authors based on DPKO and DPA mandated missions, average length of existing missions at end of each year.
5. See also "Humanitarian Assistance by Turkey," Ministry of Foreign Affairs, accessed on 17 September 2015, http://www.mfa.gov.tr/humanitarian-assistance-by-turkey.en.mfa
6. See "To Say It Like It Is: Norway's evaluation of its part in the international intervention," by Ann Wilkins, Afghanistan Analyst Network, accessed on 19 September 2016, https://www.afghanistan-analysts.org/to-say-it-like-it-is-norways-evaluation-of-its-part-in-the-international-intervention/, and "A good ally: Norway in Afghanistan," Christian Michelsen Institute, accessed on 19 September 2016, http://www.cmi.no/news/1711-a-good-ally-norway-in-afghanistan

References

Abdenur, Adriana Erthal, and Danilo Marcondes de Souza Neto. 2014. Rising Powers and the Security-Development Nexus: Brazil's Engagement with Guinea-Bissau. *Journal of Peacebuilding and Development* 19(2): 1–16.

Achilles, Kathryn, Onur Sazak, Thomas Wheeler, and Auveen Elizabeth Woods. 2015. Turkish Aid Agencies in Somalia: Risks and Opportunities for Building Peace. Saferworld and Istanbul Policy Centre. Accessed from http://www.saferworld.org.uk/resources/view-resource/893-turkish-aid-agencies-in-somalia-risks-and-opportunities-for-building-peace

Besharati, Neissan A. 2013. *South African Development Partnership Agency (SADPA): Strategic Aid or Development Packages for Africa*. Johannesburg: South African Institute for International Affairs (SAIIA).

Call, Charles T., and Katy Collin. 2015. The United Nations Approach to Peacebuilding. Paper prepared for "Rising Powers and Peacebuilding" project. www.risingpowersandpeacebuilding.org

Carmody, Pádraig R. 2013. *The Rise of the BRICS in Africa: The Geopolitics of South-South Relations*. Chicago: University of Chicago Press.

Chandhoke, Neera. 2014. Realising Justice. In *Rising Powers and the Future of Global Governance*, ed. Kevin Gray and Craig N. Murphy. New York: Routledge.

de Carvalho, Benjamin, and Cedric de Coning. 2014. *Rising Powers and the Future of Peacebuilding*. Oslo: NOREF.

de Coning, Cedric, Thomas Mandrup, and Liselotte Odgaard, eds. 2015. *The BRICS and Coexistence: An Alternative Vision of World Order*. London: Routledge.

Fernández Jilberto, Alex E., and Barbara Hogenboom, eds. 2010. *Latin America Facing China: South-South Relations beyond the Washington Consensus*. New York: Berghahn Books.

Flemes, Daniel. 2007. Emerging Middle Powers' Soft Balancing Strategy: State and Perspectives of the IBSA Dialogue Forum. German Institute of Global and Area Studies Working Paper No. 57.

Hurrell, Andrew. 2006. Hegemony, Liberalism and Global Order: What Space for Would-Be Great Powers? *International Affairs* 82(1): 1–19.

Kok, Naomi. 2014. South Africa's Peacebuilding and PCRD Activities: The Role of IBSA and BRICS. ISS Paper. https://emergingpowerspeacebuilding.files.wordpress.com/2015/08/kok-south-africas-peacebuilding-and-pcrd-activities.pdf

Lengyel, Miguel, and Bernabé Malacalza. 2011. What do We Talk When We Talk about South–South Cooperation? The Construction of a Concept from Empirical Basis. Paper presented at IPSA-ECPR Joint Conference, São Paulo, February 16–19.

Leite, Iara Costa, Bianca Suyama, Laura Trajber Waisbich, and Melissa Pomeroy. 2014. *Brazil's Engagement in International Development Cooperation: The State of the Debate*. International Development Studies (Evidence Report No. 59).

Madlala-Routledge, Nozizwe, and Sybert Liebenberg. 2004. Developmental Peacekeeping. *African Security Review* 13(2): 125–131. doi:10.1080/10246029.2004.9627292.

Mahmoud, Youssef, and Andrea Ó Súilleabháin. 2016. With New Resolutions, Sustaining Peace Sits at Heart of UN Architecture. IPI Global Observatory, New York, 29 April.

Martin, G. Eugene. 2010. Facilitating Peacemaking in Internal Conflicts: Lessons from the Philippines. *Georgetown Journal of International Affairs* 11(1): 73–80.

Mathur, Anita. 2014. *Role of South-South Cooperation and Emerging Powers in Peacemaking and Peacebuilding*. NUPI Report. https://emergingpowerspeacebuilding.files.wordpress.com/2015/08/mathur-role-of-south-south-cooperation-and-emerging-powers.pdf

McDonald, Kara C., and Stewart M. Patrick. 2010. *UN Security Council Enlargement and U.S. Interests*. Washington, DC: Council on Foreign Relations.

Mody, Renu. 2011. *South-South Cooperation: Africa on the Centre Stage*. London, UK: Palgrave Macmillan.

Mullen, Rani. 2013. The State of Indian Development Cooperation. New Delhi: Centre for Policy Research. http://cprindia.org/sites/default/files/policy-briefs/Spring_2014_IDCR_Report_the_State_of_Indian_Development_Cooperation.pdf

Nyuykonge, Charles, and Siphamandla Zondi. 2016. South African Peacebuilding Approaches: Evolution and Lessons. Paper prepared for "Rising Powers and Peacebuilding" project. www.risingpowersandpeacebuilding.org

Pouliot, Vincent, and Jean-Philippe Therien. 2015. The Politics of Inclusion: Changing Patterns in the Governance of International Security. *Review of International Studies* 41(02): 211–237.

Quadir, Fajimul. 2014. Rising Donors and the New Narrative of South—South Cooperation. In *Rising Powers and the Future of Global Governance*, ed. Kevin Gray and Craig N. Murphy. New York: Routledge.

Richmond, Oliver P., and Ioannis Tellidis. 2013. The BRICs and International Peacebuilding and Statebuilding. Oslo: NOREF. https://emergingpowerspeacebuilding.files.wordpress.com/2015/08/richmond-tellidis-brics-and-international-peacebuilding-and-statebuilding

Santos, Rita, and Teresa Almeida Cravo. 2014. Brazil's Rising Profile in UN Peacekeeping Operations Since the End of the Cold War. Oslo: NOREF. https://emergingpowerspeacebuilding.files.wordpress.com/2015/08/santos-brazils-rising-profile-in-un-peacekeeping.pdf

Schirm, Stefan A. 2012. Leaders in Need of Followers: Emerging Powers in Global Governance. In *Power in the 21st Century: International Security and International Political Economy in a Changing World*, ed. Enrico Fels, Jan-Frederik Kremer, and Katharina Kronenberg, 211–236. Berlin: Springer.

Stamnes, Eli. 2016. The European Union and Peacebuilding. Paper prepared for "Rising Powers and Peacebuilding" project. www.risingpowersandpeacebuilding.org

Stuenkel, Oliver. 2014. Rising Donors and the Future of Democracy Promotion: The Cases of Brazil and India. In *Rising Powers and the Future of Global Governance*, ed. Kevin Gray and Craig N. Murphy. New York: Routledge.

Tank, Pinar. 2013. Turkey's New Humanitarian Approach in Somalia. Oslo: NOREF. https://emergingpowerspeacebuilding.files.wordpress.com/2015/08/tank-turkeys-new-humanitarian-approach-in-somalia-tank.pdf

United Nations, General Assembly. 2015. Transforming Our World: The 2030 Agenda for Sustainable Development, A/RES/70/1. http://www.un.org/ga/search/view_doc.asp?symbol=A/RES/70/1&Lang=E

van Nieuwkerk, Anthoni. 2014. South Africa and the African Peace and Security Architecture. Oslo: NOREF. https://emergingpowerspeacebuilding.files.wordpress.com/2015/08/van-nieuwkerk-south-africa-and-the-african-peace-and-security-architecture.pdf

Vieira, Marco Antonio, and Chris Alden. 2011. India, Brazil, and South Africa (IBSA): South-South Cooperation and the Paradox of Regional Leadership. *Global Governance* 17(4): 507–528.

Wasuge, Mahad. 2016. *Turkey's Assistance Model in Somalia: Achieving Much with Little*. Mogadishu: Heritage Institute for Policy Studies.

White, Stacey. 2011. *Emerging Powers, Emerging Donors: Teasing Out Developing Patterns.* Report of the Center for Strategic and International Studies (CSIS). February. Washington, DC: CSIS.

Charles T. "Chuck" Call is Associate Professor of International Peace and Conflict Resolution at School of International Service, American University, Washington DC.

Cedric de Coning is a senior research fellow in the Peace and Conflict Studies Research Group at Norwegian Institute of International Affairs (NUPI), and a senior advisor on Peacekeeping and Peacebuilding for the African Centre for the Constructive Resolution of Disputes (ACCORD).

Index

A

B

C

C.T. Call, C. de Coning (eds.), *Rising Powers and Peacebuilding*, Rethinking Peace and Conflict Studies, DOI 10.1007/978-3-319-60621-7

www.ingramcontent.com/pod-product-compliance
Lightning Source LLC
LaVergne TN
LVHW080036210926
848481LV00011B/3209
9781013289309